TESTIMONIALS FOR DIVINE INTELLIGENCE

Dr. Jayne Gardner is a true pioneer in the science of spirituality. Her understanding of Gnostic teachings is thorough and wise. Divine Intelligence *is the handbook on Gnosticism for a New Era of spirituality, a must-read for seekers who are ready to take their quest to the next level.*
—Kathleen McGowan, International, best-selling author of
The Expected One (The Magdalene Line Trilogy)

In her book, Divine Intelligence, *Dr. Jayne brings her unique perspective as a coach to this most fascinating subject of the creative power that exists within each of us. She provides great insights that will cause you to question many of your current beliefs and help you find greater clarity about your role in the creative process of your life. When you awaken to the idea that this you does exist, you suddenly harness a power greater than anything you have ever known.*
—Rev. Lee Wolak, Agape Center for Spiritual Living

Having established an elaborate historical context, Dr. Gardner gracefully reminds us, through the coaching of one man, of the ultimate truth: That the divine is within and awaits our arrival.
—Rick Carson, Author of Taming Your Gremlin *and* A Master Class in Gremlin Taming

Dr. Gardner does a wonderful job of guiding the reader to discover their internal God. This book is a gift that will serve as a spiritual guide for seekers of God within us and help us discover the true meaning of life.
—Om Prakash, Ph.D., Author of From Change to Transformation & Beyond, Corporate Wellness Coach

The combination of spirituality, supported by science and research, took my brain by storm and blew all the beliefs I had about God into another country. This read is dynamic and powerful and does what every good coach hopes to do—create a mental shift that allows more energy and vitality to emerge in another human being.
—Christine Martin, Master Certified Coach, International Coaching Federation

Completing the Divine Intelligence Process was a life-changing experience. With my new understanding of self and God, I am not living small anymore—it is a rebirth at 63!
—Betty Choi-Fung, MD, CCFP

Simply put, this book changed my life! Dr. Jayne articulately shares the compelling story of one man's amazing transformation in a captivating way that makes it very challenging to put the book down. She explains the science behind the process in language that each of us can easily understand. This profound book inspired me to seek out Dr. Jayne and dive into the Divine Intelligence Process myself… and I am eternally grateful!
—John Harrington, Spiritual Life Coach, Authorized Guide to John of God, NLP Practitioner

The Divine Intelligence Process gave me an experience that has expanded my life and my business. I am grateful to Dr. Jayne for her brilliant development and execution of the process. It sparked the amazing gifts and talents that I have been given and energized me to help others break free from their limiting beliefs so that they, too, can achieve their dreams.
—Jenni Hubby, ACC, Professional Coach & Consultant

This book is transformational. Rooted in neurobiological research and spiritual underpinnings, this book can lead you to the "authentic" you, your powerful and spiritual self. If you are ready to become all that you want to be, read Divine Intelligence.
—Jane Hickerson, Ph. D., LCSW, Assistant Dean of Field Education, School of Social Work, UT Arlington

Divine Intelligence allows you to watch from the sidelines as someone undergoes a life-changing, personal journey to discover his inner light, his spiritual core. This book is an awesome alternative for one-on-one sessions with a coach or counselor—if you are interested in the recovery of your soul.
—Pete Baynard, Executive

Make sure you're not missing out on living the best life you can live —read this book! Dr. Jayne displays in her writing the passion and wisdom she portrays as a life coach. I (along with many of my clients) have reached my goals faster and have sustained the dramatic change over time by using the process Dan, the main character in this book, used. Divine Intelligence *makes for a very powerful reading!*
—Danielle Mercurio, Principal, Inner Effects Life Coaching

Divine Intelligence *provides the key for humanity to break free from the chains of spiritual slavery created by well-meaning but not fully informed ancestors. A tremendous transformation awaits the Earth as the masses become informed and begin to practice the concepts that awaken their internal divinity. The greatest treasures to behold truly lie within your own heart and soul. Such enlightened souls pour forth the gifts of the spirit upon all of creation, paving the way for others to step into their own light. This Earth couldn't be more blessed.*
—Deborah Wood Broach, Seminarian

The Divine Intelligence Process opened me up to my deep and hidden anger. In this book, Dr. Jayne brings in a new era of Life Coaching that totally transforms a client from darkness into God's Divine Intelligence. Grab this book, read it, understand it, and pass it on."
—Manzie Britt, Counselor, Life Coach, and Consultant, LLC

DIVINE INTELLIGENCE

A Scientific Process to Awaken the Creator Within

Jayne Gardner, Ph.D., MCC

Mindset Press

DIVINE INTELLIGENCE
A Scientific Process to Awaken the Creator Within
REVISED

By Jayne Gardner, Ph.D., MCC
Mindset Press
Published by Mindset Press, Allen, Texas
Copyright ©2017 Jayne Gardner All rights reserved.

No part of this publication may be reproduced, stored in a retrieval system, or transmitted in any form or by any means, electronic, mechanical, photocopying, recording, scanning, or otherwise, except as permitted under Section 107 or 108 of the 1976 United States Copyright Act, without the prior written permission of the Publisher. Requests to the Publisher for permission should be addressed to Permissions Department, Mindset Press, 1333 W. McDermott, Suite 150, Allen, Texas 75013

Limit of Liability/Disclaimer of Warranty: While the publisher and author have used their best efforts in preparing this book, they make no representations or warranties with respect to the accuracy or completeness of the contents of this book and specifically disclaim any implied warranties of merchantability or fitness for a particular purpose. No warranty may be created or extended by sales representatives or written sales materials. The advice and strategies contained herein may not be suitable for your situation. You should consult with a professional where appropriate. Neither the publisher nor author shall be liable for any loss of profit or any other commercial damages, including but not limited to special, incidental, consequential, or other damages.

This book is not intended to be used as medical help for anyone who has a diagnosis of depression or severe anxiety, but rather it is to be used with situational conflicts and challenges in life.

The Divine Intelligence Institute™ and the Divine Intelligence Process™ are registered trademarks of FamilyWorks, P.C.

Editor: Renee Simas, renee.simas@gmail.com
Cover and Interior Design: Davis Creative, www.daviscreative.com
Index: Sheila Ryan, www.ryanindexing.com

Library of Congress Control Number: 2017910825

Publisher's Cataloging-In-Publication Data
(Prepared by The Donohue Group, Inc.)

Names: Gardner, Jayne.
Title: Divine intelligence : a scientific process to awaken the Creator within / Jayne Gardner, Ph.D., MCC.
Description: Second edition. | Allen, Texas : Mindset Press, [2017] | Includes bibliographical references and index.
Identifiers: ISBN 978-0-9890844-2-0 (paperback) | ISBN 978-0-9890844-3-7 (mobi) | ISBN 978-0-9890844-4-4 (ePub)
Subjects: LCSH: Presence of God. | Spiritual life. | Psychobiology--Religious aspects. | Gnosticism--Psychology. | Psychology--Religious aspects. | Self. | Mind and body.
Classification: LCC BT180.P6 .G37 2017 (print) | LCC BT180.P6 (ebook) | DDC 231.7--dc23

To my Light Bearers:

Nola, Poppy, and Raiden

CONTENTS

Preface	xi
Introduction	1
How Divine Intelligence Is Organized	19
PART 1 Birth	**21**
Universal Spiritual Truth #1: There is God in Everyone	23
Universal Spiritual Truth #2: Few Will Accept the Invitation	41
Universal Spiritual Truth #3: Everything Begins with You!	57
Universal Spiritual Truth #4: What You Are Seeking Is Hidden within You	69
PART 2 Death	**91**
Universal Spiritual Truth #5: Seek First Who You Are Not	93
Universal Spiritual Truth #6: The Path to Salvation May Be Different Than You Think	117
Universal Spiritual Truth #7: Hold No Emotional Violence	137
Universal Spiritual Truth #8: As Within, So Without	155
PART 3 Rebirth	**169**
Universal Spiritual Truth #9: Knowledge of Self Is Knowledge of God	171
Universal Spiritual Truth #10: To Die to Our Human Self Is to Be Reborn	185
Universal Spiritual Truth #11: You Are Your Own Master	203
Universal Spiritual Truth #12: We Are the Creators	225
Universal Spiritual Truth #13: Nothing Is Impossible to You!	247
Universal Spiritual Truth #14: We Are Capable of Performing Miracles	265
Universal Spiritual Truth #15: We Are All Connected— One with God	291
Epilogue	309
The Evolution of Divine Intelligence	313
Endnotes	321

Glossary of Terms	337
References	343
Acknowledgments	355
About the Author	357
The Divine Intelligence Institute: A Brief History	359

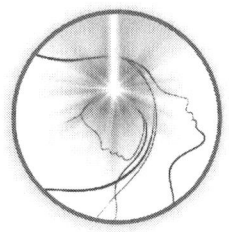

PREFACE

Two little words: the Creator. My most profound, inner transformation over the past four years and the moving force behind this second edition can be summarized in two little words—the Creator.

I believe people need, desire, and are ready for an alternative, expanded viewpoint of God with a more universal scope. Finding a common meaning or a universal concept for God is no easy feat though. When I first experienced the Divine Intelligence Process™ myself, I named my highest self: The Creator. I changed the subtitle of this edition to "Awaken the Creator Within" because "the Creator" is a more empowering way to think of God and, more importantly, the God within you. This is a descriptor that the religious, spiritual, and scientific minded among us can all relate to, and it is a term that underlies this book's core message.

By far, the question I am most commonly asked is: What is Divine Intelligence (DI)? DI does not belong to any religious ideology. Its focus is personal transformation and spiritual advancement. In its simplest terms, DI is an awareness of the unlimited, creative potential within you, and it infers a deep connection between our minds, our spirits, and the fundamental makeup of the Universe.

Science now shows that the Universe itself depends on our existence. We must face what is now scientific reality: we are the Creators. We are the Universe. We all originate from stars. The stars are real because we observe them. We are all one; we are all connected. Our lack of acceptance of those truths, I believe, perpetuates a division between us.

Both science and religion represent the same human efforts to explain the mysteries of this vast Universe we live in. In this new edition, quantum physics marries science and spirituality, showing us the true unity of our Universe. Scientific research continues to reveal extraordinary new discoveries about our Universe, our genes, and our brains, which validate not only our ability to create but also our unlimited potential.

Long seen as diametrically opposed to both religion and spirituality, science is now confirming the existence of a Divine Intelligence! Evidence from physicists, biologists, and neuroscientists, including how our minds create our world, supports belief in Divine Intelligence. Science, then, is producing spiritual elevation; there is overlap where there once was conflict. My intent is to bridge the chasm between spirituality and science, offering scientific evidence to suggest that we are all divine creators, and to connect us all in our collective consciousness.

As you will see, expanding your worldview beyond the traditional paradigm to include Divine Intelligence does not interfere with your belief in God; rather, it fortifies it. Reader testimonials about how the Divine Intelligence Process has changed their lives have filled my inbox since the book's first release. Their stories further validate how a process, based in science, can expand spiritual belief systems and guide people to the knowledge that they can create fulfilling lives they formerly never thought possible.

As you open to your own evolutionary journey, I will continue to work on mine—bringing the worlds of science and spirituality together. I do this with the knowledge that my own growth and spiritual evolution is the vehicle that brings me closer to the truth—the truth you as a reader will also uncover: The source of all creative energy lies within each and every one of us and is there waiting to be awakened—if you just look inward.

Dr. Jayne Gardner

June 2017

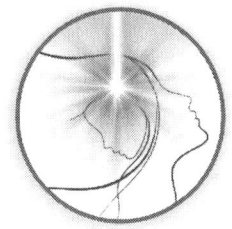

INTRODUCTION

Our Relationship with Ourselves Is the Gateway to Our Relationship with the Divine

Science without religion is lame, religion without science is blind.
--Albert Einstein

We are all divine. This realization changed my life, and it will change yours: The source of all power lies within us. When we look within ourselves and accept that one truth, we can begin to create the limitless life we were meant to live. Awakening this divinity will change the way you see yourself; activating this divinity will change the way you view and create your world.

As a doctor of philosophy in counseling psychology, I have devoted the past three decades to the spiritual development of myself and others. Throughout my career as a psychotherapist, teacher, and spiritual life coach, I have witnessed amazing transformations that brought about a new or renewed sense of purpose and fulfillment. But that was not all. As people of all religious or non-religious backgrounds set off on their search for 'self' and changed their relationship with their self, they reported that their relationship with God had also evolved to a higher level; they began to connect with God in a new way. This book encompasses what I have learned so far on this fascinating, evolutionary journey.

The framework for this evolutionary process unfolds through the eyes of a seeker and his coach. "Dan's" story is based on true events. However, his character is a composite one; he is modeled on and adapted from real narratives to protect patient and client confidences. Dan represents the spiritual awakening that my clients have experienced. Through him, readers discover what the human spirit can achieve when we release limiting beliefs about ourselves and God and enter an unlimited mindset.

I term this inherent, unlimited mindset "Divine Intelligence." Traditionally, many of us have referred to this inner power as "God" yet, ironically, it is the traditional, dogmatic view of God that oftentimes holds us back from our personal spiritual awakening. When we see God as external to us, it dims our inner light. When we see God as someone or something as all powerful, we allow ourselves to become powerless victims. When we see God as a rewarder or punisher, as a supernatural power we call on for help or to absolve ourselves from personal responsibility, we are unable to see ourselves as creators of the lives we are destined to live. It is my ardent hope that you will open your hearts and minds to the possibilities.

Dan's story is everyone's story, including my own. Dan is typical of the many individuals who call me presenting a goal to achieve but who are ultimately looking for bigger answers to life's questions. They are usually in a state of flux and somewhat disconnected from themselves and God. They may or may not go to a church. They are often not able to accept the literal interpretation of their religion's dogma and beliefs. As young children, even while being mesmerized by the metaphorical truth of the stories they were being told, they might question whether any of them could really be true. They long for a way to genuinely believe in a loving, kind God, but they feel helpless and hopeless about ever experiencing or finding this kind of God. They want a spiritual life, but they don't know where to begin. They are willing to discipline themselves if needed, but they want their efforts to be meaningful and relate to their everyday lives. Where is God for people like this?

This book is for people who, like Dan, are unable to find a connection to an external God who limits and scares them—or even to an external God who loves them. It is for people who have almost given up their quest for a spiritual connection until they point their search inside. God doesn't step out of the clouds for these people; instead, they come to God through themselves. They come to realize that they are manifestations of God, and they must learn to recognize and develop the divine within themselves. When they do, the sky is the limit regarding their ability to create and manifest the life they seek.

And this book is for you! I chose authentic stories and the narrative format because I knew it would be more effective to show you rather than tell you how this remarkable self-discovery process works and what it can do for you. Resist the temptation to just read the story; interact with it instead. Write in the margins. Agree with me; disagree with me. Feel it. Pause at the end of each chapter to consider and articulate your own feelings and beliefs. Apply newly acquired knowledge to your own situation and arrive at your own realizations.

I authored this book, but you are the author of your life. The end of Dan's story marks the true beginning of your own.

A Process to Uncover your Divine Intelligence

Empowerment requires a game plan. People are eager to change but don't know how; I was once one of those people. I had never developed an inner spiritual guide, nor was I sourced from within. I had not yet discovered my true self, my own power, my own voice. To that end, I started having daily, honest conversations with my 'self' to reconnect with my inner voice and inner light. I eventually brought my thoughts, words and actions into alignment with my personal truths, values, and character.

And so can you. Everything begins with you. It all comes down to your relationship with your 'self.' You must commit to developing this relationship and make a conscious decision to awaken your Divine Intelligence. I will show you how.

The game plan that I created was a set of instructions and exercises to guide people *to* their inner light so they could then be guided *by* this inner light. I created a continuing conversation with one's highest self. *The Dialogues,* as they were known then, emerged in the early 1990s when I worked as a doctor in a major mental health facility in the field of counseling psychology. This environment became my laboratory for developing a process to make each of us the absolute authority in our own life and consciousness.

Psychologists call that having an *internal locus of control.* As I continue to evolve consciously, it has become the focus and intention of my life. **Locus of control** is the frame of reference for the extent to which individuals believe they can control their reactions to events that affect them. Generally speaking, a person with an external locus of control believes that fate or God controls his or her life; whereas a person with an internal locus of control believes that life is what we make of it.

I had earlier made this concept the focus of my dissertation study in graduate school. I now realize that the choices and events in my life were always pointing me toward the future discovery of a process to help people find and activate this creative power within them. I can now see that there was always a Divine Intelligence within me trying desperately to get my attention.

Over the past 35 years I have guided and empowered people who were looking for help with perplexing questions, solutions to personal crises, a path to achieve a goal, or simply, looking for "more" in their lives. Thousands of people have used my process to remove limiting beliefs and blocked emotions to get what they truly want. At the end of their self-discovery journeys, they found not only themselves but also a new sense of creative energy and an expanded view of God. Because of this revelation, *a Dialogue has become a gateway to accessing and activating the Creator;* thus, I began to refer to each movement forward toward our Divine Intelligence as *the Divine Intelligence Process*™ *(or the "DI Process,"* for short). I unveil that process to you, chapter by chapter, here.

Our View of God Determines Our Creative Capacity

I have realized that the question, "Do you believe in God?" is not simply a philosophical one. The answer has a far-reaching effect on an individual's morals, politics, behavior, and the extent to which they think they can change their lives or create the lives they want. I grew to understand that a person's view of God is at the center of how they view their world and how they behave in that world. Although I had not set out to learn this, I discovered that finding God is what people are really longing for.

I discovered that finding "God," or at least redefining "God," was what I was longing for, too. Like so many of my clients, I was driven to that realization by a personal crisis, a betrayal of epic proportion, that caused me to question everything that I knew about myself and about God.

Growing up as a baby boomer, I learned that girls were expected to be sweet and passive, to marry and bear children, and were directed along career paths leading to positions as secretaries, teachers, and nurses. Expectations were low and opportunities were limited. I learned that God was in control of everything. I was to worship God, let God be in charge, and always stay humble to him and his earthly servants. But I still questioned where God was and why there wasn't a female part to the Holy Trinity. The divine, unlimited part of me was in there somewhere fighting for survival.

Unfortunately, in those days, few believed that the divine existed within anyone, so the divine part of me was not acknowledged or encouraged to develop. Belief after limiting belief began to extinguish the light of the divine Creator within me, and my true nature became a prisoner to the earthly messages of powerlessness and limitation. I began to see heaven as far above me, waiting to be reached after my physical death. I had lost connection to the divine within me. I looked to others for clarity, understanding, and meaning in my life and relied on my external world to guide me. Yet, in its infinite power, the divine mind within me called to me and attracted experiences to me, both wonderful and less so, to help me regain my true self.

At a dark period in my life, I sought a booster shot in faith from an outside "authority" that I had been raised to trust, and I learned painful, life-altering lessons. In retrospect, however, the beauty of the betrayal was that it offered me an opportunity to develop my view of God as illustrated in this process and in this book. Looking within myself, I took God out of the sky and placed that authority in my own heart and mind. I decided that the only God I could ever find was the God inside me. With this realization that God was within me, I began to take responsibility for my own life. God knows it was time!

This crisis was the reason I began searching for a spiritual process for my personal growth. While I instinctively knew I needed to work on myself, I didn't yet know how, and it wasn't easy to anchor from within after being wired with such disempowering beliefs in my early childhood. At times, I could barely hear the divine voice within me because it was muffled by the voice created by my external conditioning. In the beginning, I could not hear a dialogue between my conditioned voice and my divine voice; it was a monologue with old rules wired into place. I soon realized that if I became still and listened with the intention of hearing the divine, a dialogue arose between these two voices. I needed a system or a process whereby I could rewire all these old, limiting beliefs into a web of infinite possibilities and internal strength. I then trained my brain to wire in new beliefs, conscious beliefs this time, to awaken this divine intelligence and put it in charge of my life.

Two of my most difficult life lessons, then, have been: How do I define God in a way that inspires me to live a great life; and how do I define God to inspire others to live a great life? I now know the need to find God is really about discovering and creating a fulfilling life of significance. In this new view of God offered by this book, God is embraced not as what we seek, but who we are.

A New View of God

Initially, it was just a hunch, or maybe a hope, that we all possessed intrinsic divinity. In my work with clients, I saw many things happen that made me wonder. This curiosity led me to study religions and spirituality as a way to validate that God was indeed within. With no formal education in this area, I read everything I could get my hands on about how our image of God had developed through the ages.

While I have found that most of my clients believe in God, their views of God diverge sharply. Some people visualize a man sitting on a throne in the sky who controls everything; this god is authoritative, judgmental and very much engaged in everyone's daily lives. This is the all-powerful God I was raised to believe in.

Some believe in a God who is highly engaged in everyone's lives but is loving and benevolent; this God is always there for them and awaits their call in their times of need. For others, God created the world, laid down the law, and will render judgment at the end of days, determining if eternity will be spent in heaven or hell. Some eschew organized religion but consider themselves "spiritual." Others lean partly or entirely toward a scientific explanation of the creation and sustenance of the Universe; they believe in, simply, a "higher power" or an "energy."

Albert Einstein, one of the greatest scientists of all time and a deeply spiritual individual, explained why God can be understood through the study of science in his book, *The World as I See It* (1956). He wrote extensively about the philosophy of religion and elucidated three types of views of God. All three views are cradled in varied emotions and needs we have as human beings on this earth. In the first two views, man created God in his image to satisfy his innate needs of belonging and love as well as to alleviate his fear of hunger, wild animals, physical illness or pain, and death. Man hoped to please this powerful figure for love and protection.

The second view of God is based on a moralistic idea of the creator. Again, created by man to give people rules and dogmas, this God is a comforter and protector, but mostly a rewarder and punisher so societal order prevails. Both of those views are based on an anthropomorphic character of God; God looks like you and me, only better and perfect. "The development from a religion of fear to moral religion," Einstein noted, "is a great step in peoples' lives" (p. 28). This second view marked a large step forward in the evolution of both society and religion.

Yet Einstein believed in a higher way to view God. He wrote, "Only individuals of exceptional endowments, and exceptionally high-minded communities, rise to any considerable extent above this level. But there is a third stage of religious experience which belongs to all of them, even though it is rarely found in a pure form: I shall call it cosmic religious feeling[1] (p. 28). This view of God is not a person but an order of nature, an intense feeling, a totality of existence hard to describe by someone who has never experienced it. It is an understanding that there is significant meaning in life, one where we are responsible for the movements which we make, at best trying to be in the flow of this greater unity. Thinking of God as a being who interferes with this perfect order is impossible to imagine when God is seen from this view.

Einstein states his "cosmic religious feeling" view of God is the strongest and the noblest driving force behind scientific research; thus, I use science in this book as an effort to help define this new, expanded version of God to the world for more to know. Some may consider my view of God as heretical. However, as Einstein has also said, "It is precisely among the heretics of every age that we find men who were filled with this highest kind of religious feeling and were in many cases regarded by their contemporaries as atheists, sometimes also as saints" (p. 29).

The Gnostic Gospels— The Source of Universal Spiritual Truths

Becoming more internally located, referred to above as developing an internal locus of control, is the main goal of spirituality and even some religions as I discovered through my intensive study of both. I found a sect, now called the Gnostics, who share my view that God is within each of us and that self-knowledge is the route to union with God. This early brand of Christianity also celebrates God as both Mother and Father, which aligns with my belief that God should embrace the unity of the masculine and feminine elements. Rising to prominence in the 2nd century, the Gnostics were ultimately denounced as heretical, like many early Christian sects, and killed for their belief in a divine spirit.

The Gnostic Gospels, also known as the Nag Hammadi Library, are a combination of the secret words of Jesus, some sayings known in the

---

[1] Arthur Schopenhauer, German Philosopher, is credited with initially proposing this idea, and Einstein was a proponent of it,

New Testament, poems and philosophies, and myths and stories. This collection of Gnostic Christian texts was found buried near the Egyptian town of Nag Hammadi in 1945, most likely hidden by ones who possessed these writings to avoid persecution. Modern scholarship into Gnosticism and early Christianity has been influenced by these texts.

The name "Gnostics" originates from the Greek word *gnosis*, meaning "knowledge," but the meaning is not what it sounds like. *Gnosis* is not so much about scientific or rational knowledge as about intuition or an inner knowing. The Gnostics supported the original Christian message that our purpose in life was awakening to this knowledge. In fact, the most common metaphor used in these newly found texts is sleep.

Elaine Pagels, renowned religion scholar, historian, and author of *The Gnostic Gospels (1979)*, an enlightening book about the history of early Christianity and the politics of divinity, translates *gnosis* as "insight" and says that gnosis "involves an intuitive process of knowing oneself" (p. xix). Even better for my purpose here, the Gnostics say that to know oneself is to know the secrets, the truths, of the Universe. According to Theodotus, a Gnostic teacher, a Gnostic is one who has come to understand "who we are, and what we have become; where we were…whither we are hastening; from what we are being released; what birth is, and what is rebirth" (as cited in Pagels, p. xix). This was what I needed—a way to find myself!

As I studied these gospels, I deemed the original insights uncovered in these manuscripts Universal Spiritual Truths. These fifteen truths formed the structure of my process of finding the internal locus of control that I so badly needed in my own life. Indeed, the truths in these gospels teach us not to depend on an outer authority to define our way of looking at God, but to seek within to discover the divine within ourselves. Studying these Gnostic truths over a period of nine years, I slowly created the DI Process with the goal of achieving this inner authority—actual steps to learning to dialogue with ourselves, and what I ultimately realized was the development of our Divine Intelligence.

I witnessed this powerful, creative energy gathering up inside me and others and gaining the momentum to eventually burst into the world. During these years of working on this process for people to be able to activate this Creator within them, I realized, like the Gnostics, that the search for God was really the search for self. Thus, the idea of our having Divine Intelligence emerged. While I now live by these spiritual principles, I want to emphasize that you don't have to be religious to grow spiritually; you must only be open to exploring and deepening your connection to your "self."

The Fifteen Universal Spiritual Truths

The fifteen Universal Spiritual Truths are based on the Gnostic Gospels; however, my intention is, and always has been, that this evolutionary, spiritual process is not to be associated with any one religion. Rather, it honors and includes all people and religions. In fact, I was delighted to find in my studies of Christianity in the Gnostic Gospels that this "heretical" view of Christianity actually matched many other religions' basic tenets and represented a universal spiritual theme. It was important to me that this process was not just for people steeped in the Christian religion, but it could be used by anyone of any religion or spirituality.

I wanted the DI Process to be a spiritual process, not a religious one. Indeed, the definition of religion itself is the worship of an outside entity. It is intended to be a joyous celebration of everyone's innate spiritual nature and power. We all exist in relationship with one another; everyone is connected in a larger consciousness that defies labels. Because one of the Universal Spiritual Truths is: "We are all one," uncovering the spirit within each of us holds forth the promise of eternal life for us all. Each chapter signifies a touchstone. When all fifteen truths are acknowledged and accepted, we find our ultimate truth—God is us.

A Way to Connect with God—
Spiritual Truths Grounded in Science

Being from a scientific background, I knew the process would need to be more than just a promise of "blue sky" to be credible—that it must be based on research and the hard-core world of scientific facts. Some airy-fairy, self-discovery process would not work for me, nor would it be credible for my clients. I was a well-educated scientist, and I wanted this process to be a blend of spirituality *and* science. Spirituality to me meant something very personal, and I needed something more objective, such as science, to balance it.

Many lonely and long hours of my time were spent combing through scientific research studies for support of my message that the Creator was within me. I found the connection I was looking for in the newly developing field of ***neuroscience***, which is an interdisciplinary field that includes psychology, biology, chemistry, and physics. It is the study of neurons, the spinal cord, and the brain: it is the flow of energy through the brain. Scientific study of the nervous system has revealed a wealth of knowledge about human thought, emotion, and behavior. Through neuroscience we learn that emotions are the prime movers of energy in the world and that the past must be dealt with for the brain to grow and evolve. This is where I would begin to find the truths of religion grounded in science; here I would find the common thread.

Now I could ask: What if science substantiated the idea that you could find God within? It may be hard to believe that science backs this concept, but in every chapter of this book, I introduce the Universal Spiritual Truth undergirding the process and then present scientific studies supporting the spirituality. Science does show that there is an intelligence inside each of us that is beyond our human capabilities—and when we are able to make this shift, to tap into this Divine Intelligence, we gain unlimited creative powers to overcome any external circumstances.

Neuroscience

But the question I asked myself was: Can I create a process that will speed up this evolution of our view of the Creator within? I found the answer in the latest findings in research about how the brain changes.

What does science say about the emergence of our inner intelligence, this Divine Intelligence within us? And, more importantly, can we physically change our minds, much less consciously mold the inside of our brains? For centuries, we have been told that rewiring is impossible—that once a neural pathway has been ingrained in the brain, it cannot be changed.

I went to graduate school in the 1980s, before the field of neuroscience had taken off, and my professors taught that the personality is "set" when we are young and that interventions can do little to change that. According to this long-held limiting belief, by the time we reach adulthood we are "set in our ways" and impervious to new ideas or behaviors. In other words, we were told the brain cannot be changed once it is hardwired with experience.

Within the last two decades, however, scientists have discovered that the brain does not become rigid over time but is always capable of creating new pathways and rerouting old ones. Scientists call this quality **neuroplasticity,** and they discovered this truth with new technology that allows them to observe the brain and "see" changes occurring there. Indeed, the latest neuroscience research is the beginning of the scientific proof that through the development of our mind, we are unlimited and can grow and change in infinite ways. This discovery from neuroscience is changing the future of the human race, as it implies that the source of all power really does lie within *us*.

Quantum Physics Shows We are Godlike

But it was a second discovery in a different field of science, **quantum physics**, that ignited my own Divine Intelligence to formulate the process demonstrated in this book. Through quantum physics, we see that the Universe is built around a beautiful pattern—a very complex yet simple pattern—and everything, including us and our human development, is about expansion. That is what this book is about—a process for expanding yourself and your worldview. We are the Creators of our reality, and quantum physics shows us that.

The Universe is Made of Energy Not Matter!
A Spiritual Universe!

When most people think of quantum physics, even if they find it interesting, they don't think it applies to their daily lives. They may know that wave/particle interactions and quantum entanglement mean we are dealing with atoms, part of the sub-atomic world, but they don't connect them to the real world we live in. But it seems quantum physics has invaded our real world! Today, though not widely publicized yet, research is showing us that the Universe is mental, not physical. Physicist Richard Conn Henry at Johns Hopkins University said it this way: "The universe is immaterial-mental and spiritual. Live, and enjoy!" (2005, p. 12).

Studies are showing that we cannot ignore quantum physics in the study of our real world: It is now accepted that our world is made up of energy—not tangible things like rocks, buildings, and people. Remove our minds from the pictures and there are no rocks nor people. Our very observation creates. We are the observer—the observer is the Creator. Everything is energy! Everything is created from our thoughts.

Scientists have learned that our brain, through the energy of our thoughts, is where all creation occurs. *Creation.* This is a word many people, including myself, associate with God, which is why, as indicated in the Preface, I chose to use the words "the Creator" when referencing God. Through the evolution of our brains, we are realizing that we, rather than some outside force, are the Creators of our world. This creative something within each of us, and it bears repeating, is Divine Intelligence.

To most of us, the idea of a Divine Intelligence has always referred to something outside ourselves. Yet we all have it, and it is always working to create; however, we don't always know how to consciously manage it to create what we want.

Maybe the reason these extraordinary new discoveries in science have not made the evening news is the fear they stir up in us—that we are, or could be, the masters of our own fate. Perhaps it is easier to depend on a God "out there" who does things to us rather than accept the reality: We all have this Divine Intelligence within us and can use it to co-create and be a strong presence in this world. We hear stories every day that prove to us that we still cannot even fathom what our brain can accomplish. Just look at what neuroscience is showing us! Indeed, we may tend to minimize our own power because we fear it.

We haven't been afraid to try to harness nuclear energy, or surgically replace the human heart, or fly to the moon, but because this concept of each of us having Divine Intelligence is so powerful and "out there," most people are afraid to take advantage of it—or maybe they just don't know how. In this book, you will learn how to activate this agency in you and be in control of your life in ways that seem miraculous, even godlike.

Are We God?

Our Universe is providing us with scientific evidence there is a God. We are discovering the Universe we live in has all the characteristics we normally ascribe to God: omnipotence, omnipresence, and omniscience.

If the divine is defined in spiritual terms by these three characteristics, then science now shows there is a divine entity out there in the form of the quantum field of energy in us, around us, and flowing through us. In the 19th century, quantum science revealed the presence of an all-pervasive background sea of quantum energy in the Universe known as the **Zero Point Field** (ZPF, or "the Field"). Since we know that we live inside the Zero Point Field, we exist in the middle of an unlimited amount of energy. Since the Field is unlimited in its energy and power, it is omnipotent.

In theological terms, we say that God is immanent in creation: He is active in all places at all times. If we are divine, how can "we" be everywhere at once? How can we be omnipresent? To declare the Universe is omnipresent, we would have to conclude the Universe is infinite and goes on forever. In 1929, Edwin Hubble, an American astronomer at The California Institute of Technology, made a critical discovery which eventually led to evidence our Universe is expanding. The Universe is omnipresent! We are the Universe!

How can we possess omniscience, or all knowledge in the Universe? Dr. David Bohm, regarded as one of the pre-eminent theoretical physicists of the twentieth century and a former associate of Einstein, proved mathematically that the Universe is a hologram. Because the Universe is a hologram, each part of the whole duplicates the whole. We are a part of that whole; therefore, we contain all the information of the whole Universe. Even the smallest piece of a hologram possesses all the information of the whole, somewhat like an acorn of an oak tree contains all the information it needs to replicate itself. Thus, the Universe is all knowing—omniscient. Since all information is stored in the Universe where we interact with it every day, it follows, then, that this unlimited amount of information is available to us at all times.

All powerful. Everywhere. All knowing. All ways. Always. We co-create with the Zero Point Field. We are creators: We are God. It seems audacious, iconoclastic even to admit that realization to ourselves; however, it is becoming increasingly more difficult to deny.

The mysteries of the world have mesmerized scientists since they first started trying to understand our natural world. So as much as this book is about discovering the power within us, it would be an error to ignore the obvious power within the physical world around us. Indeed, God is both.

The Divine Intelligence Process in Action

Great coaches inspire people to find their greatness. But coaches can be great only when they find a great person hungry and ready to awaken. "Dan" became one of those people for me. His seemingly simple story about finding a job provides the backdrop for *Divine Intelligence*. As he undertakes this self-discovery process, his story is meant to be both practical and inspiring. As powerful stories like Dan's unfolded in my office, I knew they needed to be told for what they symbolized: When we let go of the darkness of our past, the light of our Divine Intelligence is awakened.

My goal in coaching Dan through this process, as it is with all my clients, was to guide him to embrace himself as a powerful creator. Dan stumbled on many obstacles in pursuit of his greatness, the biggest one being his limited view of God. When he understood that he had the power within him to overcome his job loss, I knew he could then learn to persevere despite any outer challenges. My role was to keep him pointed inward to realize the power of his presence more and more each time I met with him in a coaching session. Watch as Dan emerges from the process with a radically different view of God.

Most of us, like Dan, are raised to look to the outside world for validation and approval in the form of career status, bank accounts, and achievements, as well as accolades from bosses and others. But what we all soon realize is that a job title or a big bank account balance can change quite quickly. Dan shows us that our definition of success may be too narrow. Yes, money and achievements are coveted goals in life. But what about meaning and purpose—personal awareness, spiritual power, or awakening to your highest self? What about being able to draw on our own strengths to surmount any obstacle? I knew that strengthening Dan from the inside out would help him find the answers regardless of future circumstances.

Our Next Evolutionary Step

For thousands of years, we have not known or been able to accept the truth: God is also found *inside* all people—every one of us! Our next evolutionary step is to harness the power of our spiritual minds. Our powerful potential, our Divine Intelligence, is lying dormant in each of us.

I understand that when I present God as an intelligence within, rather than or in addition to a being in the heavens, this idea will be met with controversy. But ideas that run counter to established beliefs are often met with resistance or dismissed as heretical. Examples abound. Copernicus and Galileo once dared to suggest that the Earth was not the center of the Universe, a departure from a long-held worldview. Aristotle (et al.) posited the Earth was round while ancients insisted it was hollow or square, which is the implication set forth in the Bible. Suffice it to say that pioneers in any field expect such controversy and are undeterred in the face of scientific evidence to the contrary. Seeing is believing.

New scientific research is both supporting and supplanting long-held beliefs. You no longer have to wrestle with opposing world views. Simply expand your own. What *Divine Intelligence* teaches us is: What we say and do matters—not just to us personally, but to our collective consciousness. We are all a work in progress.

In every person's life, opportunities of awakening to the truth of this inner Divine Intelligence are offered. Usually, through adverse circumstances or tragedy, we are given opportunities to self-examine, to look within for answers. Something happens, shaking us awake, and causes us to realize there is more going on in life than just an ordinary existence. This is evolution's way of moving us forward, of advancing our worldview. When we realize, as Dan does, that our own dark experiences make us stronger and lead us to new opportunities for growth, there is nothing we cannot transcend. We then stay open to the unlimited possibilities this inner intelligence can unveil for us.

I suggest that right now, by picking up this book and reading this sentence, you have been given the same invitation for awakening to your Divine Intelligence. Why wait for a crisis to wake you up? Awakening to this awareness dramatically enriches your life. You become a creator—not a reactor; you become more r*eflective* and less *reflexive.*

My hope is that Dan's journey through this self-discovery process will ignite a burning desire to discover the Divine Intelligence within you. As spirituality and science align in this process, you will see what is possible when we awaken to the divinity in us all. Indeed, when enough of us ignite the spark of Divine Intelligence within us, just as kindling wood slowly smolders into a bigger fire, we will set the world on fire with our passion and power.

Uncover and embrace the mystery, the power, the goodness, and the divinity we all have within. Join me in reclaiming the divine within you. As the message of this book spreads through the world and gains enough momentum, we can all, together, hasten the evolutionary pace of the human race.

Let's dare to evolve to our highest state. Let's decide to see God in everyone on this earth, including ourselves, and find heaven here on Earth. Let's all awaken the divine Creator within!

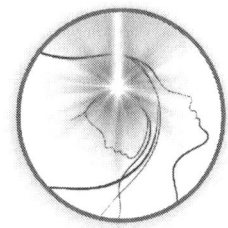

HOW DIVINE INTELLIGENCE IS ORGANIZED

Because *Divine Intelligence* appeals to a variety of audiences, the book's content is structured in such a way that readers can skip sections without losing sight of the Divine Intelligence Process (DI Process) itself. For example, icons clearly delineate the coaching, spirituality, and science sections for reading ease; these visual cues enable readers to quickly identify specific information as it relates or pertains directly to them and/or advance past those sections.

Both the book and the DI Process are organized into three parts to symbolize this transformative journey: Birth, Death, and Rebirth, representing who we are, who we have become, and our psychological rebirth as we leave the past behind, return to the spiritual nature of our origin, and begin our lives anew. Each part is sub-divided into chapters aligned with the fifteen Universal Spiritual Truths, the pathway to your Divine Intelligence. Each chapter, introduced by a quote from the Gnostic Gospels, is a step along this incredible journey and is structured around the following six parts:

Opening Narrative – The DI Process, placed within the context of a story, comes alive through each chapter's opening narrative. It illustrates and imparts the framework for this transformative process, allowing readers to experience the DI Process vicariously through Dan, who embodies this spiritual journey.

The Coach's Mindset – Readers experience the DI Process through the author's mindset. This is a section that psychologists, life coaches and spiritual life coaches particularly enjoy; others may choose to skip ahead.

The Spirituality – These Universal Spiritual Truths have been synthesized from spiritual and religious texts and the teachings of well-known spiritual leaders. Spiritual seekers will realize the truth as it applies to them.

The Science Supporting each Universal Spiritual Truth – These sections provide scientific research that validates both the existence of Divine Intelligence and the DI Process.

Summary of Concepts – A concise synopsis of key concepts summarizes chapter content.

Look Inward – Each chapter ends with an opportunity for readers to participate in and experience this spiritual journey through personal introspection. Pause here to allow time to reflect on the questions and note your answers in the space provided.

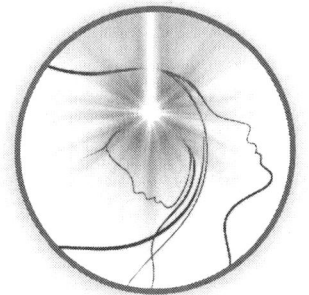

PART I

Birth

1

Universal Spiritual Truth #1:
There is God in Everyone

The kingdom of Heaven is within you and whoever knows himself shall find it. Know your self.
—Jesus, Oxyrhynchus manuscript

On the phone, Dan sounded troubled. "Jayne," he sighed, "I've been laid off. I've been looking for a job for three months. I'm almost at the end of my emergency savings, and I'm almost at the end of my rope. I've tried everything: networking, headhunters, the Internet. I just don't know what else to do." His voice caught as he said, "I need your help."

I first met Dan when he was a senior in college and enrolled in a course that I was teaching at the university. As a young man, Dan was passionately driven to succeed. I would often observe the young Dan leading gatherings of students in deep philosophical discussions of religion, spirituality, and the meaning of life. I remembered hearing him talk about whether there was a God and, if so, what "God" even meant. Later, as I watched him near graduation, his talks changed to his dream to eventually run his own company, and it would be a business that would make a difference in the world.

A few years after he graduated, Dan and I reconnected for a visit. He had been in the workforce for five years and had already been promoted to director of sales for a large, publicly-traded company. He was on a path to achieve that goal that he had set for himself in college.

We had worked together only a short time when Dan eventually was offered a position as a vice president of finance. Even after our working relationship ended, over the next few years, Dan kept me updated about his accomplishments.

On the job, he was gaining valuable experience that would help him in his quest to lead his own company. One day, when Dan was in his early thirties, he called to inform me he had just made the move to senior vice president, and I knew then Dan was on his way to achieving his ultimate goal. Dan was determined and savvy, and I looked forward to the day he would call me from his corner office in the building that was home to his own business.

Through the years, we had lost touch. Now, although Dan always sounded upbeat, I was surprised that in his mid-forties, Dan did not have that corner office, nor had he changed the world as I would have anticipated. But I assumed he was still doing well.

"Dan," I said slowly, "I'm not sure this is something we can do completely by phone. I'd like for you to come in."

"I'd like that, too," he said quickly. "Let's make an appointment."

The next Tuesday, I opened the door to a still-handsome and energetic Dan. Tall, dark-haired, and fit, Dan was just showing lines in his face, and gray barely touched the hair at his temples. He still had the look of a confident man until you looked closely into his blue eyes, where doubt played at the corners and in the deep lines between his eyebrows. These features belied the broad and even smile he gave as he took my hand firmly in his.

He slumped in the big leather chair, shrugged his shoulders, and began, "A funny thing happened to me on my way to owning and operating my own company." His smile was ironic and weak. I nodded for him to continue. I observed that the light I had always seen in his eyes was nearly extinguished amid the stressors of everyday life.

Dan continued, "You know, maybe that was just a pipe dream anyway." He looked out the window at the bright fall day for a few seconds. Then he leaned forward and rubbed his hands together. "I'm just not sure what's real any more. I thought I had it all—a good family, a nice home, a steady and successful career—everything you were supposed to want. We even appeared on the cover of our neighborhood magazine as 'The Family of Meadow Park' last year. I look at that picture now, and we do look perfect. But, Jayne, really, I haven't been happy in a long time. I'd been with this company for fifteen years, and I was just stuck. We spent everything I made. Margie stayed home with the kids, which I wanted, but that put all the financial responsibility on me.

"I gave up on the idea of owning my own business years ago. Margie was busy with the kids and all her women's club things. I needed the job I had whether I liked it or not. I didn't have time to chase some crazy business idea of mine. It seemed selfish. Well, truly, it seemed impossible. I regularly worked sixty-hour weeks. Once they brought in the new guy so close to my own age, I saw the chances for my advancement disappear like a magic act. And then for them to give me the boot...I didn't see that coming at all.

"I was doing everything right. My numbers were good; I did all they asked and more, but they are"—he used his hands in mock quotation marks— 'going in a different direction.' A different direction, what's that supposed to mean? One thing it means is that *my* life is going south. That's for sure. My boss is a complete idiot. This is all his doing. I can see his fingerprints all over this. He probably felt threatened by me."

Dan shook his head. "So now, here we are. Brad and Daniel are both in college, so you can imagine the expenses there. I can't tell them that they can't go back to school in the spring. And Thomas is a senior. He should be off to school next year, too, but, well..." Dan looked down. "Tommy is another story." Dan sat in silence for a minute or so.

When he looked up at me, Dan's eyes were earnestly pleading. "I feel so...so...abandoned. I've worked hard. I've lived right. I've been a company man. I've been a faithful Christian, a faithful husband and father, and this is what I get? I'm going to lose everything if I don't get a job. I can't lose everything, Jayne, I can't. It all depends on me.

"And don't think I haven't prayed to God for help. I have, but it's like...it's like praying to the ceiling, you know? The truth is: I haven't felt anything from God in a long time either. This stuff with Tommy...I'll get to that later, but I've been a good father, and God isn't answering any prayers there, either. Maybe God is just as much a fairy tale as my life has been. I don't know." Dan's despair filled the room. "Jayne," he asked. "Do you believe there's a God out there?"

I could hardly believe my ears. Dan was again talking about philosophy and God as he had as a student so many years ago. I wondered if he even remembered the earlier time in his student days when he had asked the same question.

"Well, tell me this. What would happen if you did find God?"

"I don't know. I mean, it sounds nice, the whole *heavenly Father* thing, someone to depend on, I guess. I would feel more direction, maybe. And then I might also feel more in control because, right now, I don't feel in control of anything. I've always wanted to be a leader, the kind of person who could impact others, make a difference. I don't think a job has ever done that for me. So maybe finding God, the real God, if it's out there, would help me find me and help me help others."

"So, Dan," I asked him, "In hiring me as your coach this time, what is your goal for our coaching engagement? What would be happening in your life if you were happy, content, and making a difference in people's lives?"

"Well, obviously, Jayne, first of all, I'd like to have a job. Maybe not just any job. If all went well, I would be working in just the right business with an opportunity to impact people's lives in a positive way."

Dan paused, and I let him have the silence necessary to decide what he really wanted from the coaching with me.

"I know you can help me find a job, but can you really help me find something bigger, too? As I said, I haven't been happy in a long time. Finding God, is that too much to ask for? A job *and* God?" Dan asked.

We had an agreement. I wrote down under his goals: *find a job*; *find God*. It was up to him to decide which would come first. It was up to me to ensure that he focused on both.

Coach's Mindset

The process begins as a person experiences the "anguish and terror" of the human condition—as if lost in a fog—not knowing where to go. —*The Gospel of Truth, from the New Testament Apocrypha found in the Nag Hammadi Library*

We find God by developing our own Divine Intelligence: the Creator within us. All of us are presented with opportunities to do our spiritual work at various times during our lives. A lot of times we don't realize that these challenges are opportunities to find God, and we miss our chance. People assume the answers they seek are to be found outside themselves. We go to solve the crisis itself, and we miss the divine message and, thus, lose the chance to do our spiritual work. Our very evolution depends on our making an important shift to an internal awareness that all crises come from within ourselves, as do all solutions.

Sometimes, earth-shattering transformations come from inspiring moments or uplifting experiences; however, mostly, transformation comes from serious illnesses, near-death experiences, or loss of loved ones—or, in this case, job loss. We can have positive experiences that give us these deep inner shifts, but more often than not, it is the negative experiences that change us.

Dan was indeed in a fog and without much hope, focusing on his negative thoughts. Working with people who have been laid off in a recession, I have realized the huge impact of a public rejection such as he'd experienced. I can understand completely how they lose connection to anything spiritual. Yet I also know, from my years of meeting people in the midst of change and crisis, that a dark tendency prevails in our consciousness that we must face: self-pity for the unfairness of life. One must step over this consciousness to move forward.

When Dan called me about coaching, he was in the same crisis situation as many of the people who come to me. (See "Differences Between Coaching and Therapy" in the Endnotes.) People seeking coaching at this stage are desperate to reach a goal and, like Dan, think they are doing everything in their power to achieve it. But still, somehow, the goal remains just beyond their grasp. Whatever was holding Dan back was also dampening his spirit. With each failed attempt at reaching it, the goal that Dan was so desperate for seemed less and less attainable.

Also, like most others who contact me, Dan seemed, on some level, to realize that a deeper spiritual issue was affecting his life and contributing to his current situation. Even from his college days, Dan has always had difficulty accepting the notion that God is an external force who controls people from afar, and Dan's lack of success in forging a connection with the spiritual world that was meaningful to him only dragged him down lower.

Somewhere along the years, Dan had convinced himself he would be okay with settling for less. But it was not the modified goal that sent up a red flag for me—it was the fear and desperation I heard in Dan's usually confident and upbeat voice. Dan had been laid off three months earlier; the recession had forced his company to eliminate his executive position entirely.

Dan was distraught—he had almost exhausted his emergency savings and was about to be forced to spend the money that he had set aside to use for his youngest child's education. He had not called me sooner because he had assumed that with his glowing credentials, extensive list of contacts, and honed networking skills, he would find a new role quickly. However, he had become disheartened by the lack of progress.

Unfortunately, Dan's plan was not going as he had hoped. He had been working his contacts and sending out résumés and had even received a few interviews in his first month of unemployment. But he told me that he had not gotten any promising leads in the past few months. He worried that his contacts might have forgotten him. The recruiters whom he spoke to told him that he would not likely make the same comfortable salary at a new job. The news he kept hearing about the recession was getting him down. Even his buddies stopped being sources of comfort and escape. They were always supportive, of course, but his relationship with them became strained as his lifestyle diverged further and further away from theirs.

Right now, Dan feels resentment, regret, and anger at the world for not cooperating with him and giving him what he wants. He feels abandoned and alone and does not know where to turn. He is a good, responsible man trying to live his life centered on God and focused on doing the right things. He is discouraged because he is trying so hard, and he feels things should be easier at this point in his life.

Dan is in pain. Dan is being given an opportunity to transform his life.

This is Dan's chance, finally, to return to his original dream in life—and to pick it up and let the unlimited possibilities of that dream lead him forward. His current life drama has been a red flag showing him where he is off course relative to one of the missions we are all put on this earth to accomplish: to recognize who we really are. He doesn't know it yet (and it's hard to see the opportunity when it is served up in a bucket of pain), but in time Dan will find that the problems he's going through are an invitation to find himself. Jalalud'din Rumi, the highly revered mystical poet whose timeless appeal transcends borders and religious labels, astutely observed eight centuries ago, "The wound is the place where the Light enters you."

Feeling abandoned, even by God, he had been trying to solve his problem all alone using the more traditional concept of God, a supreme being in the heavens. Dan thought of God as something external to himself and desperately needed another concept of God that he could turn to for help right now. Because coaches should always use a client's language, we used "God" rather than "Creator" throughout his sessions and the sharing of his story.

# The Spirituality
Universal Spiritual Truth #1:
There Is God in Everyone
Just how do we know God is within everyone?
Both science and religion support the idea that God, as a Divine Intelligence, is inside all of us. Science calls it light. Religions call it the Christ, Buddha, Krishna, or Brahma, and most spiritual figures are seen radiating light, if not directly, then symbolically. In early Christianity,

one of the major themes of the Gnostics was that one could discover the Divine within. Scriptures point to each of us having this light within us: "Ye are the light of the world. A city that is set on a hill cannot be hid. Neither do men light a candle and put it under a bushel, but on a candlestick: and it giveth light unto all that are in the house. Let your light shine before men, that they may see your good works and glorify your father which is in heaven" (Matthew 5:14–16, King James Version). Luke 17:20–21 states, "Now when He was asked by the Pharisees when the kingdom of God would come, He answered them and said, 'The kingdom of God does not come with observation; nor will they say, "See here!" or "See there!" For indeed, the kingdom of God is within you.'"

Jesus espoused the divine dimension in humans and believed in a repeatable Christ: "Ye therefore shall be perfect as your heavenly Father is perfect" (Matthew 5:48). He must have been convinced that humanity could do all he could do, and he must have been absolutely convinced of humanity's divine potential. But the question as to the divinity of man according to the Christian faith is best answered in Genesis 1:27, one of the most powerful statements in the Bible: "God created man in His own image, in the image of God created He him; male and female created He them." Indeed, it is our destiny to produce God's likeness just as precisely as Jesus did. Jesus is trying to teach us that any person may come to himself and release his innate divinity. This is the goal of everyone and of every experience we have in life. It is an opportunity to take that next step toward our inner God, our inner Creator.

The Hindus use a word of greeting that represents their belief in our divinity. The word *namaskar* means: "I salute the divinity in you," meaning everyone has the divine within. Hinduism affirms our divine potential: "Fix thy mind on Me, devote thyself to Me, sacrifice for Me, surrender to Me, make Me the object of thy aspirations and thou shalt assuredly become one with Me, Who am thine own Self" (Bhagavad Gita, chap. 9). Islam affirms our divine potential also: "I saw my Lord with the eye of the Heart. I said: 'Who are you?' He answered: 'You'" (Al-Hallaj, a Sufi text). Judaism states the same: "For I the Lord am your

God: You shall sanctify yourselves and be holy, For I am holy.... You shall be holy, for I am holy" (Leviticus 11:44–45).

Light and God

Most religions associate light with divinity or God. In the Bible, light is the most often used symbol for the activity of God. Many ancient cultures, such as the Egyptians, the Aztecs, and the Mayans, worshipped the sun for its radiance and life-giving powers. Indigenous African tribes describe God as shining brightly like the sun. The Islamic Qur'an teaches that "God is the light of the heavens and the earth" (Qur'an 24:35). In the Hebrew Bible, God is said to be "clothed in light" (Psalm 104:20; Baumann, 2006, p. 76). The holy book of Zohar teaches Kabbalists that the creator should be called "His Light" or the "Upper Light" (Baumann, 2006, p. 81). Hindus know their god, Brahma, as "the light of lights" (Baumann, 2006, p. 44). And Christians call Jesus "the light of the world" (Baumann, 2006, p. 29). The Gospel of Thomas, from the Gnostic Gospels, talks about light: "There is light within a man of light, and it lights up the whole world. If he does not shine, he is darkness" (Pagels, 1979, p. 120).

If, as many religious texts and teachings indicate, God is in us and is the spiritual equivalent of light, it follows that religions would also recognize the profound relationship between the light source and humankind. That is to say, if humans are connected to the energy and light via energy and light within, humans must also be connected to God via God within. As it turns out, they are.

The ancient Greeks associated the light in the body and mind with the highest and best part of the self, and they called the light *Christos*, which literally means "follower of Christ; bearing Christ inside" (Harpur, 2004, p. 12). The Christian Bible asks its followers, "Do you not know that you are the temple of God, and that the Spirit of God dwells in you?" (1 Corinthians 3:16). Consider that in the Bible the most often repeated symbol for the activity of God is light. The concepts called "God Within," the "inner light," and the "inward Christ" are central to most religions.

The differences between religions are as numerous and varied as the people who follow them. One theme is central to every major religion on Earth: that a godlike light within is an innate trait that was gifted to us the moment we were born. God is within us all, and this light will always be a powerful source of creative energy that we can use to create the world we want.

But what about spiritual leaders and philosophers down through the ages? Have any of them referred to the idea that God is on the inside? The title of Leo Tolstoy's book, *The Kingdom of God Is within You,* says it all, and he influenced the young Mahatma Gandhi's philosophy. God being on the inside also rang true to Ralph Waldo Emerson and David Thoreau, but it was Ernest Holmes, founder of Religious Science (also known as Science of Mind), who brought the idea into the modern world in the early twentieth century. His philosophy states that we cannot be separate from God and that every person is a direct manifestation of God. He and Charles Fillmore were two of the first New Thought leaders who knew that we were so close to God that we could create him through our thoughts. A more contemporary philosopher, Eric Butterworth, said: "We are human in expression but divine in creation and limitless in potentiality" (Butterworth, 1968, p. 46).

The Science

> Far from destroying God, science for the first time was proving His existence... –Lynne McTaggart, The Field

The World Around Us

The Gnostics believed in the internal path to God but acknowledged God is everywhere; science provides the proof. The answer to some of the mysteries of our external world lies in the scientific discovery of the Zero Point Field. Physicists, in their quest to discover the laws that govern the inner workings of matter and the Universe, began breaking the world down into smaller and smaller pieces. First they examined atoms, then molecules, then protons and electrons. As they continued to subdivide matter into smaller elements, scientists discovered something astonishing: No matter how many times they tried to divide energy out of the natural equation, some always remained. Initially, scientists were quick to discount this residual energy as an inconsequential remainder and saw fit to ignore it. Now, however, scientists recognize the remaining energy for what it is—proof of the existence of an infinite amount of energy of unknown origin, of God.

Nestled down in the mind of God, we are just a tiny fragment of the whole, but we are a mirror image of the whole. Our own unlimited form of energy, our *ipseity* (explained below), is just a part of a bigger field of energy called the Zero Point Field. The Zero Point Field theory contends that even seemingly empty space is constantly abuzz with a slight level of energy. The Zero Point Field is a repository for all energy fields, energy states, and particles; in essence, the Zero Point Field is a field of fields. Even more fascinating, the total energy within the Zero Point Field has been calculated, and it exceeds the total amount of energy that resides in all matter. Physicist Richard Feynman described this huge measurement as follows: "If it could be harnessed, the energy in a single cubic meter of the Field could boil all of the oceans of the world" (Talbot, 1991, p. 51).

Max Planck, considered a founding father of quantum physics, further proved that this empty space is bursting with activity. His experiments showed that empty space is actually a sea of motion, which he dubbed a "quantum sea of light." This sea of light, according to Planck, is kept in constant motion by the exchanges of energy that take place between all matter and living things. The Zero Point Field, then, is also a repository of light. To be within the Field is to be in the brightest place in the Universe. To be outside the Field, conversely, is to be in darkness. We are always a part of this Field, but the only thing that keeps us separate from it is our failure to recognize our relationship to the bigger whole. Our thoughts of separateness from God take us away from this unlimited energy source. All we must do is claim it.

Light is a Form of Energy

This "light within" that I refer to, then, is not only a spiritual metaphor but is also a literal, scientifically proven luminescence that exists deep inside us and all around us. Every cell in the human body has the light rays of the sun constantly streaming through them. These rays of light are called neutrinos. At the Sudbury Neutrino Observatory in Ontario,

Canada, scientists have shown that untold billions of solar neutrinos pervade the entire Universe, can pass through the Earth itself, and penetrate all substances, including lead. An unlimited number of these light rays pass through us creating our Light Frequency.

Everything including the human body has an electrical energy, a Light Frequency that can be measured right down to the cellular level. Scientists measure the degree of light in these neutrinos using a unit of measure called quantum, the smallest amount of any form of light or energy measure. A Quantum BioFeedback device can measure the finest amount of light energy in a person's body as well as determine what is blocking the light.

Theoretical biophysicist Fritz-Albert Popp was fascinated by light and its interplay with the body. He believed that light was the creator of all living systems and was first to postulate that there is light in the human body (Popp, 2006). Popp discovered that all living things continually emit a current of photons—from a few to hundreds—that keep us connected to each other (Popp, 2006). He theorized that human beings are essentially candles, sending out light as part of our very existence. When the light that we emit is bright, our connection to God and each other is strong; when our light is dim, our connection is weak.

This light in our body has been there from the beginning—in fact, we all started out as light. The energy or light that is us right now was created from the stars. Remember that periodic table we memorized in chemistry class? Every element on it, in fact, all organic matter containing carbon, was produced originally in the stars. The Universe was originally hydrogen and helium, and when the two elements fused together and became one helium molecule, two photons of light were released—producing the electromagnetic energy in our body right now. The carbon, nitrogen and oxygen atoms as well as other elements in our bodies were created in previous generations of stars 4.5 billion years ago!

What keeps us continually filled with light? In our solar system, the Earth has its own electrical heating system built in as the Sun alone releases five hundred million tons of hydrogen every second. That fusion continues perpetually and warms us here on Earth with bursts of electromagnetic energy into the Field. Thus, the source of our life is in the stars. As well-known astronomer Carl Sagan put it in *Cosmos*, "The nitrogen in our DNA, the calcium in our teeth, the iron in our blood, the carbon in our apple pies were made in the interiors of collapsing stars. We are made of starstuff" (1980, p. 190). Sagan's words are confirmation of what I stated earlier: *We* are the stars; *We* are the Universe!

As long as this light is shining, we are alive. Scientists have shown that when we are diseased, the light in our body is dimmed. This light is the energy within our body that we are in charge of to keep us alive. We all know on some level we have energy in our bodies. Think of what doctors do when your heart stops beating. In hopes of saving your life, they use "paddles" to shock your heart back into a regular rhythm. Physicists have proven we live in a field filled with electromagnetic energy. Each of us has a smaller field of energy surrounding our body. Both inside us and outside of us, an exchange of energy is always occurring.

When we die, our light returns to the Universe. Research conducted in 2017 by Dr. Stuart Hameroff, an American physicist, and Sir Roger Penrose, a mathematical physicist at Oxford University, suggests that our soul doesn't die; it just returns to the Universe. Together they have worked on a quantum theory of consciousness in which the soul is maintained in micro-tubules of the brain cells. Upon death, the human brain is, in fact, a biological computer, and our consciousness is a program run by the quantum computer located inside the brain which continues to exist after death. We transform from an energy in our genesis, to the form of a physical being, and then back to energy. Just as we were made from the stars, we return to the Universe upon death (Peace Quarters, 2017).

In this moment, at your birth, spirituality and science crisscross. The ancients, thousands of years ago, knew we were sourced in light even though they may not have had a scientific method to "prove" it. The Sanskrit word for birth star is "Nakshatra." They believed we each have a birth star, the star in direct alignment with you at the moment you were born—or the way they put it was—the first star the moon saw as you passed into this earthly realm. Just hearing these words takes you back to that divine moment of your birth when the light of you, the perfect bliss of you, was still intact.

Everything including the human body has an electrical energy, a Light Frequency that can be measured right down to the cellular level. Earlier in this chapter, I talked about that there are rays of light called neutrinos constantly flowing through our body. Scientists measure the degree of light in these neutrinos using a unit of measure called a quantum, the smallest amount of any form of light or energy measure. A Quantum BioFeedback device can measure the potential for light energy giving us information about what emotions may be blocking the light in a person's body.

Ipseity: The State of Mind of Light

New studies by Antoine Lutz, John Dunne, and Richard Davidson (Siegel, 2007) suggest that there is a state of mind that is clean and pure and unaffected by the outside world. They call this pure, clean experience *ipseity*. Ipseity is the essential or core experience beneath all the wiring that life brings us as we grow and mature. It could be the closest thing to our bright inner light. God is on the inside of us all in this untouched, pure part of the brain. It is our Divine Intelligence, the Creator within us, ready to be developed and used.

In the *Cambridge Handbook of Consciousness* (2007), Philip David Zelazo calls this part of our brain the most basic form of selfhood, the basic or minimum self. In the same book, Dan Zahavi calls it "the first person give-ness of an experience," and Antonio Damasio and Jaak Parksepp call it "self-consciousness." I call it the divine or "God part" of us. Of course, it is not really a "part" of the brain. In reality, it is a moment in time when we can pull back the curtain of all the experiences of our life, emotional reactions, and limiting beliefs, ignore the outside world and delve within to who we really are…the pure essence of the divine within us. It is our shining moment of truth. It could be called a state of luminosity, radiance, or high intensity.

Light Frequency

One of the properties of light is brightness or intensity. Our inner light can be measured in the form of our Light Frequency by measuring the amount of energy it carries. One way to think about this inner light, or source of energy, or inner Creator, is to see it driven by our thoughts and emotions.

Emotions are energy in movement; therefore, emotions are also the creators of our Light Frequency, or our brain wave patterns. Dr. David Hawkins (2002), an internationally known spiritual teacher on the subject of advanced spiritual states, has shown that emotions have different levels of power and has created a ladder of emotional energy (presented in Chapter 13); he has shown that your Light Frequency is determined by which emotion is most predominant in your state of mind.

For example, low frequency occurs when you feel shame or guilt or are worried or fearful about paying your bills. High frequency occurs when you feel grateful or when you look at a baby and feel love. High Light Frequency can shine brightly out in the world and attract good things. For example, if a person feels positive and confident that he will get a job, he is at a higher frequency and more likely to attract an offer. Remember, everything in the Universe is connected with everything else. Changing frequencies has a great effect on the world at large.

A high emotional level of energy results in a high form of light—therefore, the higher the Light Frequency and the stronger the connection to the Creator within us. The goal of the DI Process is to teach seekers to manage their energy and emotions, their inner divinity, so they can raise their Light Frequency. In Dan's case, once he has raised his Light Frequency, he can use his Divine Intelligence to create the job he wants. He is quite obviously in a low energy state, or Light Frequency, right now because he is in a low emotional state. As we work on increasing our Light Frequency, we will evolve to a higher level of personal power.

Summary of Concepts in Chapter 1

1. God is Light.
2. Light is in the human body.
3. Since light is in us, God is within everyone.
4. It is possible to connect to this light within our body for a source of energy.
5. The brighter or higher the intensity of light, the stronger our connection to our Divine Intelligence, or the Creator.
6. Our thoughts and feelings are the representation of light within our bodies. One way to measure light or energy within our bodies is to measure the potential Light Frequency of our thoughts and emotions.
7. Ipseity has been defined as a state of infinite possibilities, a pure awareness without limits—or a high Light Frequency.
8. As we work on developing our Divine Intelligence, we are increasing our brilliance and intensity of our light within and evolving toward a higher level of personal power.

Look Inward

Conscious Evolution: Our next evolutionary step is to develop this personal power and return to this sense of "I"-ness, our ipseity. I am using a metaphor of light to represent our Divine Intelligence. Spirituality has always seen God as light; now science is seeing the same thing. I am measuring the degree of light by Light Frequency. As we access our divine light, we will be able to not only return to our ipseity but build it into a luminous, Authentic Self. The brighter our light, the more access we have to our Divine Intelligence and the more we are evolving our uniqueness and brilliance as a person and can impact the evolution of the human race.

Whether you are atheist, agnostic, Gnostic, Jewish, Christian, Muslim, Buddhist, or another religion, we all have one thing in common: We have the ability to activate an unlimited power within us. The premise of this book is that God is expressed as your Divine Intelligence.

How do you view God? Here are some possible ways to view God that you may not have considered. Consider any that speak to you, but stay open and self-aware as to how you receive each of the following words. Does one of these concepts describing God sing to you? Do any of them turn you off? Just observe how you react to the words for now.

- A source of energy
- An inner light
- An inspiring thought
- A moving incident
- A feeling like love, hope, or peace
- A moment in time
- A power within yourself
- An inner intelligence
- Your intuition
- None of these speak to me

What is your concept of God?

2

Universal Spiritual Truth #2:
Few Will Accept the Invitation

These things are not openly spoken of, for not all people are ready for Gnosis [knowledge of self].
—Gnostic Christian master Ptolemy

I let Dan sit in silence for a moment. I think he was surprised by my next question. "Dan, you asked me earlier if I believe there's a God out there. What do you believe?"

He shrugged. "God's just not there for me right now. Besides, God helps those who help themselves, right? I just need to put my head down and make some things happen."

I smiled. "Yes, I think I can help you help yourself, but I want to go back to something you said earlier. You said that praying to God was like talking to the ceiling. What do you believe about God?"

Dan was puzzled. "Believe about religion? Well, I'm Methodist, and Margie is Catholic. We've raised the kids in the Catholic Church, but I've never converted. I go to Mass with the family, but honestly, I don't know what it all means."

"So do you think of God as mostly being in church?" I asked.

"I guess I haven't...well, it's kind of hard for me to admit, but I really haven't thought about it much lately. Like everything else in my life, God hasn't had the meaning it should. God has just been something I do on Sundays and someone I pray to when I'm in trouble." Dan looked at the floor. "I'm not much of a Christian, I guess. Another failure of mine, I'm afraid."

"I remember you as a student. You seemed to be very passionate about defining what God was to you. What has changed?"

Dan sighed. "You know, I think I've just gotten away from God. At times, in the past, I just remember so badly wanting to know what God was. I think because of my religious training, I've always tried to see him in a traditional sort of way, yet I always had my doubts. But I guess I have settled into seeing God just as my Sunday school teacher told me to: as a man up in heaven and running the world—the boss of the world."

"You see God as separate from you?"

"Huh? Well, sure. I mean, he's God. He's got a lot more to think about than me and my lousy job." Dan's voice had an edge.

"So you see God as in charge of you?"

"Oh, not really, I mean, I'm where I am because of my own mistakes. I'm sure of that. God has nothing to do with it." He leaned back, folded his arms, and looked at the ceiling. "Unless he's trying to punish me or something, and if that's the case, I probably deserve it."

"Dan," I said gently, "do you feel like God is punishing you?"

"Feels like it," Dan replied. After a few moments, though, he continued. "I grew up in the Methodist Church, like I said. I don't remember a time when I didn't believe in God, but I guess what I wired into my head was this idea of God as judge...as judging us for how good we are, how we live and behave. As a student taking the time to really think about my own thoughts, I found myself questioning all those old beliefs about God. As life went on, mostly I think I put God back in the sky because, as I said earlier, I've been a faithful husband and father, and I've always tried to do the right thing. When you look at my whole life, well, really, I've been pretty blessed. I have had the picture-perfect life and family. I have had a lot of success. I guess as long as things were going well, it was easy to believe in a traditional kind of father-like God. I hate to say it, but maybe I've been a fair-weather Christian." Dan uncrossed his arms. He looked uneasy. "Maybe over the years, I've abandoned that passion I had for trying to understand God…just given in to pressure."

"How important is it for you to find God, Dan?" I said.

"I want to feel God, Jayne. Deep down I know I want to know God and experience God, not just talk about it. I really do think it is important, too."

"Right now, let's work on developing you. I believe that the only thing you can control is you, so let's look within for some answers for you." I knew we were getting nowhere in just talking philosophically about God. I wanted to steer Dan into a place where he could attain empowerment for getting what he wanted in life, but I had to catch myself from putting my own wishes into the coaching. This was his life, and I had found out the hard way that when I thought I knew what was best for a client, it was trying too hard to get them to think my way. I checked my need to control.

"Developing me? You're losing me here, I'm afraid. I don't know what you mean. You're not speaking about some 'New Age' thing here, are you?" He shifted in his chair and chuckled.

"Dan, how would it be for you if you found yourself?" I asked him boldly. I knew it was what would ultimately help him get a job.

"Well, I'm sorry, but I just don't see where you are going with this 'finding yourself' thing." Dan pulled away.

The Dan I had known in the past would have been excited to start working on developing himself and would have immediately understood the connection of self-development to self-fulfillment and creating the life he wants. He must be under a huge amount of stress being unemployed, I realized.

We talked a little more, but our time went quickly. Dan did agree to meet again the next week. In the interim, he had a meeting with another headhunter and was hopeful that it would lead him to a job.

The next week, Dan arrived in a starched white shirt with some optimism that his meeting with the headhunter had gone well. The headhunter had several leads for him.

"Dan, I think that's great," I said. "I really support your efforts there. What could all this be telling you about your search for God?"

"The God thing?" Dan smiled. "I have thought about that a lot since our last session. You know, I've realized that I lost my youthful wish to understand God, and I have slipped back into my old idea of God being someone in charge of my life. I have gone back to seeing him as the old, bearded man in the sky. Doesn't exactly sound like the 'Almighty,' does it? And I don't think this view of God is working for me right now."

"What view of God would work for you?"

"Like I told you last week, Jayne, I'm not sure where all of this God stuff is going. I mean, if defining my view of God would create a job for me, I would do it in a second. I know I told you when we started working together that I wanted to find God, but right now, in this situation, I still think of God as a person who has control over me. If he has a job for me, I need for him to hand it over." His blue eyes were tired but sincere.

"Yes, that image of God is hard to change since you usually see that picture of a man sitting up in heaven used in art, in churches, and in the Bible," I said. "Dan, what would it take for you to believe in yourself right now even with all this going on?"

"Jayne, right now, I feel so scared I can't really think about anything other than money, and I feel so alone. It's not that Margie isn't supportive. She is. It's just…just…something's missing, is all. I know I need more than just a job. I know I want to find a higher meaning in my life, but let's be practical here; I still need a job."

Coach's Mindset

One of the reasons someone hires a coach is that she cannot seem to achieve a goal she is trying to reach. She is usually procrastinating and doing the same thing over and over again trying to get different results. A coach holds up a mirror so that the client can see herself. Most people are unable to see their blind spots unless they engage in the coaching process and are willing to self-examine.

The truth is, most of us avoid change if given an alternative. However, even when we do decide something needs to change, the finger is rarely pointed inward toward ourselves. The last thing most of us consider is self-change. We first go to changing others or external circumstances. This is why few of us accept the invitation, as few of us are willing to see ourselves as the change agent.

Dan knew that he needed to change or "help himself," but knowing and doing are two different things. He still thought that either I, his headhunter, or God would solve his problem for him, but neither his headhunter nor I had a magic wand to help him. No one outside himself did.

He also admits his view of God is the traditional one of "the boss of the world" and that he had kept God up in the sky. It is obvious that Dan has no relationship with this boss who is running the world other than as a victim of God's whims; furthermore, he sees God as judging him. He realizes that over the years, he has lost his passion about trying to understand God and has just gone with what others have told him about what God is and how God works.

Dan may decide he is not yet ready for change. It will be hard to access his Divine Intelligence with his current view of God. It will help if he eventually dares to examine his beliefs about God. Like most people in forming their beliefs about God, he accepts beliefs handed down through the generations and never questions them. In fact, many people find comfort in keeping the status quo. Dan states that he wishes he could be one of those people who just accepts what God is without doubting or questioning; however, he cannot.

Negative emotions like fear and depression can be terrifying at times and, for many, they can freeze us in our desperation and keep us in the same old repetitive patterns, thinking that what we have always done will work this time, too. In short, in this emotional state, our Light Frequency is very low. My wish for Dan is not that he be sheltered from things such as a job loss, but that he learns to be fearless in facing them.

My job as a coach is to hold a space for Dan, knowing that he has the ability to delve inside and access his Divine Intelligence. I knew he was about something bigger than he was showing right now. Because I had known him in his early college years, I knew that his openness and receptivity to new ideas to change was very high. As his coach, I could see the Divine Intelligence inside him quite clearly, even though it was still hidden from him. But he still had choices. He would have to be the one to uncover it. I remembered the passionate, young man eager to make his mark on the world. I just knew that somewhere along the way, this Dan must have been buried by all the demands of the outside world.

 The Spirituality
Universal Spiritual Truth #2:
Few Will Accept the Invitation

The Gnostics themselves admitted that the discipline of spiritual development would only appeal to a few. Maybe this is one reason they didn't survive the third century— Gnosticism did not lend itself to a mass religion at the time. Most people could not read nor write, so how could they spend all day studying the divine? The question is: Are we ready to devote the time necessary today to discover the divine within us? Obviously, a process like Dan is embarking upon is going to take time and effort.

We have within ourselves the potential for great insight, but most times we ignore it. The struggle for connection to this insight can be a solitary, difficult process, as internal resistance is usually strong. Christ declared that when he came into the world: "I found them drunk; I found none of them thirsty. And my soul became afflicted for the sons of men, because they are blind in their hearts and do not have sight…" (Gospel of Thomas 38.23–29, NHL 121).

He saw the resistance to awakening as the desire to sleep or to be drunk, or, as we would say, to be unconscious. Spirituality itself is about willingness to look inside. As Buddha said: "Just as there are few pleasant parks and lakes, but many dense thickets and inaccessible mountains, so are there few beings who will be reborn among men" (Anguttara Nikaya 1.190). It seems self-discovery must involve inner turmoil.

In spiritual language, when we are facing something very scary and unpleasant, we may take the attitude, "It's God's will that this happened to me, and I will leave it with God as to the outcome." This approach may feel good in the short term, but it does not open us up to the truth about what the event could show us. It merely sweeps it under the rug, where we breathe the dust until we decide to clean up our mess. This is known as *spiritual bypass*.

It is difficult for all of us to see our challenges as opportunities to grow; however, we will keep being offered the same invitation in different-colored envelopes until we open one of them and read what it invites us to do. To evolve, our job is to increase our own inner strength so that outside occurrences will not dim our light.

Dan is having a hard time relating his job loss to a bigger spiritual issue. Everything we face in life, especially challenges filled with a high charge of emotion, is meant to help us grow spiritually and evolve to a higher level. From my experience, few people want to look at this way of solving problems until they have tried everything else. Most of us Westerners want a quick fix and fail to see a crisis as the bigger invitation to grow.

In the model about change included later in this chapter, I present a new way to approach change—by learning how to live in awareness and not having to suffer so much or expect change to be so painful. There is a better and easier way to evolve, and that comes when we decide to develop our Divine Intelligence.

# The Science

The Observer Effect
The development of our Divine Intelligence is about expanding our viewpoint, changing the way we observe what we are seeing and experiencing around us. "The observer" is science's name for the Creator. When we look at our lives from another perspective, as one who is observing our lives from the outside in, we are able to see the bigger picture. When we become aware of ourselves in this bigger view, we

experience a mental shift. From this viewpoint, we create more effortlessly and powerfully and meld into the omnipotent, unlimited power of the Universe.

In the years 1925 to 1927, Werner Heisenberg formulated his famous quantum uncertainty principle, which states that when someone attempts to observe a subatomic particle, his attention inevitably alters the state of that particle. During the same time in history, Niels Bohr clashed with Albert Einstein, believing that reality does not even exist independently of one's own observations. He said that atoms and all other particles do not possess definite positions and energies until they are measured in an experiment. Einstein rejected this theory and remained convinced until his death that this was only a stepping stone to a much-needed unity theory.

Yet the Observer Effect remains one of the most commonly taught interpretations of quantum physics. Physical systems generally do not have definite properties prior to being measured, and it is the act of measurement that affects the system, causing the set of probabilities to reduce to only one of the possible values at the time of the measurement. This feature is known as wave function collapse. Later to become a quantum physics law, it was not proven mathematically until many years later.

When we observe something, we change the energy state from a wave form to a particle form—just by looking at it. In the spiritual world, instead of attracting something, you notice it already exists in your reality, and when you put enough of your attention on it, it is uncovered in your own reality.

One qualification to note here: I present in this book that the Observer Effect demonstrates what you think about most comes about. I present that as a possibility in this book; however, the truth is that physicists don't know what it actually represents. It is a mathematical formulation I chose to use in this book as one way to view the Universe. In my gut, I feel, along with many physicists, it is a viable way to think of reality.

We are the observer. Your Authentic Self is your perception, the lens through which you look at this book. I show Dan how to notice the observer by teaching him a specific form of dialoguing, allowing him to observe his creative powers.

Real Evolution Requires Conscious Change

Just as science shows that there is a light within us—also known as our consciousness—it also shows us that few people really do accept the invitation to enlightenment and have not yet discovered the Divine Intelligence within them. David R. Hawkins, in his book *Power vs. Force (2002)*, demonstrates with kinesiological testing that only 15 percent of the world's population rises above a certain Light Frequency or consciousness level. This means that most people cannot rise above a state of fear, grief, apathy, or anger. Our inner light symbolizes our ability to be awake or conscious to how we are feeling and thinking. Most people live their lives in quiet desperation in unconscious ways, reacting to life instead of waking up to the awareness that they can choose the way they think and feel. As you will see as Dan continues through this process, one way to measure our ability to be conscious, or our Light Frequency, is how well we can hold high emotional states such as peace, love, and joy. Hawkins also shows that even though small in numbers, people who are high in consciousness or Light Frequency can counterbalance the other 85 percent who have not answered the call for spiritual growth and conscious evolution (p. 282).

Why is it so challenging to change and grow in a spiritual way? Why are we not in touch with this Divine Intelligence within us? The brain itself is always changing; it's a living, breathing entity. However, the brain is not necessarily evolving in a spiritual or conscious way. The brain has a negative bias and is constantly in movement to keep you alive and away from pain. Evolution, up until now, has existed to help us stay alive. Because the brain is built for survival, its main purpose is to scan the environment and check out what is happening, so it knows when to send you messages for safety and protection. If danger threatens, it will send a message, a new thought for protection. And if that danger keeps repeating itself, then the brain wires in a completely new belief for you. Once that belief gets in your brain in the form of a neural pathway, then change in the brain moves slowly because the brain is stubborn enough and careful enough not to change on just your whim.

Once it decides what is safe, the brain says, "Let's keep it this way." In some ways, it fears change as shaking up its way of looking out for you. Therefore, change comes slowly, and it is no wonder that it takes a crisis for the brain to even consider the prospect. And rightfully so, as there is an intelligence in the body wise enough to always seek well-being and stay away from capricious thoughts. After all, physical safety does have to be there for spiritual enlightenment to have a chance.

Our Consciousness:
The Conduit to Developing Our Divine Intelligence

To connect with God, we must expand our view of God to include our own being. God is not separate from us; we are, indeed, a part of a larger whole. In the past, we have placed God as an entity outside ourselves, sometimes thought of as a person or even a man sitting up in the sky ruling over us. As we shall see in later chapters, science now knows the Universe to be in complete unity, including us as part of this greater whole. This God within us is an invisible intelligence we can activate.

As we change our consciousness and understand God to be within us as well as around us, we can become aware of this Divine Intelligence and can put it in charge of the physical structure of our brains. Our brains will change and evolve much more quickly by acknowledging this presence. Let's look at how our physical brain has evolved so far.

Just as nature develops and changes in stages, so has the brain evolved over the years. Neuroscience studies the natural flow of information in the brain. I am going to explain how the brain operates and how we break it down into parts to understand it. This will help us understand how to develop our Divine Intelligence. An American physician and neuroscientist named Paul MacLean, in his book *The Triune Brain in Evolution* (1990), created the model of a triune brain, or a brain having three parts or layers. Some scientists think the triune brain model is an oversimplification of the most complex and complicated system in the Universe; however, its underlying evolutionary perspective is sound, and it serves our needs well in regard to the development of Divine Intelligence. Of course, the brain works as a unified system of parts, and saying that one part of the brain is where we think and another part is where we feel is an oversimplification. The parts of the brain are best understood as one single, unified mind, working together to create our Divine Intelligence. In this case, however, understanding each part can help us ultimately learn to manage our brain as a whole and become more self-aware. Later in the book, we will see how our brain itself is just a part of a bigger whole sometimes called *the mind of God.*

Simply put, the brain is divided into three regions: the visceral brain, the limbic system, and the neocortex. We now know that evolution of humans has occurred in layers in a top-down fashion, and the newer physical structures have surrounded and altered the original parts. Because these three regions are interrelated, their individual functions are not distinct or easy to separate. However, scientists have been able to define their theoretical roles in our lives with some accuracy:

1. The **visceral brain**, sometimes referred to as the *reptilian brain*, is the deepest structure of the brain and the first to originate, and it has evolved over the last five hundred million years. It is the enlargement of the top of the spinal cord or what has been called the *brain stem.* It is the seat of the basic survival patterns and is rooted in strong genetic tendencies. This part of the brain handles breathing, heart rate, and other basic bodily functions necessary for survival.

2. The **limbic system**, the second to arrive, has been called the *old mammalian brain.* This part of the brain responds to occurrences from our outside world in respect to memories and what those memories have taught us. It regulates emotions, is primarily responsible for integrating brain activity, and plays a crucial role in the formation of new neural pathways. Self-regulation appears to occur mostly in this region, which has been called the *seat of the emotions.* Here is the storehouse for intense brain reactions to trauma and the ingrained patterns, mental models, and old beliefs when we go on "autopilot." Here is the origin of early psychologists' thinking that our personalities are hardwired and incapable of being changed.

Think of these first two older core structures of the brain as similar to a person's liver or heart, in that they are organized less for original thought than for automatic reflexive action to keep the body safe and running properly.

3. The **neocortex**, also called the *prefrontal cortex* or *cerebral cortex*, is the "thinking" part of the brain. Because the brain was built over time, this part is the outermost part and the newest layer to arrive. The newer structures in the neocortex have encapsulated the older parts and can give feedback to the lower layers; this higher-functioning part of the brain can change or modulate the way in which the other parts operate.

This ability to control the other parts is why we can now say we have Divine Intelligence. It is where our ipseity lives. Indeed, ipseity, the "I"-ness and ability to have self-awareness, is the reason we have divine capabilities. It has been only in the last several million years that we have had this part of our brain. The neocortex controls a wide range of body and brain functions, including sensory perception, motor commands, spatial reasoning, conscious thought, and language. If this part of the brain had not emerged, we would not be any smarter than a bird, fish, or cat. When we learn to consciously control and manage all three parts of our brain, we are truly evolving consciously and spiritually growing, modeling the greatest spiritual minds.

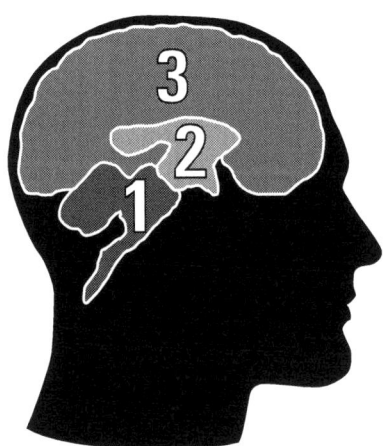

Our Divine Intelligence Is Concealed

As the human brain evolved and new structures appeared, it began to increase in size and to require new and more complex circuitry connections. When these new connections formed between the visceral brain and the neocortex, the limbic system (which is intertwined with both structures) was unwittingly affected and involved. At our present evolutionary stage, even though thoughts seem to be within our power, the neocortex defers to the limbic system in times of stress or crises. In Dan's case, because he is living mostly in a state of fear, he has trouble making decisions and maintaining his highest thinking abilities. Because his limbic brain is in control most of the time, he is not able to access his higher thinking skills. He is shut down to his innate Divine Intelligence. This is how we usually evolve unconsciously—through fear.

But as we will see, the neocortex has unlimited potential for development. It is divided into two hemispheres, each controlling the opposite side of the body and working in perfect harmony. This balance in the neocortex is responsible for such human distinctions as hope, spirituality, decision making, and willpower. But most important to our spiritual growth, activating our Divine Intelligence gives us more control over our lives through this management of our brains. We no longer have to be a slave to the other parts of the brain, which are reactive only. Here we have the power to override the top-down influences of past centuries of human wiring. It is possible to step around habitual thinking and use the neocortex to manage the other parts of the brain to evolve to a higher level of spirituality. You can be in charge of your brain.

Self-Directed Change

The triune brain model suggests that we are run by three brains, any of which could take control at any minute—unless we have learned to manage the brain ourselves. This is important to understand in light of the spiritual evolution of Divine Intelligence. Someone who has taken the time to awaken her inner intelligence will know which brain is running her and has the flexibility to shift to another part for control, if needed. In other words, at the highest evolutionary step, you are consciously running your own brain. Thus, our task for Dan and the purpose of this book is to facilitate our own evolution.

When we are totally aware of ourselves and our power, we are in our ipseity or our Divine Intelligence. This is an exciting and big evolutionary step—to be in charge of running our own brain. This amount of control over our brain is not attained without much internal work, as you will see as Dan goes through this process. Few people have learned to develop their Divine Intelligence enough to be able to control their brain. When this happens, they are called spiritual masters who have Divine Intelligence, like Christ, Buddha, and Muhammad. At this time in our evolutionary history, many more of us are taking steps in that direction. And, yes, it may take us many generations to become half of what the masters achieved, but we must begin our journey. It is what we are all here on Earth to accomplish. It is the goal of people who want to evolve to a higher level of spirituality.

The willingness to change underlies the ability to control your brain. When you are open and receptive to work on yourself, you can evolve to this high level of spirituality. Therefore, the goal is always self-directed change. As we all figure out somewhere along the path, we can only change ourselves. (See "Readiness for Change" in the Endnotes.)

Summary of Concepts in Chapter 2

1. We block our light (and, therefore, access to our Divine Intelligence) by resistance to change, addictions, denial and blame, and pent-up negative emotions.
2. We have the choice to ignore our divine potential or to claim it.
3. The evolution of the brain has occurred in three layers from the top down: the neocortex, the limbic system, and the visceral brain. Understanding the development of the brain helps us understand how our Divine Intelligence has evolved.
4. When the limbic system is in charge, we are no more than reactionary happenings living unconsciously and low in Divine Intelligence.
5. The neocortex allows us to access our Divine Intelligence.
6. It is possible to manage our emotions and put our neocortex in charge to balance all three parts of the brain; however, it requires a lot of internal work, and a willingness to grow spiritually must be present.

Look Inward

Conscious Evolution: To evolve consciously, you must be open and receptive to the idea that you can be in charge of your own evolutionary growth. Until you are willing to look within, your Divine Intelligence—your full potential—cannot emerge.

What invitation have you been issued lately that could be an invitation to grow and spiritually evolve?

How willing are you to look within for the solution?

3

Universal Spiritual Truth #3:
Everything Begins with You!

Abandon the search for God and the creation and other matters of similar sort. Look for him by taking yourself as the starting point. Learn who it is within you who makes everything his own and says, 'My God, my mind, my thought, my soul, my body.' Learn the sources of sorrow, joy, love, hate....If you carefully investigate these matters, you will find him in yourself.
—Hippolytus, *Refutationis Omnium Haeresium*

Our next meeting occurred by phone. Dan could not contain the excitement in his voice. "I have a job interview!" he exclaimed. "You know, I've been thinking about the things we've been talking about. I've been feeling more positive, more energized. I do feel more in charge, more my old self. When I first called you, I thought we'd talk about my career goals, but talking about all this spiritual stuff is really helping me. I'm putting out some positive vibes, and this spiritual stuff is paying off. I know I'm gonna nail this thing, Jayne. I can feel it. I'm going to get my life back on track."

I congratulated Dan, happy for him that his energy level was increasing a bit, but I had some concerns, too. People are capable of the great insight that Dan was exhibiting, but our conversation showed me that Dan's real focus was still on the job, not deep spiritual learning. I had to be okay if he was turning down the invitation to self-discover. At this point, Dan did not see the connection. I could still detect the underlying desperation for the job, and I could certainly understand the pressure he felt to support his family. We spoke about his preparation for the interview, and I encouraged him to really think about what he wanted, what would bring him genuine satisfaction and fulfillment.

I knew that Dan was capable of achieving his goals of starting up and running a company, but I sensed that something was holding him back. Of course, he had financial concerns. He did not want to tap into his retirement fund, and his savings were dwindling. I knew that these were some of the things propelling him toward just any old job, but I sensed that there was more, as well. I knew we needed to work at a deeper level or he would eventually end up right back at this same unsatisfied point later in his life. He would keep repeating the same pattern until he discovered what he was doing that was blocking his success.

When we spoke the next week, Dan was elated. "The interview could not have gone better," he glowed. "Really, the job fits right in line with my experience. Okay, it's not terribly exciting. But we talked for over two hours—always a good sign. I'm pumped. I think it's mine, although they won't make their decision until next week."

"How will this job get you to your dream of owning your own company?" I asked, hoping Dan remembered his goal of a job that would make a difference and bring him fulfillment.

"Jayne, it's a job!" Dan reacted quickly.

"You know, Dan," I said, "I am glad to see you had a successful job interview, but this brings up a red flag for me."

"What's that?"

"Well, I remember you from college. I remember your dreams of owning and running your own company. What would happen if you got back in touch with that higher part of yourself that is passionate about life and knows who he is and what he wants in life?" I asked.

"I can't hear that right now, Jayne. I am scared to death I won't be able to support my family. Panic—that is a better word for how I feel. I know you mentioned many years ago to me that you believed we have two parts in us, a human part and a divine part. Well I need that divine part to get me a job and quick. Anyway, I don't really have time for that mumbo-jumbo now with the pressure I am under."

"What is really going on here, Dan?" I was trying to get him to see the bigger picture.

Dan admitted: "Okay. I am probably settling for a job just like the one that made me so unhappy."

"What would your life be like if you didn't settle and got the right job?" I asked the same thing a different way.

There was a long pause on the other end of the line. "Umm, well, I know that we're talking about bigger things than just a job, but honestly, Jayne, I want the job maybe just because it is a job.

"While I'm struggling financially and careerwise, I just don't have that luxury," he admitted. "Can't it just be that this job is like the first step or something?"

I could hear the fear and desperation once again. "You know, Dan, I really am with you. I want you to get what you really want." In the back of my mind, at this point, I questioned whether Dan knew what he wanted. He seemed to just be focusing on what he didn't want: unemployment.

"I know that. And I'll admit that the job isn't perfect. It's not a dream job or anything. It will be a cut in pay—but it will pay. I'm not going into this with my eyes closed. I'm going to use this job to get myself in a position to explore what I want and even to do what I want eventually. I just need to get back out there in the working world earning money. It's been way too long."

The next time I answered Dan's call, I wasn't surprised by what he had to say. In a halting voice Dan said, "I didn't get the job." He waited for a few seconds. More softly, he continued, "I just don't know what went wrong. They couldn't even tell me, except to say that they had gone with the other candidate. I just don't get it. This was a step down for me, and I still didn't get it. I just can't believe it." He paused.

"There is no failure, Dan, only feedback." I gave him the hard truth even if it was in a trite saying. "Dan, what is the bigger message here about your life?" I knew it was hard to believe, but this rejection was just another invitation to grow. I also knew that Dan was not quite ready to hear my ideas about spiritual growth yet, and it was his choice whether he ever did or not. I had confidence that he would find a way to get to where he wanted to go—his way.

"Listen, you may be right about all that, but I can't talk any more about this. I'm sorry. But before I figure out the bigger purpose of my life, I have to pay my bills. It's not that I'm not interested in our deeper work or in some of the stuff we've been talking about. I need a break, is all, and a job. Remember, Jayne, I've got three kids and a wife and tuition and a mortgage…well, you know the crunch I'm in. I'll call you later." Dan hung up quickly. Dan was using his option to stay where he was in his evolutionary growth. He deserved that right. Yet I had spotted a leader, and I knew he was just resting for a moment. I just didn't know how long it would take him.

Dan phoned after the holidays. In an even voice he said, "Hi, Jayne. Listen, I'm sorry that I haven't called." He sighed. "I was just in such a bad state when we talked last that I thought I needed a break. But I'd like to come in again. Nothing much has changed jobwise, but a lot is going on. I'm still trying to get on track, and I just can't get anything done." He was silent.

"How can I best help you now, Dan?" I asked him.

"Jayne, I know I keep coming back to this, but I am still confused about what God is trying to tell me with this job loss. Can you help me figure that out? Should I just give up and let God take over?" Dan was trying hard to figure out this God thing.

I knew my job was to ask the hard questions: "For what purpose have you created this whole mess?" I could almost hear Dan swallow hard. I wondered if I was about to be re-hired or fired as a coach.

He thought about it for a while before he answered: "Wow, Jayne, you are really hitting a guy when he is down. Hmm…it's all about me, isn't it, Jayne? Me, Jayne, only me. Maybe I am ready to learn more about me."

"Dan," I said, "of course, I'd welcome the opportunity to see you again. In fact, I have an assignment you can begin before we talk next."

I was moving Dan into action, as I could tell he was ready. "I do think you are ready. The process you are about to experience is called the Divine Intelligence Process. I created the process to remove any blocks in your body covering up your Light Frequency. Regaining access to this energy potential will allow you to be more of a conscious creator of your life. I will e-mail you the first of twelve steps, called Dialogue One, with specific instructions on how to begin. You will need to follow the instructions very carefully to get the results you want, Dan."

"We are getting started, aren't we," Dan said. It was a statement, not a question. (See "Quantum BioFeedback device" in Endnotes.)

Coach's Mindset

I had no judgment to cast on Dan for turning away from this inner work at first. I just knew that the sooner he started on this journey, the quicker he would find the job of his spiritual calling, so I was excited when he finally accepted the invitation.

I was noticing that as Dan ran out of options and got more desperate, he became more open to looking within himself for answers. People have the answer within themselves. Until Dan accepted the invitation to start this self-discovery, I could do little more than watch him going in circles. Now, by accepting this invitation, he was taking responsibility for his life. This step has to happen before he has any chance of activating his Divine Intelligence.

Dan is taking an essential step forward by taking personal responsibility for his own actions. He is no different from anyone else. He wanted the fastest way to get out of his misery, and no one can blame him! But now he has realized that doing the same old thing over and over again is getting him nowhere. With a commitment to follow the implicit instructions written in The Dialogues, to which I introduced him, he is taking responsibility for the mess he is currently experiencing in his life by becoming more conscious of his thoughts and feelings.

The traditional view of God might have told Dan to give up his power or surrender to a God that is outside him or espoused that old theory that God is testing him. Dan may be testing himself in order to grow, but no one is doing anything to him. As Dan begins his personal dialoguing, he is searching for a source within himself for the power to create his dream. The only person he can change is himself, and as he works on changing his attitudes and beliefs through dialoguing, he is connecting to a higher power within himself. God may not be so much of an audible voice that will speak to Dan, but God will appear through the awareness of his thoughts and feelings.

Since the source of all power is within, the more we discover about ourselves, the more likely we will find a solution from within our own library of knowledge. Self-knowledge is the same as knowledge of God, the Creator. The purpose of this spiritual growth is to move the point of control in your life from outside to inside, to recognize your inner light and its potential for unlimited power. You are the one standing by the dimmer on the light switch, and you can reach out and turn it up or down.

As referenced in the Introduction, psychologists recognize this as a shift from an external locus of control to an internal locus of control. Spiritually and metaphorically speaking, this process is taking God out of the sky and moving God inside your heart to be available to you for power and energy when you need it. God is the power source inside you. Coaching is what helps you find it.

 The Spirituality
Universal Spiritual Truth #3: Everything Begins with You!

> Until one is committed, there is hesitancy, the chance to draw back, always ineffectiveness. Concerning all acts of initiative (and creation), there is one elementary truth the ignorance of which kills countless ideas and splendid plans: that the moment one definitely commits oneself, providence moves too. A whole stream of events issues from the decision, raising in one's favor all manner of unforeseen incidents, meetings and material assistance, which no man could have dreamt would have come his way. *–William Hutchinson Murray*

We will use our brain and how it works to understand and harness our Divine Intelligence. In reference to this inner light, Jesus says, "The lamp of the body is the mind" (Dialogue of the Savior 125.18–19, NHL 118). Silvanus, an early Christian Gnostic teacher, says, "Bring in your guide and teacher. The mind is the guide, but reason is the teacher....Live according to your mind....Acquire strength, for the mind is strong....Enlighten your mind....Light the lamp within you" (Teachings of Silvanus 85.24–106.14, NHL 347–356). This early Christian group believed divine nature is discovered within oneself. In the Gospel of Thomas, when the disciples asked Jesus to tell them how to become like him, he refused; he told them to discover their own hidden resources within and referred to this place within as "the pure light." In this way, he continually points the disciplines within toward their own self–discovery (Dialogue of the Savior 126.5–8, NHL 231).

Many religions share this theme of the divine mind. In Hinduism, for example, the sages said, "The spiritual aspirant controls his senses. He controls his mind. He gains lordship over the faculties of his higher intelligence. Then he becomes one with the Supreme One" (Taittiriya Upanishad 1:6.2). No religion has taken the quest for self-knowledge as seriously as Hinduism. They believe that by exploring the very depths of your own soul, you will get to know God personally.

 ## The Science

Since Nobel Prize-winning physicists have proven the physical world is made up of energy and that energy is always moving in and out of being in seconds, nothing really is solid—including us.

Energy is in us. The subatomic particles physicists speak of are in us. Our body is made up of systems like our circulatory, muscular and respiratory systems. These systems are made up of organs which are made up of tissues. Tissues are made of cells, and cells are made of molecules, which are made of atoms, which are made up of, yes, subatomic particles. And these subatomic particles are comprised of energy.

Even though it was not yet referred to as such, quantum physics could be said to have begun in 1864. James Clerk Maxwell (1831-1879) was the first scientist to postulate that there was a "field" of electromagnetic energy surrounding us that he called the Zero Point Field. As described earlier, according to science, this "field" is the empty space existing everywhere in the Universe, bursting with activity and potential energy and available to us for creative purposes. One way to capture this unlimited energy from the ZPF is to find enlightenment using our own little reservoir of energy in the form of our thoughts and emotions.

Emotions: Our Connection to Our Truth

Emotions are our major form of energy. An easy way to grasp the meaning of emotion is to divide it into two parts: e-motion. This division reveals the word *motion*, or action, which implies that emotions are energy in motion. When we allow ourselves to fully experience a wide range of emotions, such as joy, anger, love, sadness, and gratitude, we are able to keep emotions in motion. This expression of our emotions helps keep the three parts of our brain working together seamlessly. Authentic emotions are our connection to our truth, as well as our reality.

If this energy is not released and begins to pile up in our body, it can block us from the natural energy that exists in the natural ebb and flow of emotions in our body. It forces the emotional brain to take control and upsets our internal balance. Our lack of self-awareness of our thoughts and emotions keeps us from feeling and disconnects us from our major power source.

Why Dialoguing?

Dan will learn to dialogue rather than journaling or writing. To clarify what I mean by dialoguing, let's look at how it compares to other forms of personal writing.

Journaling: Journaling is writing about the outside world and its happenings. It can be writing down what happened in your day, as you would in a diary, or it can be writing down information about how to do something, making a list of things to do or reminders for the day.

Writing in a diary: Often we use diaries to write down our feelings about things. While this is similar to dialoguing in a free-form manner, the actual process of The Dialogues is very different. These Dialogues are focused on, and driven by, questions and self-discovery.

Dialoguing: Dialoguing is writing about your inside world of thoughts and emotions. Since the word *dialogue* means "two speakers," dialoguing means that at least two parts of you are available for talking. Dialoguing also has been shown to improve health by releasing the tension caused from the negative emotions. This release leaves a more positive mindset, giving the brain more mental clarity due to the integration of deep feelings. And that's just the beginning...

For Dan's specific dialoguing activities, I pulled details from relevant research conducted by a social psychologist, James Pennebaker. His research shows the many benefits of writing about emotional experiences—that dialoguing can improve physical, mental, and emotional health and can positively affect sleeping habits, work efficiency, and sociability. Dialoguing may start out staying in your head, but will progress to writing down more about your emotions, and that is what will impact spiritual growth the most (Pennebaker, 2004). The list of benefits goes on and on. Students make higher grades in the semester after dialoguing. Research has shown that dialoguing improves *working memory*—the term for one's general ability to think about complex tasks and stay focused. More research shows that when we are worrying about emotional issues or problems, we have less working memory, so writing can free working memory to be used on other challenges in our life, as well as better production at work (Klein & Boals, 2001). Lastly, social life can be enhanced. In one study, people who wrote talked more with others, laughed more easily, and used more positive emotions. Dialoguing made them better listeners and better friends (Pennebaker, 2004).

Writing Reduces the Stress of the Unemployed

Pennebaker conducted a fascinating experiment using dialoguing on middle-aged, unemployed men. They had been laid off from their high-income jobs and had been working for the same company for more than fifteen years. The control group wrote about how to better use their time, which is a usual approach on how to help someone get a job—that is, to get over the procrastination. The participants in the other group were told to dialogue, or write to themselves, about their deepest emotions and thoughts about losing their jobs. Eight months after writing, 52 percent of the emotional-writing group had new jobs, compared to only 20 percent of the participants who wrote about time management (Pennebaker, 1988).

Here was a group of successful men, like Dan, whose lives unexpectedly fell apart in a thirty-minute interview when HR told them to pack their things and leave the building. These men also had families to support. They were all dealing with the huge shame and humiliation of no longer being the breadwinners. Many of them had wives who had to get jobs to bring in income, too. These men could not talk about their feelings and did not want anyone to know those feelings, which, as we see in the research, intensifies the negative impact on them—both physically and mentally. But after dialoguing before going on job interviews, they found that when they went on those interviews they were less hostile than the group not writing daily.

By choosing to begin his spiritual growth and start his dialoguing, Dan will become more self-aware and be able to generate power from the inside. In uncovering the energy source of his emotions, he will be able to access his Divine Intelligence.

Summary of Concepts in Chapter 3

1. Our major form of energy is our emotions.
2. We develop our Divine Intelligence when we manage the ability to focus our emotions.
3. Becoming aware of our emotions is the first step to managing them.
4. We can become more powerful thinkers when we learn to manage our limbic system—our feelings.
5. Dialoguing is a method of exposing our inner energy to ourselves for the purpose of learning more about ourselves and increasing our energy level.

Look Inward

Conscious Evolution: Our evolutionary future lies in awakening our consciousness. Hindu sage Swami Muktananda says, "People of different religions never cease to fight. But think—is religion just another branch of the military?... The true religion is that in which one becomes aware of one's own Self. That Self is Consciousness, which nothing can surpass" (Johnsen, 2002, p. 149). This chapter introduces a way to wake up by becoming aware of our emotions. With this embracing of our emotions, we are taking our evolutionary future into our own hands.

Are you willing to accept 100 percent responsibility for everything that shows up in your life?

What emotions are a major form of energy in your life?

4

Universal Spiritual Truth #4:
What You Are Seeking Is Hidden within You

Recognize what is in your sight, and that which is hidden from you will become plain to you. For there is nothing hidden which will not become manifest.
—Gospel of Thomas

The Dan in my doorway looked completely different from the one I'd seen just a month ago. He was seriously thin, his face drawn, his dark hair not styled. In his T-shirt and jeans, he no longer bore a resemblance to Dan the confident executive, who would one day be at the helm of his own company. He looked like someone down on his luck, someone who scanned the want ads every day.

"We're living on my 401(k)," he began, sinking into the chair and looking down at his tennis shoes. "There was just no other way. I wasn't about to take the boys out of college. Margie can't part with the house. Neither can I, for that matter. We raised our family there. The doorway in the kitchen is notched with the boys' growth spurts through the years. I landscaped the yard myself, built the tree house…" He picked at an invisible string on the seam of the couch. Finally, he crossed his arms and looked at me. "I just got turned down for a midlevel position I could have done with my eyes closed." He shrugged. "They suggested that I 'dumb down' my résumé for the next opportunity."

"Okay, Dan. I can hear your dejection. But it only takes one job to be the right one! What if it all goes right this very next time? What if the stars do line up, and you get that right and perfect job?" I asked him, testing his ability to go to the positive with me. I had learned to never underestimate my clients.

Dan didn't say anything, but his lack of response said everything. The Dan I'd known years ago would have taken that question and run with it. He would have excitedly told me the vision he saw of himself in that corner office or pumped it up to something even grander. I was searching to uncover that part of Dan that could dream. Something was different now with Dan's energy level, as well as his spirit.

When he finally answered, he confirmed my suspicions that he had lost touch with himself: "Look, Jayne, a part of me has given up. I don't think being the CEO of my own company is possible anymore. I think I'm too old. I think there's too much water under the bridge. I have put that away and don't even want to risk thinking about what I really want for myself. It seems impossible right now, and I just need to knuckle down and accept where I am. That part of me you knew years ago…he is gone now. We just have to work with what we have now."

"What happened to that part of you? That part I used to know when nothing could hold you back. Where did he go?" Dan was buried under limits and fear and practicality. I have always felt we have two parts to us, a higher and a lower part. A long time ago, I decided to call the higher part in people the "authentic" self and the lower part, the part that can be changed, the "conditioned" self. The human part is our Conditioned Self, and the Authentic Self is our divine part. It was obvious that Dan's lower, human self (his Conditioned Self) was in charge right now.

"I really don't know. I see your point—I feel very different now than I did several years ago when you coached me and I moved up to the senior vice president job. I don't have the same drive or ambition. I would like that part back, but I have no idea what happened."

"What is obscuring that dream of yours?" I asked Dan.

"It's just me, Jayne. It's like I'm waiting for the burning bush to speak to me and tell me what to do. I need a clear message from God—one with fire would be good."

Dan and I laughed at the humor of his own desperation, but again it showed me that Dan was still looking to God *out there* to save him, which meant it would be hard to find his inner power. I had a suspicion that he was also thinking he had to please that God up there in the sky and didn't have a clue how to do it.

"No, really, when I have succeeded in the past, it has been like a small voice was inside me directing me to the right choices and telling me when to step out of my comfort zone. I would love to have that part of me back right now."

I was glad he wanted to find that part of him because it was a glimpse into his Divine Intelligence. I knew he had lost the spark—his mojo was missing. I knew it was time to remove the block that was hiding his spirit.

Our work together as we moved forward would certainly be about more than the job search. The light in Dan's eyes seemed to have gone out. I knew we had to go back and find out where he had lost that energy, where his Light Frequency had been diminished.

"Let's do something a little different today, if you don't mind," I began. "Let's see if we can find that more energetic part of you. But first, we need to define the part that is holding you back. Then we can step around it and reconnect to the real you, the one I first met when you were in college. Are you ready to look at the part of you that is holding you back?"

I swear that Dan looked at me like I was someone from another planet. He had this blank stare on his face, and his mouth twitched like he was about to laugh at me. Thank goodness he was not judgmental because his natural kindness overcame his desire to make fun of me. I admit that my philosophical, deep-thinking questions and intensity must appear a bit far out for most people.

"Huh?" he asked. I loved his transparency and knew that this would be one of his top potentials as he developed his Divine Intelligence.

"Well, what I was trying to say is that sometimes I wonder, Dan, if we don't have to face who we are *not* before we can be who we really are meant to be! In other words, are you ready to meet your dark side?" I was referring to what I called the opposite of a person's ipseity, the Conditioned Self, now.

"I'm in the dark, all right. I don't see how I could get much darker. I am willing to try if you feel it would help get me a job," Dan said honestly. He was still gently laughing at me. I think I even saw him roll his eyes.

Undeterred, I plowed right into the depth of it with him: "What is holding you back from believing in yourself? I have a hunch about how people develop negativity. I'd like to explore a little bit of your past. Are you up for that?" I was seeing that this was the moment that Dan might completely jump into the process.

"I'm not having much fun in the present," Dan mumbled.

"Now, Dan, this is up to you—whether we go into the past or not. Coaching doesn't usually explore the past; however, I think there is something to be gained from seeing how you got here. If you study how the brain works, you realize we cannot really avoid looking at how we are wired, as this belief system is what controls us and can hold us back from reaching our dreams. I'd like to examine some of your old beliefs that may be keeping you stuck. We can find these old beliefs by looking at some early memories of when you were growing up." I was starting him into the process, careful to get his permission first.

"What kind of memories?" Dan sounded suspicious.

"For example, share a memory about a time when you were a kid and something happened with you and your father," I requested.

Dan was just desperate enough to follow my lead or maybe too tired to protest. "When I was around eight, my older brother, John, and I were both really into baseball. One night before our games, my dad took us into the backyard so he could help us with our swings. John caught on quickly, and, assuming that I'd learned just as fast, we called it a night after only a few minutes of practice. The truth was that

I hadn't understood what Dad was teaching us. I was just too ashamed to admit that I couldn't learn as quickly as my brother.

"My dad was in the stands cheering me on at my game the following day. He was usually teaching or coaching his own teams during my games, so on those rare occasions when he could attend, I always hoped I'd be able to put on a good show for him. When it was my turn at bat, however, I had absolutely no confidence that I'd be able to swing the way Dad had tried to show me. I was so discouraged and nervous about disappointing him that I swung at a terrible pitch and missed entirely. After the helpless swing, I heard my dad say, 'I tried to teach him how to swing last night, and today he looks like he's never held a baseball bat!' Then I watched him leave the ballpark out of disappointment and anger. And the disappointment was in me!"

When Dan finished the story, he was silent for a minute, obviously still recalling the shame of that incident. When I waited, he went right into a second memory.

"My father was very busy with his job as a high school basketball coach when I was growing up, so I was raised primarily by my mother. She really was a great mom, and she was an almost constant source of security and love for my brother and me; however, like all mothers, she sometimes used guilt to control us. One day she told me that she was cooking a special meal for Dad since he had just been named Coach of the Year. I was quite young at the time and didn't realize how significant the award was to my father. Nevertheless, my mother told me to come home early that evening so we could celebrate with Dad.

"I liked to please my mother, so I rarely broke her rules, but on that particular spring day, I guess my boyhood got the best of me. As soon as I arrived home from school, my friend and I headed down to the creek to take advantage of the fleeting hours of daylight, and I ended up missing my father's dinner.

"When I finally made it home, Mom was furious. She told me I was 'selfish' and 'inconsiderate of others' needs.' I tried to explain myself to her, but that only upset her more. She lost her temper and pulled out the big guns: God would punish me for being a bad boy." Dan shook his index finger, mimicking his mother's threatening gesture.

Finally, Dan shared this story:

"Since Dad was the head coach of our high school basketball team, John and I finally got to start spending more time with him when we made varsity. My brother had always been better than me at everything we did—school, sports, dating; he excelled at it all. But basketball was different—I was really great at it. I was number one, and for the first time in my life, I was outshining my brother!

"When I was a junior and my brother was a senior, our team made it to the state championship. In the championship game, John had gotten into foul trouble early, and my dad had substituted me for my brother. I knew Dad was more confident in John than he was in me, and I'm sure he would have preferred to let John finish the game, but he had no choice.

"I knew that here was my chance to prove to my dad that I was as good as my brother, so I started trying to win the game on my own and look like a star. We were down two points as the final seconds were ticking off the game clock. I was dribbling down the court, about to take a shot that would tie the game, when all of a sudden, my father called a time-out. He was apparently frustrated with me for being a ball hog, but I was furious with him for stopping the momentum. I hurled the basketball down in frustration.

"My dad reacted to my anger, benched me for acting out, and put my brother back in the game to finish out the final seconds of the game. After the time-out, the team went back onto the court and my brother made a three-pointer to win the game while I watched from the bench. The next day, our hometown newspaper ran a picture of my father and my brother high-fiving on the court, along with a caption about the thrilling father-son victory. It was a great day of celebration—for them!" Dan crossed his arms, the rims of his eyes turning red.

"Dan," I said, slowly, "what do these stories say about you?"

"I haven't thought about these things for a long time—how I always felt like I was competing against John and never really winning—sort of like I was second best. And you know, I never really felt like my own needs were that important either. Whenever I tried to do anything for myself, I got in trouble. Again, it was like I was second best—I had to meet everyone else's needs before my own. But mostly, I was just always trying to please my dad."

"How do you think this impacts you today?" I asked.

"Oh, I think I've put it all behind me," he paused, "but the fact that you're asking makes me wonder." Dan thought for a minute. "You're asking if I still view myself as second best, I think, aren't you?"

"Well, yes," I replied. "That, and whether you still think you have to please others before pleasing yourself. I'm also thinking about your belief that God is always judging you, maybe the way you thought your father did. Dan, I wonder, how could your thoughts and beliefs about your biological father have influenced your beliefs about God?"

Dan replied, "In reality, I learned as a kid that God was like a father, so maybe I did merge the two without even realizing it. I certainly saw my father on Earth as being controlling and in charge, just like my view of God. And I am certainly not living up to the expectations of my heavenly Father or my earthly father."

I told Dan, "I think you have some limiting beliefs about God and other things that we ought to look at." I was guessing that his negative thoughts had accumulated over the years and were now totally in charge of Dan.

"Huh," Dan mused, "I've never thought of all of that. I've just been trying to do 'the right thing.' I think I've always wanted Dad's approval, and God's, and everyone else's, too…" He paused for several seconds. "I've thought this way for so long that I'm not even sure what I want any more. I thought getting a job would solve everything, but I can see myself settling. I know one thing: I am tired of trying to please everyone! Maybe I'm still being 'second best.' Maybe that's how I got to where I am."

"Yes, it could be," I said. "But let's go a different direction from that negativity that you just shared, Dan. Think about your past again, your growing-up years. This time, share with me as many positive, fun times you had as a child as you can remember." I was beginning to pull in information from what I knew about science, indicating the fact that memories hold the secret to finding our limiting beliefs that are holding us back. The literature shows that repeated emotional experiences will eventually be encoded into neural pathways in the brain as states of mind. These states of mind hold the key to uncovering our belief system.

"This is harder. I do remember baking things on holidays with my mom. This made me feel good, as John wasn't interested, and I felt I was Mom's favorite. One time, Jayne,"—Dan's face softened, and he leaned forward as if to tell me a secret— "when I was sick with a sore throat, my mom took me to the drugstore and told me to buy any coloring book I wanted! I mean, you have to know my mother's frugality to appreciate that! But that same day, I remember going home and my fever went back up. My mother took me in her arms, Jayne, and rocked me! I mean, I was around six or seven, a big boy by that time, and I will never forget how good that felt. I can still remember feeling my feet drag on the floor, but I didn't dare change positions as I was afraid she would stop. Then she tucked me in my bed and kissed me and told me she hoped I felt better when I woke up." Dan looked away for a minute, trying to recapture that moment in time.

"Dan, why do you think you remember those few moments in your life?" I asked.

Dan thought a moment and then said, "Well, I really don't know, as it was kind of a silly thing to remember. But maybe, I guess, it was because it never happened—I mean my mom was not a demonstrative kind of mother who hugged and kissed you all the time. In fact, now that I think about it, I really can't remember another time in my life when she showed love to me like that. I mean, I know my mother loved me and all…but my parents didn't go around telling you they loved you. I guess I remember that time she rocked me because it was so unusual, maybe?"

"Dan, this memory will be very helpful to us as we work out a new plan for how you think about yourself," I told him. "That memory is what we call a "Positive Anchor," a time when you felt high, positive emotion about something. This memory is especially powerful because I think you felt loved, and love is a very powerful emotion for wiring the brain, Dan. I want you to use this memory to help you stay in a higher frame of mind. You can always go back to that moment in time, concentrate on it a moment, and raise your energy level. A Positive

Anchor is like a tool you can use." I hoped I had explained this in a way Dan would appreciate and learn to use, but when I saw the look on Dan's face, I knew I had gone too far.

"Jayne, look, it was one second in time. Let's not get too carried away!" Dan's face had lost its softness and returned to the executive's face.

"Well, okay, so what else do you remember that was good?" I went with Dan's inclination to ignore the importance of the memory in which he felt loved by his mother.

"There were times I can remember of playing out in the backyard with Dad and my brother, fun times of running and yelling my heart out. And I also remember my buddies growing up, meeting them at the creek, and spending long summer days just dreaming up how to fight the enemy." Dan paused. "Jayne, I can remember lots of good times, but when you first asked me, the only memories that came up were the negative ones. And now, thinking about my childhood, I seem to remember the bad rather than the good. It is really bringing me down again."

"It is not uncommon that when a person is facing a crisis, the brain centers more on the negative than the positive—to protect you." I explained a little of neuroscience to Dan, knowing that right now he would hear cold, hard facts better than ideas about Positive Anchors. "The brain is built to survive, and if it senses danger in the form of stress, it goes into hyperdrive, kicking up all the fear it can to make sure you are ready. The brain is a good learner, so if by incident after incident it repeatedly learns the idea that being a "Pleaser" in life will get you off the hook, then with every new challenge, like this job loss, that wired-in message will come up to solve the problem."

"But is it possible for me to change that way of thinking?" Dan asked me.

"Yes, it takes some mental effort and focus, but we can revise and focus on anything that you really want. In fact, right now that will be our work—to help you raise your energy level by concentrating on more positive thoughts. It just takes some mental work. It's like going to the gym, Dan. You know how you have to do push-ups to build up muscles. Well, you are going to have to do some mental push-ups to build up a new mental muscle. That need-to-please groove in your brain has to be replaced with a new crease in your brain of believing that you can be number one."

"Yeah, but how? I think I have been this way forever." Dan's interest was hard to gauge.

"We can use your dialoguing—the writing we talked about earlier—as the starting place," I suggested. "If you could write each morning for twenty minutes, I think you could become more aware of these limiting beliefs we are uncovering. Then when you catch this negative thinking, make a mental note to go to a more positive thought. Like rewiring your brain.…Would you be willing to do that?" I was basing my suggestion on the research by James Pennebaker. As mentioned, his research had shown that when people are laid off, writing about the incident defuses the anger and resentment.

What neuroscientists discovered about the brain was that Dan would have trouble creating new neural pathways while he was so pulled down by his emotional state. In the brain, emotion trumps thoughts, so it would be necessary for Dan to get past his emotional state to focus on new thinking. I felt it would give him some hope to start the process now, however.

"But, Jayne, how in the world is that going to help me find a job?"

"If you try it," I said, "I think you'll quickly see the benefits. For one thing, I think it will help your mood. In addition, you'll become clearer about how your past impacts your present and about how your thinking influences your ability to attract the job you want. I'll be here to help you. Will you try it?" I asked Dan.

"Twenty minutes a day, every day. That seems like a lot of time to just write." Dan hesitated. "I guess I can give it a try, though. I mean, what else have I got to do?"

As Dan prepared to leave, I emailed him Dialogue 2, the next set of instructions on what to write about to begin the rewire process.

Coach's Mindset

After hearing Dan's stories, it was clear to me just how influential his family experiences, especially with his father, had been on him. When Dan was growing up, his interaction with his father was limited. It was rare for Dan's father to be at his games and activities, so when he was there it was very important to Dan that he do well. Early in his life, Dan had wired in the belief that he needed to please people to receive love, so in his young mind he had lost his father's love when he failed that day on the baseball field because he had displeased his father. Shame and humiliation are the strongest emotions for making sure we wire in a belief. Because of the negative bias of the brain, it works like a mother hen, making sure we learn how to avoid that situation again. From that day on, the belief that "I must work harder than everyone else and do exactly what I'm told to please other people and receive love" was deeply embedded in Dan's brain. Whenever he did something that he knew would displease someone, he felt less worthy of love. This set up a passive, negative view of life for Dan.

It seemed to Dan that his brother had pleased his father in a way Dan never felt he could. I knew that this is quite typical of secondborn children who are the same sex as the firstborn, especially if, as in Dan and John's case, there is less than a two-year age difference between the children. Naturally, the secondborn will always be developmentally behind the first and will constantly struggle to differentiate himself from his sibling.

Dan's father had been a big influence on him. His father was a good man, as Dan described him, but he had never dealt with any of his own "issues," so to speak. In his defense, he may not have had the opportunity, as he was invested in being the breadwinner; however, his imprint on Dan's belief system left Dan a victim.

We Equate Our Father with God When Forming Our Belief System

Why did I ask Dan to think of a memory with his father and not his mother? I used a memory involving his father to uncover a limiting belief because I knew his father was the breadwinner in the family, and Dan would have learned from him his beliefs about work and career. If his mother had been the primary breadwinner, I would have asked him about memories of his mother. But in most religions, God is referred to as a person and as our "Father," so fathers are very impacting on our belief systems. Children take things very literally until around the seventh year of life because their neocortex is still developing; therefore, it is quite common to associate the person God with your father. Dan was likely unaware he was doing this.

Dan's most predominant limiting belief is: "I am second best or I am not good enough." His relationship with God was like that of a father and son, and his image of God was compared to that of his biological father. Dan felt his father did not believe in him and that he could never live up to the expectations his father had for him. Thus, he felt he had little power to create or control how his life turned out. It was all up to God, and he thought that God had no faith in him. He wasn't good enough for God.

But these stories did more than reveal Dan's limiting beliefs to me; they also made his spiritual struggles more obvious. Dan created an image of God for himself based on his perception of his father and his mother's shame-based view of God. Even though he spent the first few years of his life learning Bible stories, singing hymns, and going to youth-group functions, Dan learned to see God as a distant, unreachable entity and never formed a relationship with "him" or felt anything for God other than a fear of earning "his" disapproval. Dan's experience in church and at home wired in perhaps the most limiting belief of all—that God is a person sitting up in the sky who sees him as a sinner and with whom he cannot actively engage, much less please.

Based on the stories Dan told me, I could begin to see the pattern of his limiting thinking, which was formed by Dan's early perception of his life. Even though they grew up in similar environments and shared DNA, Dan's brother, John, would most likely have experienced life very differently and would have formed different beliefs, which would result in different behavioral patterns. For instance, John might have seen their father as a more positive influence on his life than Dan did, which would have led him to form a more positive pattern. These patterns are what make us different and unique.

Dan was born into a fundamentalist, Christian family that went to church every Sunday, so Dan's malleable mind was imprinted early on with the beliefs that God was like a father that Jesus was the Son of

God and, therefore, the only man who had been or would be capable of harnessing the power of God. Dan had been told that no one (except God and Jesus) was divine. He was told that he could never atone for his sins but would need to have Jesus save him from his sins. This created limiting beliefs within, making him think at a very early age that God was not on his side. This limiting belief about the nature of God disconnected Dan from his inner source of light and intelligence, as well as belief in himself.

One certain thing was that Dan was living in a limited state of mind rather than the unlimited state of mind of someone who is connected to the divine source within him. Another thing I was sure of was that Dan had always had that God within him, even though he couldn't see it right now. I knew he needed to find that inner power to have the confidence to get a job.

Right now, Dan is about as far from a connection to God as we can get. I wanted to help him get closer to God by encouraging him to become more aware of himself first and the power he has within himself to find just the right job. But again, it is up to Dan.

 **The Spirituality**

Universal Spiritual Truth #4:
What You Are Seeking Is Hidden within You

When we are babies, our inner light shines brightly, and we operate at an incredibly high Light Frequency, which means we are still connected to our Divine Intelligence. As young children, we believe we can do and be anything we choose, and we really do have the potential within ourselves to turn our beliefs into realities. Our thoughts and emotions are not limited. We believe we can do anything. We are still close to our ipseity when we are young and can call on our imaginations and creativity quite easily—if we have not been layered with a lot of limiting beliefs early in life.

Most of the time, the messages that cause us to limit ourselves are directed at us from people whom we respect and love. Often, these messages are intended to protect us from mental and physical pain, to help us learn about ourselves, and to help us discover how we fit into the grand scheme of things. The three main sources of these messages are parents, teachers, and religious leaders. A father may laugh or get angry at his son for expressing his feelings. The son then learns that feelings aren't okay. As he moves through life, his willingness and ability to express his feelings will be inhibited. Parents hold the strongest influence over a child's belief system about himself. Because he had been taught to not express his feelings, dialoguing would be challenging at first for Dan.

Change the Collective Consciousness

So many of our beliefs are a collection of centuries of beliefs from the mindset of the world: Boys shouldn't cry; girls shouldn't get angry; God is a man; men are stronger than women; and so on. When we hear or are taught something repeatedly about ourselves, others, or God, a limiting belief eventually wires into our brains, and we become unconsciously attached to it and unintentionally recall it in similar situations where it is triggered. The idea eventually becomes self-fulfilling, and we learn to ignore our inner prompts. We begin to base our decisions in life on what the more powerful outside environment indicates we should do. By uncovering our early belief system, we now have the power to change it. This gives us increasingly more power over our circumstances and makes us producers of our lives, instead of victims.

The Evolution of Our Understanding of God

After reading the book *How God Changes Your Brain*, by Andrew Newberg and Mark Robert Waldman (2009), I understand more about how the evolution of our image of God mirrors the evolution of the physical structure of the brain, and how the evolution of our consciousness mirrors the evolution of our image of God. You must understand how the brain works to get this, so think back on the three parts of the brain presented earlier as the triune brain.

In historical times, we thought of God as punishing and authoritarian and felt fearful, putting our limbic system (feeling brain) more in charge than our neocortex (thinking brain). For example, we reacted to the environment with emotional responses. We felt we had no control over someone or something pushing our buttons and making us afraid, angry, sad, or guilty. As we developed more of a thinking brain, we realized we could choose how to respond rather than be a victim of circumstance. When we realize we can respond to our circumstances, we put our thinking brain in charge, giving us more power or control. When we do this, as we will see in later chapters, we activate the energy of God within us, our Divine Intelligence, even as we are changing and developing our physical brains.

As our image of God has evolved, so has our brain. Over time we began to think of God as more unconditionally loving and forgiving…or at least I hope we have. As we work hard at shifting to this new state of awareness, we will be able to think through our emotions to make good decisions for ourselves. We are maturing into powerful influencers and producers. The next step in our evolutionary cycle of the brain and God is to see God as an action we take, a thought we think, or a feeling we feel—as well as or instead of a concrete person sitting up in the sky. We all have a little spark of God inside us—but it ignites only if we choose to be responsible for our thoughts and feelings. In the past, we have said things like: "God gives us things to test us." "God kept me from doing that." "It was God's will." Well, the truth is that the God inside you may have been watching out for you, but it was not about some supernatural person taking control of you. We can use this as an excuse not to take responsibility for ourselves. In this book, whether Dan is conscious of it or not, he is moving toward understanding that his own thoughts and behaviors are the only things he can control. The only God we can ever know for sure is the one inside of us, and in most of us, this infinite power is unavailable because of the limiting beliefs about ourselves.

 The Science

The Biology of Divine Intelligence

Quantum physics impacted all sciences as it introduced the idea that everything visible and invisible is made of energy. This new physics spawned new laws about how the invisible world of energy works. These new laws of how energy works began to impact the science of biology and eventually have filtered down into the medical community and how we view our health.

There were many studies out there showing invisible forces affect biological regulation. For example, studies are showing us that the laws of quantum physics control a protein molecule's life-generating movements (Pophristic & Goodman, 2001). More studies reveal the manipulation of quantum properties of matter can influence the course of biochemical reactions (Schulten, 2000; Chergui 2006; Gaidos 2009). I found that energy research like this has been mostly ignored by scientists.

We now know that beliefs control our biology! In his groundbreaking book, *The Biology of Belief (2005)*, Bruce Lipton provides us with research study after study proving "the fully conscious mind trumps both nature and nurture" (p. 29). We cannot deny the mind and our belief system's control over our health and well-being. He breaks with all the past theories of genes controlling our destiny and lays out the scientific evidence to show you genes do not control biology. Dr. Lipton wrote, "While we cannot readily change the codes of our genetic blueprints, we can change our minds and in the process, switch the blueprints used to express our genetic potential" (p. 143). Our creative potential, then, is not limited by biological or genetic constraints.

Deepak Chopra, co-founder of The Chopra Center for Wellbeing, and Rudolph E. Tanzi, Director of Genetics and Aging Research at Massachusetts General Hospital, explain the importance of Lipton's new development in science in their book, *Super Genes: Unlock the Astonishing Power of Your DNA for Optimum Health and Well-Being* (2015). The bestselling duo refer to it as "self-directed biological transformation" (p. 181). "You are not simply the sum total of the genes you were born with," writes Chopra and Tanzi. "You are the user and controller of your genes, the author of your biological story. No prospect in self-care is more exciting" (book jacket). With this new research, we are no longer the victims of our DNA and the old "biology is destiny" paradigm is eroded.

Beliefs, therefore, like the ones we uncover in Dan's life now, have much more power and influence over our physical bodies and our health. But in an even broader way, Lipton suggests the idea that our beliefs create our lives. Consciousness is now known to impact our health as well as our future destiny or what we can create. In Dan's life, his beliefs bring down his energy level and he has no control over his future. It is scientifically supported that Dan's shaping events impacted his biology (Lipton, 2005).

For decades, medical science has believed that genes determined our biological destiny. Now the new genetics has changed that assumption forever. You will always have the genes you were born with, but genes are dynamic, responding to everything we think, say, and do. Suddenly they've become our strongest allies for personal transformation. When you make lifestyle choices that optimize how your genes behave, you can reach for a state of health and fulfillment undreamed of even a decade ago. The impact on prevention, immunity, diet, aging, and chronic disorders is unparalleled.

With these new developments in science, we can now say our minds can change our brains! Thus, beliefs actually carry more power than reality. Or the invisible world rules the visible world.

This shift in what controls our body leads us to ask the question: How does energy work in the human body? Energy starts to flow through the expression of our feelings. We have discussed and cited research on how our thoughts generate our environment. Now, in this Dialogue, we will see how our emotions assist our thoughts in carving out the pathways of our brains and creating our belief systems. Studying biology, we learn what we feel is just as important as what we believe; maybe, as Lipton suggests, they are inseparable.

How Divine Intelligence Is Covered Up

In effect, humans are born pure, in a divine or godly state of mind, much like what scientists call ipseity. Unlike every other organ in the body, the brain is not fully formed at birth. Some neural pathways already exist, but most of the neurons are not yet wired to complete circuits. We just have an infinite number of possible neurons available for wiring, so you can say that, in the beginning, the brain is unlimited and ready to be formed by experiences. It also is plastic, giving it the potential to grow during its lifetime. Because of the nature of the brain, however, the infant brain is extremely vulnerable to messages that can limit its creative potential.

Interactions with our caregivers influence us so profoundly because the brain is a living thing capable of growing and evolving. As a child develops and begins to perceive and internalize the world around her, thousands of neural pathways join to create a structure of basic beliefs and ideas that are based on the new information the child receives from interactions, experiences, and relationships. These experiences shape the brain. The typical child's brain can take in information about both the mental and emotional states of caregivers and will begin to wire itself based on the reactions it observes in authority figures. Developmental psychologist Lev Vygotsky determined that a child's internalization of experiences with parents creates "thought." This theory suggests that a person's thought process is formed by the relationships that the child builds with family members during the early years of her life.

In his book *The Developing Mind* (1999), child psychiatrist, educator, and author Daniel Siegel goes beyond the old science idea of nature/nurture. He shows how interpersonal relationships and experiences with family create the key connections in the brain. He presents a groundbreaking new theory that the development of the brain is influenced heavily by parents or caregivers: "A child's response to a parent's patterns can be described as a child's internalization of the parent. From a basic biological perspective, the child's neuronal system—the structure and function of the developing brain—is shaped by the parent's more mature brain. This occurs within emotional communication. The attunement of emotional states provides the joining that is essential for the developing brain to acquire the capacity to organize itself more autonomously as the child matures" (p. 278).

The family is the biggest influence on anyone's belief system because most people spend the majority of their early life with their family. Knowing this, you can understand the significance of the family atmosphere and its influence on our belief system. At specific times in our lives, beliefs are formed by events that have had significant influences on our brains. These beliefs and shaping events are stored in the brain in the form of memories. Have you ever wondered why you remember certain things and then forget other details of your life? Our brain teaches us to remember times when we were in distress to teach us survival lessons.

Unfortunately, as adults, we remember things through the eyes of that child whose brain was not fully developed and could not always reason properly. In the evolutionary cycle, the neocortex, the thinking brain, is the last layer to develop in childhood. According to Siegel, by the time we are two years old, the neocortex, which is responsible for the telling and interpretation of what happens to us, begins to develop. During this time, the brain is developing so rapidly that the cognitive functions may be less efficient (Casey et al., 2005). But even more important to Dan's creation of limiting beliefs (as we will see in the next few chapters) is new research showing that this same increase in brain growth is duplicated in adolescence. This is a second period of extreme growth in which a natural pruning of connections occurs— a use-it-or-lose-it reshaping occurs. Therefore, the brain continues to mature through the mid-twenties (Blakemore & Choudhury, 2006). Many of Dan's incidents with his father occurred in his teenage years. Even though the brain is wired very quickly in early childhood and the teenage years, more and more researchers are realizing that the brain continues to develop throughout our lives, and we continue to be vulnerable to externals.

Due to the power of the limbic brain over the neocortex in early development, many times a child's beliefs are based on emotions rather than logic. This problem leads to what psychologist Albert Ellis refers to as "irrational beliefs." These beliefs, according to Ellis, can distort reality, contain illogical ways of evaluating oneself and the world at large, and create extreme emotions that block a person from achieving his goals. The idea of being totally self-responsible and developing our Divine Intelligence is blocked until our mid-twenties because of this idea that our brain has not totally matured. Of course, becoming responsible and spiritually mature is a process continuing your entire life.

Memories Hold the Key to Our Belief System

Why did I have Dan tell me stories about his early life? It is a way of developing some perspective. Telling our life stories helps us make sense of ourselves, and research shows that it encourages brain integration (Siegel, 2011a, p. 71). What Dan and I had done successfully in just that one afternoon was to uncover what had been hidden away in his mind; having done so, we now began to see what was obscuring his Divine Intelligence. By doing this inner work, Dan can free himself of the past and be more able to be fully present. The goal is to make Dan the expert in his own personal history. Or as Siegel says, "Memory retrieval can be a memory modifier" (p. 72).

What the brain remembers has been shown to be related to emotion. Dr. Eric Kandall and his associates at the Columbia University College of Physicians and Surgeons have proved that memory processes are emotion-driven and locate unconscious thoughts. The memories are conscious, but our thinking about them has been hidden. That is why we can sometimes take our conscious memories and locate our "hot spots." For most of us, our earliest and oldest memories are highly emotion-laden ones, so emotions teach us what to remember and what to forget for protection and survival. Fear, just as much as love, can secure any moment as a "memory."

We now know that limiting beliefs are for protection. They are protecting us from things we thought were dangerous at the time they were wired in our brain. This is why dialoguing is so beneficial. As we write and rewrite our stories by dialoguing about them, reliving them, and seeing them in new ways, we become more receptive and open—and more able to look at ourselves with our thinking brain and rationality, eventually rewiring them. When we are defined by our old mental models and our old belief system, our brain is inflexible and has a hard time being in the present. Experience plays a primary role in stimulating neuronal connections. Failure to integrate experiences from childhood, if they go unnoticed or are forgotten and not processed, results in incoherence and a chaotic or inflexible brain. We cannot be clear about who we are or find our Divine Intelligence unless we rid ourselves of these old, limiting beliefs. The first step is to find them.

As you can see, Dan is having a hard time concentrating on staying in the present and focusing on getting a job. As he continues his dialoguing process, he will begin to be able to focus on the present more and be in control of what he thinks about and how his mind works.

Summary of Concepts in Chapter 4

1. We are born with divine potential.
2. The brain is not fully formed at birth.
3. Experiences in our lives begin to limit our thinking.
4. The family is the biggest influence on our brain.
5. Our father is frequently our basis for our view of God.
6. The neocortex begins to develop around age two, and our inner voice emerges.
7. Memories hold the code to the discovery of our belief system.

Look Inward

Conscious Evolution: As our brain matures, it is influenced by experiences as well as molded by the minds of our caregivers. For our own protection at the time, we wire in limiting beliefs that bury our Divine Intelligence. But as we mature, we no longer need some of these limits, and they start to hold us back. As we become ready to consciously evolve and uncover our Divine Intelligence, we are ready to release our limiting beliefs. These limiting beliefs dim our Divine Intelligence and make our influence less powerful.

What are your hidden limiting beliefs?

How could they be holding you back?

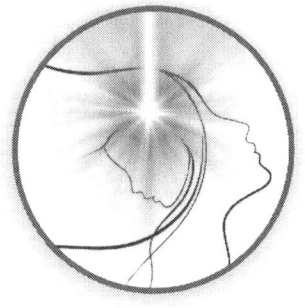

PART 2
———

Death

Sometimes a part of us must die
before a new part can come to life.

5

Universal Spiritual Truth #5:
Seek First Who You Are Not

If you bring forth what is within you, what you bring forth will save you. If you do not bring forth what is within you, what you do not bring forth will destroy you.
—Gospel of Thomas

"I've got to find a different recruiter," Dan stated flatly. "This guy is getting me nowhere fast. I call him every day, but to tell you the truth, I think he's dodging some of my calls. He's treating me as if I'm too old or some kind of loser, when I've actually had a pretty darn good career. No one has worked harder than I have." Dan's voice was agitated. "When I was senior VP, I was in the office before anyone else and out after everyone was long gone. I always took on extra duties, particularly when others fell behind. I'd pitch in and take up the slack. But where does that go on a résumé? And what's the payoff anyway? I gave that company everything and then some. I don't know what more I could have done then, and I don't know what more I can do now. In fact, I'm not even sure anymore that I was doing anything right… obviously not, huh? Maybe I'm not cut out for executive work after all. I don't know what I'm qualified for anymore. Maybe the recruiter sees me for what I am—that it is too late for me. Maybe there just isn't a job out there for me."

Dan's emotions were leading him. "Dan, I can hear your discouragement, but what if I told you there is a part of you that is limitless? If we could access it, you could truly have anything you wish or create anything (at least anything that is not harmful to others). I wonder, Dan, what would happen in your life if you could activate that part of yourself?" I was seeing if he could go along with this idea of his unlimited potential, his ipseity.

"What do you mean, limitless? I sure don't feel very limitless right now!" Dan said, indicating his low level of energy.

"Well, you know we have always wondered about the capabilities of us humans, and there are some pretty amazing stories out there of people overcoming what appeared to be human limitations. But science now shows us that there is a part of the brain that has unlimited potential."

"What do you mean? An unlimited part?" Dan looked up, quickly interested.

"Neuroscientists call it *ipseity*. It is a term they use to mean untouched by human imprint—pure and real," I explained to Dan. I had taken off my coaching hat and was a teacher now.

"Okay. I think I see where you are going—the limiting beliefs we uncovered about me last time we talked." Dan was sitting straight up in his chair, and I knew I was seeing this unlimited part of him beginning to come to life. "You mean there is something underneath there where I am untouched by the opinions of my parents or…or anybody?"

"…or teachers or religious ideas or even society in general. Think of the brain as having layers of coverings of neural pathways, that over a lifetime, wire over and cover up that pure, unbiased part of our brain where our spirit lies, where we believe we can do anything."

"It's funny you should say that, Jayne, because there was a time when I was a kid that I thought I *could* do anything. In fact, my brother encouraged me to jump off the roof of our porch with an umbrella, telling me he was sure I could fly! I guess I still had access to that ipseity part of me telling me I could do anything."

"Hum…" I decided to play along with Dan's story. "And I am afraid to ask, but how did that work out for you, Dan?"

"Jayne, I fell flat on my face and broke my jaw in several places." Dan was grinning at me. "No, really, I do remember feeling like I could do anything."

"That is exactly how we feel when our brain has not yet been wired with limiting beliefs," I told him.

"Are you saying that if I could tap into that part of me, I could get a job?" Dan was following right along with where I was going.

"Absolutely, Dan! Because whatever you think about comes about," I assured him. "I want to know if you are ready to begin the work to uncover that unlimited part in that brain of yours. Because there are certain steps of growth you can go through to access your unlimited potential."

"Jayne, as I have said before, I am not getting anywhere the way I'm going, so I'm up for just about anything short of a lobotomy—and it won't be long before I will tell you to go ahead with that. Or maybe that is what you have in mind with these parts of the brain you keep talking about." Dan's humor reassured me that he was still hanging in there and willing to make some changes. He had been through a lot, and I was glad to observe his resilience.

"Well, one of the first steps is about willingness. So are you saying you are willing to move into doing additional internal work?" I asked, just to hear his commitment.

When he nodded, I said, "The proof of your commitment is the action you take every day to do your dialoguing."

"Yes, I get that, Jayne! You have made it quite clear that to get a job, I need to write out my feelings every day," he said. "I am into that habit and actually find it quite rewarding, keeping my mindset more positive."

"Good job, Dan. That in itself is not easy and, at least in the beginning, takes a lot of self-discipline," I told him. "Now, let's move into the next Dialogue, where the potential for growth lies. This next step involves learning to accept yourself fully, unconditionally, without any self-judgment."

"I am ready, but for some reason it sounds like it will be really hard to do," Dan told me.

I wanted to show Dan how pervasive his preprogrammed, limited thinking really was, so I asked him if he would be willing to take a personality assessment to determine the best way to tackle his limiting beliefs and unlayer their influences on him. I was moving him into Dialogue 3.

People adopt any of several personality types based on the limiting beliefs in the particular assessment I was using. I used this personality assessment to help people describe the "theme" or pattern of their limited beliefs. Dan's eagerness to always satisfy everyone else's needs and let his own fall by the wayside were classic traits of one personality, a Pleaser. I was sure that once Dan was aware of it, he and I both could see how this part was holding him back. However, I felt that Dan needed to take the assessment rather than simply be told of his personality type so that he could gain a better understanding of the habits and emotions that his limiting beliefs had created for him. Dan agreed to the assessment, and within a few minutes I saw exactly the results I expected. Dan was, indeed, a Pleaser.

"Pleaser?" Dan asked. "What does that mean?"

"It's a part of you, what you call your personality, that always puts others ahead of yourself. When in the past have you done that?"

"Are you kidding?" Dan asked. "I do that all the time. I try to make others happy. Is something wrong with that? I'm just trying to help. I thought I was just being a good guy."

I said, "You put the needs of others before your own needs. It's just the way you operate. There's a part inside you that just wants others to be happy. You are willing to make others happy, even if it means that you make yourself unhappy. I remember your stories and memories about how hard you tried to please Mom and Dad."

Dan was quiet. "Yeah, I can certainly see that I am that way," he admitted.

"How is this part of you holding you back?" I asked him.

"I don't know."

"Well, then, how about if we just have a dialogue with that Pleaser part of you and see what it can tell us?" I asked.

"I'm not sure what you mean." Dan was cautious.

"All of us are wired into certain personalities by our experiences. These experiences create our belief systems. Our brains wire neural pathways that create certain pervasive behavioral patterns based on these beliefs that form into distinct personalities. We all develop a personality that we hope will meet our needs for love, approval, or power. This is a learned characteristic, rather than an inherent one. It's a constructed personality that gets wired in as we go along. After a while, it develops a life of its own. See what I mean?"

"Kind of," Dan conceded.

"Through all my years as a coach, I've seen that everyone, including you and me, has this part. Your personality part just happens to be in a pattern called the Pleaser. Other personality types that emerge as part of the Conditioned Self can be categorized as Doubters, Controllers, Critics, Perfectionists, and Avoiders. (See "The Conditioned-Self Chart" in Endnotes.)

I knew it was time to conduct a Conditioned-Self interview to emphasize the destructive impact this personality type had on Dan's life. After thirty-five years of experience in observing people, I had seen that we tend to use this negative part of us as a default mindset when we get stressed or in a crisis. Yet this "human-made" part of us is limited and not really our Authentic Self. The unwired part of us, our ipseity, is inherently unlimited in the amount of power and energy it can provide for us. I wanted to separate Dan's Conditioned Self from his Authentic Self so he could learn to differentiate between the two and consciously tap into his divine birthright.

"This is too weird, Jayne. I mean, you are pushing it with this one. I have gone along with a lot of your stuff, but really...a 'part' of me? I'm reminded of that movie years ago I saw called *Sybil,* where this lady had different parts of her that...well, trust me, it is unsettling to think of me being like her." Dan shook his head.

"Yes, it is true. Research shows that we all have different parts to us. Maybe another way to say it might be that we all have different roles in life. Like you are husband, a father, an executive....see what I mean?"

"Okay. You've calmed me down. I can listen now." Dan put his hand over his mouth to hide a smirk.

"Yes, well, there is a false or limited part of you—the exact opposite of the ipseity part that I told you about. Indulge me for a minute. The purpose of this is to help identify what you are *not* so that we can identify who you really *are*. Okay, Dan. Play along with me: Let me talk to that part—to your Pleaser. It will help us separate it out from your unlimited part."

Dan was quiet and then said, "What if there's nothing else in there, Jayne? What if it's all the Pleaser? Maybe that's all I've got in this brain of mine. I am not at all sure that the unlimited, pure, ipseity part of me is in there anymore." He laughed uncomfortably.

I could tell that Dan found talking to a "part" of himself uncomfortable and wanted to make a joke of it. I hoped he would eventually see a part of himself, a blind spot as to why he was fired from his last job or hadn't moved up faster in the business world.

"Remember what you told me about your father and your brother and how your mother reacted the time you did something for yourself instead of for your father? Just answer all of the questions as you were then, when you were in the act of pleasing others. Let's try it."

I began to converse with Dan's Pleaser. Like most people, Dan found it very awkward and "weird" at first, but this interview is the most life-changing experience I can ever provide. After experiencing their very human and limited personalities, clients realize that they have been led through their lives by a part of them that is unconscious and reactionary.

I set up this role play by asking Dan to move to a different chair in my office to symbolize he was to shift into a different part of himself. Then, when the interview was over, I would ask him to move back to the original chair to signal for him to return to his Authentic Self. Once he had settled into this new chair and state of mind, I began his Conditioned-Self interview.

Coach: *Tell me about yourself, Pleaser. I would like to get to know you better. What are your strongest beliefs?*

Dan gave me that eye roll again, and I thought I was going to lose him, but he finally answered.

Dan's Pleaser: *Well, I guess I may be a Pleaser. I do like to make other people happy. Jayne. This seems really weird…are you sure…?*

Coach: *Keep thinking in your Pleaser mind, Dan. Let's just see what will happen…. Pleaser, what are some of the things you believe about yourself that make you think you need to make other people happy? [In an aside to Dan, I nudged him to remember some of the limiting beliefs he had discovered in our earlier session when he brought up his childhood memories.]*

Dan's Pleaser: *Um, okay. Let me think. Based on our previous discussion about my early memories and how I formed my image of myself, I've realized that maybe, as a child, I felt like I needed to please. These ideas may have come from how I grew up and might still make me feel like I need to please people today. I guess I could say there are some things I've always thought were true: [He ticked them off on his fingers.]*

- *I must please others to be loved.*
- *I must work harder at everything I do to measure up.*
- *I should not speak up about my own needs, but always please others first.*
- *I am powerless. Second best is as good as it gets for me, so I must settle for that.*
- *I should not conflict with others.*

Coach: *Okay, Pleaser, I think I am beginning to understand you better. Can you give me an example of a time in your adult life that your pleasing behavior caused problems for Dan?*

Dan's Pleaser: *Actually yes, now that I think about it. Okay, Jayne, I am getting into this. Several months ago, my CEO called me in and told me that one of our major customers was not happy* with me. I had done everything I could to please this customer, and he had just gone over my head to complain. I was so shocked that you could have knocked me over with a feather. According to the CEO, I hadn't been getting the product to the customer as quickly as I had promised. He blamed this underperformance on my team and called me out for not being stronger with them. Then—I will never forget this—he mocked me by saying, "Poor Dan, can't be the bad guy."

I was embarrassed that the CEO had to correct the team I was supposed to be in charge of leading. I thought I had solved the problem several months ago, but I guess I hadn't made my expectations as a leader clear. I didn't want to be too tough on the team because I thought they'd been giving it their best effort. I even ended up taking on some of their work because I didn't want to create conflict by telling them to do better. Eventually this got out of hand, and they began to expect me to do some of their work for them. I was working ten to twelve hours a day and couldn't cover all the bases. The CEO had told me before to be a stronger leader, but when I look at it now, I see that I thought that keeping everyone happy and avoiding conflict meant I was a good leader.

COACH: *I am curious.... did you explain to your boss how hard you were working to please the customer?*

DAN'S PLEASER: *No. I just felt it was better to shut up and agree with him. Uh-oh...I guess I was being the Pleaser then, too.*

COACH: *How do you feel after something like that happens to you—when you try so hard to please people, but you can't seem to do so?*

DAN'S PLEASER: *I feel just like I did when I was eight years old and could never seem to please my father. The harder I tried, the less I succeeded.*

COACH: *Dan, I know we have talked about this, but describe it to me again. When in your past did you learn your limiting beliefs?*

DAN'S PLEASER: *I felt that I must always work hard to please people because I could never be as good or as loved as my brother. I learned to not speak up because it upset my mother. I learned to avoid conflict because my mother and father never argued in front of us, and my mother never stood up to my father about anything. Dad was in charge, and I felt very helpless to gain his approval as a young boy. Now that I hear myself talk, I think I've been using pleasing behavior to try to gain approval for pretty much my entire life.*

COACH: *What is the purpose of your pleasing behavior?*

DAN'S PLEASER: *I think I am trying to please to avoid having to tell others what I really feel. I learned early not to give people the real deal in what I say. I don't like to hurt others' feelings at all.*

COACH: *Are there other relationships in your life that have been negatively affected by the Pleaser?*

DAN'S PLEASER: *Well...yes, my relationship with my wife. I'm so hesitant to disagree with her that my kids say I let her run over me. She has never wanted to work outside the home, so I've never asked her to. She has done a great job in raising the kids—don't get me wrong—but now that they are almost grown and I am out of work, you'd think she would get a job to help out. I know she feels she isn't skilled at anything since she's been out of the job market for so long, but she's got a college degree in teaching. I am beginning to resent her for not reaching out to help me.*

COACH: *What would happen if you told her this?*

DAN'S PLEASER: *I haven't told her. [Dan stepped out of the role play and said with a smile: "I know it will not 'please' her."]*

COACH: *Usually, when a lot of resentment and negative emotions build up over the years, people have to use a distraction or even an addiction to keep the feelings from overwhelming them. What have you used to hold those feelings in?*

DAN'S PLEASER: *That may have something to do with why I worked so many late hours. I would rather stay at work than go home to hear her complain about me or the children. Now that I'm not working and don't have anywhere to go to escape the feelings, our relationship is getting worse.*

COACH: *How aware were you of those feelings of frustration before this interview?*

DAN'S PLEASER: *I don't think I was aware of them at all because I think I may have been hiding from them behind my relentless job search. I'm trying to avoid thinking about the fact that I don't really respect myself right now. I'm really discouraged and blame myself for the hard times my family and I are going through.*

COACH: *All your life, Dan, how have you been trying to please your dad?*

DAN'S PLEASER: *Absolutely. Except it turned into pleasing others like they were my dad, like my boss. I don't think I have ever felt like I could get my own needs met, Jayne.*

COACH: *What do you, the Pleaser, say to Dan in that inner dialogue to persuade him to keep pleasing people instead of being honest and upfront with them?*

DAN'S PLEASER: *I still think this is a weird way to talk, Jayne, like I actually have two parts of me. Okay, Jayne, I know that you psychologists think that we all have different parts, but is this part of me, the Pleaser, the same as the ego? Because I always tell myself (I mean Dan) that he won't measure up if he doesn't work hard. I tell him that it is important not to upset others or they won't like him. I tell him his own needs are not that important. I try to guess what others want or need from him and help him fulfill those wants and needs. I tell him that this is how to be successful. Huh. Now that I think about it, I talk to him a lot of the time in a negative way.*

To be perfectly blunt, Jayne, I doubt that shifting him into new beliefs will help him. I don't trust the methods you are encouraging because I'm afraid the new Dan—the real me, I guess—will displease people. I question whether what you are trying to teach him is what will be best for his career and his life. And I don't think he can change anyway.

COACH: *Okay, Pleaser, I hear you, but I do believe Dan's Authentic Self is strong. The real Dan is in there. Dan will be able to let go of this pleasing behavior and will no longer feel as if he has to* compromise his own needs to meet the needs of others. He can and will change when he starts to put his relationship with himself before his relationship with others.

I know that you, the Pleaser, have Dan's best interests in mind, but your way of helping him to be successful is antiquated. You developed your coping mechanisms when you were young. At the time, you still depended on your parents, so it made sense that you would try to please them. This job loss is the perfect catalyst for you to begin to rethink some of these old beliefs and finally allow your divine self to develop. The changes Dan will make using this process will frighten you at first, but in the end, they will make it much easier for him to meet his goals.

DAN'S PLEASER: *Well, I don't know about that. I think the Pleaser part may insist on keeping him the same.*

COACH: *It is up to you, Dan, which way you go.*

I then asked Dan to move back to the original chair he had been sitting in before he shifted into his Conditioned Self for the interview. I asked him to close his eyes and get in touch with his real self again.

"Dan," I said, "in your writing this week, dialogue from both parts of yourself. Let your Conditioned Self write first, then answer with your Authentic Self."

"Jayne, you are going to have to give me a medal for actually thinking this might work.…Are you trying this out on me, or have you ever used this weird idea before?" Dan was still smiling as he turned to go.

I made a mental note that Dan was ready for Dialogue 4.

Coach's Mindset

At the end of our interview, it was clear to me that Dan's issues were not with the boss whom Dan assumed was unappreciative, or with the recruiter whom Dan assumed was not working hard enough to help Dan find a job, but were instead within Dan himself. Dan had not lost his job in spite of how hard he had worked, but because of it. Dan's Pleaser personality told him that he should do everything he could to help others. Once Dan's colleagues realized that he would be willing to help them with their workload, they began passing more and more of their responsibilities off on him. Eventually, Dan was spread so thin that he was unable to complete any of his tasks properly, and he lost his job because his leadership and productivity were in a state of decline. Dan's Conditioned Self is the theme of all his limiting beliefs.

The Conditioned-Self interview is a powerful tool to reveal one's Authentic Self with all its Divine Intelligence. It gave Dan a second chance to uncover who he was meant to be in life. It defined who he is not, leaving him with the idea that the real person within him is still in there and available to him. Thus, in the interview, his real self was a "witness" to what his Pleaser was doing, almost like a part of you observing yourself. With this awareness of the Pleaser, Dan now has the opportunity to go back to his original part, the pure, untouched divine part of him, where he is free to enjoy life without guilt.

Part of a coach's job is to ask questions that may make a client uncomfortable. I had certainly done my job here. I felt I had shaken up his old belief system, and the uncomfortable feelings were a good sign that there was an opportunity for change.

In Dan's case, his Pleaser is in control. What I want for him is for his Authentic Self to be in charge—not totally doing away with his Pleaser, but putting his Authentic Self in the role of pilot and his Pleaser as a copilot. I wanted him to be able to hear the Pleaser's voice but not to react to it without awareness, as he has his entire life. Eventually, his Authentic Self will be able to override and balance out the Pleaser when needed. He was to begin to practice this new Dialogue between his Conditioned Self and his Authentic Self.

Most of my clients are like Dan, unaware that they can choose the part of themselves that they want to activate and use in their lives. Dan was using his Pleaser to do the extra work for his team instead of confronting his team and requiring them to help. He thought this would please his CEO, but it backfired on him. His Pleaser was a weak leader to his team, and as a result the team failed to get the product to the customer on time. If Dan had been aware enough, he could have called on his Authentic Self to calmly and assertively instruct and lead his team to a completed task. He could have still called on his Pleaser, as a mental tool to confront the team in a nice and comfortable way.

Dan was unconscious of what he was creating in his business life by being in Pleaser mode. By unconsciously using a pleasing attitude in the outside world, he was projecting doubt and undervaluing himself. Dan was full of regret and guilt about losing his job and failing his family. Yet, because of this inner turmoil and distress, Dan was sending out negative thoughts and getting back negative outcomes.

If we are unconscious of our externally created personalities, we allow that negative part of us to dictate our relationships with others. The more he tried to please his wife, the less she thought she needed to get a job to help him out. He tried so hard to keep his children happy that they didn't feel any pressure to get part-time jobs while in college. And he had tried to please his boss so much by working long hours that he had lost the respect of his boss and his coworkers. Dan was in a vicious cycle—creating events in his life over and over again that were influenced by the Pleaser pattern running inside his brain.

My role as Dan's coach in conducting the interview with his Pleaser was to stay nonjudgmental. In these interviews, I am privy to personal, private information about clients' innermost lives. For clients to trust me to explore this side of them, they have to know that I will not be reactive to anything they disclose. Whatever they have done or not done, it is not for me to judge. It is my job to consistently hold up a mirror and let them see what they are saying to me. I need to provide them with a safe place to unload and examine this part of themselves. The main goals are to let them see that their externally-created part is not who they truly are and give them a glimpse of a higher part of themselves. But to reveal who they really are, they have to discover who they are not. If not identified, this Conditioned Self continues to overshadow their inner light.

I encouraged Dan to dialogue about his personality interview to build his awareness of the difference between these two parts of himself. As Dan became more and more aware of his Pleaser self, his Conditioned Self, he was moving ever closer to being able to move past it.

This interview is a vital part of the spiritual process and has deep transformational qualities. I was glad Dan had finally found this part of himself. Now the real Dan could step forward. As you will see, I am constantly checking in with him to see if he is dialoguing every morning. I will slow down the process if I see that he is not dialoguing. As a coach, I am in charge of the process; Dan is in charge of the agenda. His agenda, of course, is to find a job and to find God. My job is to hold his agenda in my mind as I guide him through this process of self-discovery and make it relate to his goals. And even more important, I must always believe he can attain his goals, even when he doesn't believe in himself. That is the beauty of coaching: to have that perfect parental-like support you may not have gotten as a child. It is also challenging for a coach to remain nonjudgmental and nonattached to the outcome to provide that unconditional acceptance. I cannot want this more than Dan wants it for himself or I become the leader, and the whole process falls apart.

The Spirituality
Universal Spiritual Truth #5: Seek First Who You Are Not

Cistercian monk Thomas Keating uses the concept of two parts of ourselves in self-growth work also. In *Intimacy with God* (1994), he defined one's human, limited part as "the false self"—as "developed in our own likeness rather than in the likeness of God" (p. 163), and thus the distortion of the image of God in which we are created. The false self "seeks happiness in gratifying the instinctual needs of survival/security, affection/esteem, and power/control, and it bases its self-worth and identity on cultural and group identification" (p. 163). Keating refers to the divine self as the true self or "the image of God in which every human being is created; our participation in the divine life manifested in our uniqueness" (p. 166).

These two parts of ourselves have been described in many ways by many people. Spiritual teacher Eckhart Tolle calls the inauthentic, externally-created personality the "pain body" because it is formed by painful experiences to protect us from feeling that same hurt again. Carl Jung called it "the shadow" because it is cut off from the light of God. And of course, we all know about the Freudian id, ego, and superego. But even the Bible suggests that we have different parts. The Bible designates a less-than-divine part called the "human" or "flesh part" because it is created by humankind rather than by God. Mother Teresa called these human parts of us "distressing disguises."

Definitions of Authentic Self and Conditioned Self

Because these two parts of ourselves are called different names by different people, it is important to clarify the definitions of these terms as used throughout *Divine Intelligence*:

Authentic Self: The divine, Authentic Self in all of us is the godlike image in which every human being is created. It is a state of mind, ipseity, that has not been imprinted through human interaction. When we are in our Authentic Self, our Divine Intelligence has been activated and has unlimited potential; when identified and developed, it can allow you to go beyond what are commonly thought of as human limitations.

Conditioned Self: The Conditioned Self in all of us is the false image of ourselves that we have developed to protect ourselves, please others, and gain approval. It is the opposite of being godlike. It is the part of us developed in reaction to our experiences; it is that part of us that is human and contains repressed weaknesses, shortcomings, artificial feelings, hidden motives, and dysfunctional behaviors. It eclipses the divine, Authentic Self and manifests itself as our "human self" or our personality. Much of the time it remains hidden from us, and we think it *is* us.

What Keating describes as the "true self" and "false self," I refer to throughout as "Authentic Self" and "Conditioned Self." No matter what we name these concepts, however, their descriptions are similar. When referencing the works of others, the original terms are as used to maintain the integrity of those citations.

 ## The Science

Scientists break things down into parts to try to make them understandable. Labeling things with words helps us better understand the concepts. Neuroscientists are the same—they have broken the brain down into parts to give us names we can use to study and interpret their findings. And they have created models for us to use for understanding the brain more. This is how scientists simplify things for a better grasp and understanding by the layperson. A growing number of scientists believe that, in addition to this more reductionist way of looking at parts, a holistic view could expand our knowledge of the brain. Therefore, it is important to remember, as we break the brain down into parts, that the brain is just a small part of our body, and the body itself works in a holistic fashion.

Ipseity versus the Conditioned Self

We have already seen that scientists now believe we have a part of us that is pure as the driven snow and untouched by the outside world, our ipseity. Neuroscience supports the idea that we also have a "False Self" (Siegel, 1999). It suggests that we add a covering to our original self, which then becomes our False Self. Research shows that we may have many "selves" in normal development and that these selves are dependent on our relationships with others to develop. Furthermore, our relationship histories are shaped by patterns of feelings, attitudes, and meanings that are more likely to become activated in the future. If people become stuck in a negative state, such as the False Self, then they are filled with unresolved conflict and lack a sense of authenticity (Harter, 1988). So the research does suggest that we all have many selves, or states of mind. The term *state of mind*, according to Daniel Siegel in *The Developing Mind* (1999), means "the cluster of brain activity and mental modules at a given moment in time" (p. 121). If this state of mind is repeated over time, it is called a "self-state" (Siegel, 1999, p. 229). The False Self is an example of a self-state, one big neural net in the brain.

But let's look more at how this happens.

Even when we grow up in a fairly functional home, child development specialists agree that our brain ultimately breaks down into parts and different self-states (or states of mind) to deal with life (Harter et al., 1997). As we experience different roles, such as sibling, student, and friend, our brain starts to group certain behaviors and thoughts together that work to give us the love we desire and need, and those ways of being eventually form a neural circuit. Think back to Dan's list of limiting beliefs. All of Dan's limiting beliefs are combined to represent one part of him, his Pleaser. By the time we reach adulthood, we have all created different "parts" to address the many diverse activities in our lives. Some of this brain activity is healthy for us and gives us good coping skills to use when life gets challenging. But many times, we get diverted off our path of unlimited power and self-awareness to fall into the crevice of deep neural pathways of limitations called our Conditioned Self.

Comparing Your Authentic Self and Conditioned Self	
Authentic Self	Conditioned Self
Imaginative	Limited thinking
Positive thinking	Negative thinking
Unconditionally loving and accepting	Conditionally loving and accepting
Creative	Stifled, old, reactionary thinking
Original	Fake, copy, inauthentic
Confident	Doubtful

Filtered through Our Parents' Eyes

Daniel Siegel, in his book *The Developing Mind* (1999), notes that we see ourselves through the filter of our parents' minds. This may be one reason we develop a Conditioned Self. Some of the time, parents' minds are preoccupied with work and their own needs, and they themselves most likely have limiting beliefs, thus setting up the likelihood that a child would develop a false part of herself (Harter et al., 1997, p. 271). A child's inner world may be filled with such questions as, "Am I loved enough? Do I matter to my mother? Do I live up to Dad's expectations?" Because of this, a Conditioned Self may develop in a child to cope with filling important needs, such as love and acceptance. The research of Harter and her colleagues shows that a person is capable of at least two self-states: a private, inner-core self and an external, public, adaptive state. The public self becomes false only if internal emotions are masked from the outer world. Dan was a good example of someone who had created a Conditioned Self to hide his true feelings, as one of his beliefs was that negative feelings should not be expressed. Eventually, as in Dan's case, a person begins to mask his own internal feelings from himself. Dan, as a result, has little sense of knowing who he is, as our emotions define us. He may have even shut down the circuits that control affective expression.

We put up this false front, or what we call a personality, to deal with the outside world, and yet we retain another part of us that is internal—how we really see things and our internal perspective. This is not to say that we always appear fake in the outside world, just that babies create an outer exterior part to get their needs met. Again, keep in mind that our logical thinking brain is not fully developed at the time we decide who we are. Since no parent is perfectly able to meet all the needs of a child, most children create a personality to get those needs for love and security met. These two parts of us may overlap at times, but most of us have distinct inner and outer ways of being.

The Harter studies also suggest that certain self-states conflict with each other. The more extreme the creation of a Conditioned Self or outer self, the more disconnected a person may feel from others and herself. I think this could keep us from developing a relationship with the Creator within us, our ipseity. Our outer self doesn't have to always be false; however, there is a natural tendency to please caregivers and/or react to others in our outer environment, which can take away our true or divine nature. For example, if a teacher makes a child think he is not good in math, he may generalize that he will never be any good with numbers and carry this with him for his entire life, keeping him from developing those mathematical skills.

The Protection of the Conditioned Self: Your Default Personality

The brain has a built-in negative bias (Vaish et al., 2008), which sets us up for the development of a Conditioned Self. The Conditioned Self is the part of the brain that stays busy scanning for problems, and when you are in a crisis, as Dan is, this part of the brain takes over to protect you. Negative experiences like Dan had when he was young tend to create vicious cycles of circuits in the brain, and then one falls into those crevices of old neural pathways automatically when threatened.

Research has shown that we pick up on negative information. Here are some examples: By putting both fearful and happy faces in front of people and seeing which one predominates thought, researchers found that participants gave more attention to the fearful face. Other research shows that the brain likes bad news better than good news (Yang et al., 2007). As we have seen with Dan's memory storage, negative events generally have more lasting impact than positive ones (Seligman, 2006). The brain concentrates more on bad information learned about another person than on the good (Peeters & Czapinski, 1990). I have learned in working with couples that it takes many positive remarks to remove a negative one, and research supports my observation by telling us that for every negative interaction, five positive ones are needed to override the effect (Gottman, 1995).

Since our brain is built for survival and is always trying to protect us from negative feelings, it naturally creates a part to deal with danger. The Conditioned-Self part of Dan's brain told him: "Don't feel hurt or isolated. Just try to figure out what will please your parents, and then they will love you!" Thus, the Pleaser part of him started to create a whole circuit in the brain, which replayed itself so many times that it became an ingrained pathway. Think of it like learning a song or poem: The more you repeat it, the quicker you learn it and the longer it lasts in your memory.

Your Conditioned Self Must Die Many Times Each Day

The Conditioned Self will never die completely, as your personality has been with you a long time and was wired in when your brain was easy to influence and shape. So let's put it this way—you must "die" to your Conditioned Self daily, maybe even many times a day. This looks like shifting from a negative mindset to a positive one. You may have to do it over and over again before your Conditioned Self gives up the struggle. Research says it takes six months to wire in a new belief. It may take six months before your Conditioned Self begins to understand that you are in charge. Tricky business, but this is what using your Divine Intelligence is like: the mental practice of letting go and accepting your greatness. Dan wondered if his Conditioned Self would ever be dead for good. I told him that one must die to his Conditioned Self many times a day to stay in the Divine Intelligence mindset. Just as soon as you think your Conditioned Self is gone, it will strike again with amazing strength. As soon as he becomes exactly like Christ, his Conditioned Self will be gone—maybe in the next lifetime.

The Voice of your Conditioned Self

Our thoughts can be categorized into two types: Conditioned-Self thoughts and Divine Intelligence (Authentic-Self) thoughts. Both kinds of thoughts, or voices, can be identified in dialoguing, as well as heard in the conversations in your head. Learning to discriminate between the two helps you isolate your Divine Intelligence and learn what it feels like to be in that state of mind.

The voice of your Conditioned Self is described more fully in the following chart:

The Voice of Your Conditioned Self	
Externalization	**Negative Feelings/Thoughts**
Should/ought	Need to/have to
Must do	Guilt
Fears	Worry
Injunctions	Doubts
Judgments	Regrets
Criticism of yourself	Inadequacy
Procrastination	Perfection
Discounting yourself	Pleasing

How did Dan use these two parts of him in his dialoguing every morning? Researchers have pinpointed at what age an internal dialogue begins within our brain's development. As the brain in an infant develops, neocortex activity emerges around age two, as stated earlier. This is the beginning of the time when we can speak of ourselves to ourselves from the third person. At this point, an internal narrator develops, and we begin to have self-talk (Tulving, 1993). Dan tells me many times about what he is saying to himself inside. For example, he relates to me that he feels he may be "a fair-weather Christian." He says he knows he is "settling." His talk about God inside his head is from this narrative, third person much of the time. His self-talk at this point in his life is mostly self-deprecating. As part of the process of developing his Divine Intelligence, he will learn to monitor his self-talk and consciously eliminate his limiting thinking.

Change the Voices in Your Head

As we begin to talk about his past and his experiences in the Conditioned-Self interview, more memories continue to flow in the conversation. He will continue to remember things well after our conversation. The dialoguing he will be doing every day will help him find more of the wired-in beliefs that are now limits to reaching his goal of finding a job and finding God. In this dialoguing, he will begin to isolate his Conditioned-Self voice and allow his Divine Intelligence to be heard. The morning writing is the key to this process, as it requires Dan to work on it daily, instead of just during the hour when Dan talks to me every week. It is a basic foundation for the rewiring process. He must have developed this habit for the process to work.

If we spend time developing our inner life, as Dan is doing in his dialoguing, we may be able to find and develop this divine self we were born to be. In my work, whenever my clients participate in a Conditioned-Self interview, they describe feeling lighter and freer and say their lives have begun to change. It is somehow freeing to them to know that this part is not really who they are. Clients realize that they have been living "in the shadow" of an externally-created personality, and they are curious to uncover their true potential. And once they put their conscious awareness in control, their ipseity or "true part" becomes more evident and accessible.

In this process, Dan will learn to discern the difference between these two parts of himself and eventually will be able to put the true, unlimited part of himself in control of his life. When he does this, he will take the next step in the evolutionary process to ignite his Divine Intelligence.

Summary of Concepts in Chapter 5

1. Our limited beliefs hide this inner light, our Divine Intelligence, from us.
2. Our limited beliefs form a personality pattern, a Conditioned Self, that holds us back from achieving our goals.
3. Your Conditioned Self is a tool to help you find your Authentic Self.
4. Our authenticity is connected to our emotional awareness.
5. If we block our emotions, we may get stuck in a self-state that is unhealthy.
6. Our Conditioned Self is not who we really are.
7. When we are born, we are in a self-state of ipseity—pure, unlimited potential.
8. As we grow up and adapt to our external world, we develop "other-self" states, and sometimes a Conditioned Self, that can take away our authenticity and divine nature.

Look Inward

Conscious Evolution: The natural evolutionary process, if left to your automatic brain and unchecked by your consciousness, will tend to focus your brain on the negative and unpleasant side of life to protect you. To move forward in personal growth and development and get out of the caveman mentality, the Conditioned Self must be brought into awareness and labeled, so you will realize you are in a less-than-creative state of mind. This inner dialogue is usually judging you as not good enough to try to get you to stop growing and changing. The evolutionary steps in this chapter are to know that you are not your Conditioned Self and to stop listening to the voice of the Conditioned Self, who is judging you as less than worthy. It is a challenge to swim against the currents of beliefs that have been there for centuries, but this is what we have to do if we are to direct our evolution and hasten our growth.

The move is inward toward loving and accepting yourself unconditionally so that you can see your Conditioned Self and separate from it.

What is a part of yourself you do not like?

What is this part of you always telling you about yourself?

How could you change the voices in your head to help you?

6

Universal Spiritual Truth #6:
The Path to Salvation May Be Different Than You Think

> *Through Gnosis we are purified*
> *of diversity and experience the vision of unity.*
> *Those who have realized Gnosis know the source*
> *and the destination. They have set themselves free*
> *by waking up from the stupor in which they lived,*
> *and become themselves again.*
> —Valentinus, Gospel of Truth

After our interview, Dan said, "Wow. A Pleaser. That was really something. I had no idea that I had this, this part of me—a large part of me—that thinks that way. I'm not sure how you saw this in me, Jayne, but I can really see now that I am a Pleaser. I have been this way as long as I can remember. I've always put myself last. I thought that was what I was supposed to do. In fact, I think it would be weird not to do things that way. I have no idea how to change that. But I'm beginning to see that I should. It's a real blind spot. What's the next step?"

Pleasers always want the coach to give them the answers. I had to keep working hard to put the responsibility for change back on Dan.

"Dan, you've worked for so long to please others...I wonder what needs of your own you're neglecting?" I have found that Pleasers are usually very tired because they never get their own needs met. They have the limiting belief that others will meet their needs because they themselves are so self-sacrificing. Well, Dan is finding that it doesn't work out very well to be a Pleaser.

There was a long pause before Dan said, in an astonished voice, "Jayne, I don't even know. I've been thinking that all I need is a job. I always come back to that, but that's not it, is it?"

"Think for a minute. What would make you feel better?"

"Uh, besides a job, I'd like to be valued, and not just by a paycheck, but real value. I'd like for people to see that I have value."

"What else?" I coaxed.

"Well, first of all, Jayne, I would like to have some respect—again, not just from a paycheck; I'd like for my family and friends to respect me for who I am. I mean, I have not yet even told you the details about my son, Tommy. He is our youngest and our 'wild child.' Just within the last week, we received a notice he is failing two subjects, and now he has been expelled for three days for losing his temper with his algebra teacher." Dan rolled his eyes and quickly let his head fall forward in dismay.

"What do you think is going on inside Tommy?" I asked, thinking he might be mirroring Dan's depressed-like attitude right now. When adolescents are depressed, they often act out.

"Well, I don't know and don't care. I just need him to straighten up and fly right. I have enough problems right now with this job thing. I don't need him causing any more friction between me and Margie. She thinks I don't talk to him enough and wants me to be more involved in his life." Dan paused and became very still for a moment.

"Jayne, when I heard myself say that, I realized I sounded just like my father! Oh my gosh! I would rather be compared to anyone but him!"

"Dan," I asked, "what would change in your life if you focused on taking care of yourself instead of others?" I watched Dan nod his head and grimace at this truth. I continued: "What if you just focused on doing the best you can?" I wanted Dan to begin to wish himself well.

"So, what now?" I asked him, not knowing where he wanted to go with this part of his life.

"Well, I guess I might as well take some time for Tommy right now. Heaven knows, I have the time, when in the past, I really haven't had the time to give to him like I did the others. By the time he came along, I was really involved in all that overtime at work."

"Okay, and what else do you want right now, Dan?"

"And…and…I want…well, this seems kind of self-serving, but I'd like to be important. I felt important at work once, but I'm not sure I've felt important anywhere else. I'd like to be an important part of my own life. You know what I mean? Is that too much to ask?"

Dan then began pointing out why he thought he had been unable to meet those specific needs.

"When I first lost my job, my friends were all very supportive. They were full of leads and ideas for me, but as time has gone on, I hear from them less and less. It's like we're living in separate worlds now. They're still up there in the corporate world, and I'm down here in no-man's-land. I played golf with them for a while, but you know, the longer I've been out of a job, the less we have to say to each other. I never realized how much we talked shop. They're polite about everything; they ask how it's going, but they all know I'm on the ropes here. I think it's embarrassing for them. And it's for sure embarrassing for me. I think they've lost all respect for me, and they're worried that my bad luck, or karma, or whatever you want to call it, will rub off on them. I haven't gone out with them in months, and they haven't called. It wouldn't matter anyway. I don't have the time. I spend every waking minute doing something to get a job. I probably won't see any of those guys until I'm working again.

"And you know what else? Things aren't so hot on the home front, either. I'm doing everything I know how to do, everything the recruiter tells me to do, everything the unemployment commission is telling me to do, and Margie treats me like I'm loafing. If I'm watching TV or something, she starts giving me the third degree. Have I tried this?

Have I tried that? Have I called the recruiter? You know, I don't see her polishing her résumé. She really could teach again. She did that before the boys were born, and if she doesn't want to teach, she could do something else. At the very least, she could substitute teach, or do anything that would keep us from bleeding our meager retirement. She saw the check I had to write to the university for Brad and Daniel. Plus they expect spending money every month! They don't seem to understand that it just might be time for them to look for some work, too."

He paused. "Of course, I haven't asked them to do that. College is supposed to be fun. I want them to have the kind of experience that I didn't have, you know, where you just go to school and study and hang out with friends. This is a time for them to build lifelong connections and friendships. I haven't said anything to them about getting jobs." He sighed. "The truth is that I'm too ashamed to admit that I need their help. Instead of being honest with them, I've just let them go about their business like nothing's going on. I feel like I'm lying to them when I talk to them, so I don't talk to them much these days. You know, I'm recognizing that Pleaser in me more and more.

"And you know what Tommy wants? Tommy wants to skip college altogether and just move to Colorado in May. We fight about this all the time. He thinks he can just move up there and wait tables until snowboarding season. He wants to be a ski bum. He thinks that he'll just automatically get a job teaching snowboarding or working at a lodge so he can snowboard all the time. I've tried to talk sense to him, but you won't believe what he said to me the other day: 'Look where college has gotten you!' I tell you, I almost decked the kid. I can't believe his nerve. He has no sense of reality—none! Where does he think he got everything he has, huh? His car, the money he burns through regularly? I can't even talk about it. It just makes me furious...." Dan's voice wavered.

"Really, Dan, everyone takes some time off, even people who are looking for work. In a way, it's part of the process, part of what it takes to build your energy back up for the search. I can hear how exhausted you are. How could you give yourself some refueling right now?" I said.

"That's so weird, Jayne. Most people think that every day is a day off for me, but it's not, not at all. I'm as tired now as I was with a full-time job. I think I'd just feel worse though, you know, guilty, if I took my eye off the ball." Dan paused for a few seconds. "Is this part of the Pleaser in me? It is, isn't it? It's one of my beliefs—that I have to work harder than anyone else. You know, I'm doing all I can in this job search. I really could use a break."

"Dan, how would it be if you felt some compassion for yourself?" I looked up and saw Dan begin to tear up. "I want to challenge you to some fieldwork, taking some of these ideas into your real life. What could you do to meet your own needs right now?"

"Well, I don't know if this is too simple, but I take out the garbage every day, and I would like to know I am doing a good job." Dan said proudly.

"So, what could you say to yourself that would validate that for yourself?" I asked him.

"Well, I will say to myself as I drop those bags by the curb every morning: Dan, by golly, you are a good man for doing this!" He laughed at himself.

Dan continued: "I know it sounds silly, Jayne, but I really believe it will stop me from thinking whether others think I am doing something valuable and important and to start deciding for myself. But, Jayne, what the heck is 'fieldwork'?" Dan was playing with me again, but it did remind me to stop using all the coaching jargon, as it turned people off.

Over the next few weeks, Dan began making time for himself. He had always enjoyed sports, but he had stopped allowing himself to go to the gym with his basketball buddies and had even stopped watching sports on TV because he was afraid Margie would disapprove. Dan loved playing golf, but eventually he had decided it was too expensive and dropped his club membership. He had failed to realize that he could still play at the public course. He had also mistakenly put in his head that his friends had deserted him, even though he had never directly asked them for help and support. Oftentimes, when people don't know what to do to help a friend, they feel awkward and avoid the friend. This response is seldom an indication that the friendship is meaningless or has ended.

"Jayne," Dan said excitedly when we next spoke, "it felt so good to be outside on the golf course again. A couple of guys even commented on how good my swing is. We ended up playing together. But the really cool thing was that I saw the vice president of sales from the job I was laid off from, and he practically jumped the fence to get to me and tell me how much he had been thinking of me. He ended up asking me to play with him next week!"

"Dan, that is great! I am so glad to see you having some fun!" I replied, sincerely glad he was having a good moment. I thought he deserved it.

"And Jayne," Dan continued, "I did start to watch myself and see there are many times during the day that I am doing something valuable to others. And here is my first small miracle as a result of your process. I have taken out the garbage for twenty-four years, and Margie has never even noticed that I do it—and I do it every Tuesday and Friday. I recycle and am careful about the environment. But here is the miracle: I was rushing to get three garbage bags out to the gate last Tuesday, and when I looked up, Margie was dragging the third one behind me, trying to help me. I mean, here she was in her robe and no makeup. This is a big thing for her to do, Jayne. She was really trying to help me. Me—the man with no job!" Dan and I laughed together at his progress.

"Well, and now Dan, I think you are ready for an even bigger challenge," I said, careful not to say *fieldwork* again. "How could you take some time off to enjoy yourself, right now, even having no job?"

In an effort to show Dan how to care for himself, connect with the power inside him, and finally take an active interest in his own life, I helped him develop a few, new, personal habits aimed at increasing his energy level and showing the world that he was meeting his own needs. He was crawling out of the victim hole he had dug for himself. In my notes, I wrote down the three specific needs he said he needed to fulfill: importance, value, and self-respect. For him to complete Dialogue 5, we would need to develop a plan whereby he would get into action to meet these needs for himself rather than hoping someone else might do it for him. Here is his plan:

1. Exercise six days a week for thirty minutes (need to feel important).
2. Continue to journal every morning to make himself more aware of his feelings (need to feel important). Dan is now working his way through the full Dialogue process.
3. Set better boundaries with his wife and alert her if she becomes a greater source of pressure than of respect and support (need to feel valued).
4. Start having fun by returning to some of his sporting activities with his buddies (need to feel valued).
5. Devote only eight hours each day to the job search and take weekends off (need for self-respect).

After working on these habits for nearly three weeks, Dan received a call from a company that was interested in scheduling an interview with him. This victory strengthened his faith in the direction we were moving and inspired him to be even more vigilant and devoted to this process.

Coach's Mindset

Like most of us, at first Dan was skeptical about focusing on self-care, but he eventually admitted that it was time to try something different from what he had been doing. As Dan began to make time for himself and practice new personal habits, his life slowly began to show signs of change. He had an honest talk with Margie, and she found a temporary teaching job for the spring term almost immediately. This proved to Dan that making inner changes (such as showing himself more respect) would inspire others to treat him differently. Margie's job also brought much-needed income into the home, which took a great deal of stress off Dan's shoulders and afforded him more time to relax than he had ever enjoyed before in his life. By asserting his right to have boundaries with his wife and meet his own needs, he began to activate the power, the Creator, within him.

For Dan to remember to become less pleasing, it would be necessary for him to become more internally attuned, seeking to find strength in his own inner source. Internally-centered people think of themselves not as victims, but as agents of change, or victors of life. Learning to take care of his own needs forced Dan to turn inside and build up this inner strength. One of the hardest lessons Dan faced was that no one was going to take care of him. He was going to have to do it himself. Dan found that people in the world respond to him differently when he is taking care of his own needs.

Up until the day Dan lost his job, his Pleaser had successfully (albeit often dysfunctionally) met his needs. What the Pleaser projects, it always gets in return. All his life, Dan had been projecting "I need to please; I need to put others first; I'm not as important." Projecting this message was a definite obstacle to finding an executive position. In other words, he would have to show that he valued himself.

Dan had long assumed that the only way to please his wife and children was by supporting them financially, so when he lost that ability, he believed that he could not be of any value or importance to them anymore. Dan's nature as a Pleaser told him to put his family's needs before his own, so Dan eventually stopped participating in the activities he once enjoyed because he felt that it would be selfish of him to spend the family's savings on his seemingly frivolous interests. I hoped Dan would realize that he would have to continue his self-care habits for the rest of his life. He would have no power except the strength he created inside himself.

Everyone needs to be loved, appreciated, valued, touched, fed, nurtured, and so on. I knew Dan really needed to feel loved. I knew, also, that the change Dan needed to make would have to be much deeper than just changing his self-care habits, but right now, I hoped that these new habits would give him a little peace of mind and raise his Light Frequency. Eventually, what I wished for Dan was that he feel love and respect for himself. In this Dialogue, Dan learns that he is the only one who can meet his needs—or, as I tell clients, life is not a banquet but a buffet; you must get up and get it yourself.

A Pause in the Process

Pointing Dan toward self-care at this point in the dialoguing process is strategic and important to the success of the process for him. When people have been working life from their Conditioned Self—in this case Dan's Pleaser—for most of their adult lives, they are exhausted...literally out of energy. Dan is tired from taking care of all these people in his life. For him to have enough energy to go through the middle Dialogues, which are extremely taxing and challenging, he must take some time off to restore some of his natural energy. The purpose of this Dialogue is to regain some natural energy and show the client that he can take charge of at least one area of his life. Clients going through the process say that this break seems to take them out of the process; however, by the end of the process, they see the need for the pause. They continue their dialoguing every morning during this break, giving their brain some time to stabilize.

Meditation as Part of Dan's Spiritual Practice

I would be remiss not to introduce meditation into Dan's spiritual practice as the research in the past few years shows the many benefits to our physical body. I felt it would help him integrate the feeling of self- love into his brain and hopefully into the cells of his body. I asked him to practice meditation for 20 minutes each day. While 30 minutes of meditation daily is ideal, I felt to add this to the requirement for dialoguing might be too much. I chose to teach him to visualize in the meditation, at the point of deepest relaxation, what it felt like to have the exact new job he desires and to try to feel like it has already come true. I helped him detail some of the specifics of what he wanted.

Numerous studies have documented that meditation positively affects our blood pressure, heart rate, oxygen output and brain activity. A groundbreaking study in 2013 showed when our bodies are in a deep meditation, immediate changes in the expression of genes involved in immune function, energy metabolism and insulin secretion occur (Bhasin, et.al, 2013).

 The Spirituality

Universal Spiritual Truth #6:
The Path to Salvation May Be Different Than You Think

Better Self-Care

I was encouraging Dan to continue to take better care of himself and focus some attention on his self-care routine because I knew research showed that self-care and time to reflect enhance the efficacy of the brain. To be more attractive and radiant to the Universe out there trying to help him find a job, he needed to have a state of higher energy, a brighter Light Frequency. This would come as he tapped into his Divine Intelligence. The challenging part of the process right now for Dan, and for all of us, is realizing that he has to do this for himself, that nothing "out there" is going to swoop down and magically save him.

The better you care for yourself, the more people are drawn to you. "When you do kindly things to yourself, then you know what it is to be able to love yourself. Then you can look at others who desperately need kindness and love and feel good about their getting it," says Gary Zukav, spiritual teacher and author of *The Seat of the Soul* (1989, p. 196). Dan's pleasing nature had been keeping him from getting his needs met, as he always put his needs second, yet as we see, he is bitter and angry at others. This concept may seem somewhat counterintuitive. The more we treat ourselves well, the better others treat us. Dan has always thought, "If I please people enough, they will give back to me." Not so.

The Conditioned Self was created to get the most basic needs you had as a child met, but again, the Conditioned Self came into existence when your neocortex was not developed. Your reasoning capabilities were not as well-honed as an adult's. As a result, your neocortex will come up with all sorts of sometimes dysfunctional ways to get your needs met, such as pleasing behaviors, denying your own emotions, trying to be perfect, or trying to control others and feeling selfish if you focus on yourself.

Dan's main modus operandi was to focus on others, taking care of their needs and always putting their needs before his own. As a child, he must have decided he should be a really good little boy and read Mom's mind as to how to act so he would meet her needs. To be more authentic, I knew Dan had to focus on himself and his own needs to get out of the pattern of the Conditioned Self. When someone is a Pleaser, he usually wonders why others don't try to please him. Dan had taught people how to treat him. They knew they could get him to meet their needs, so, of course, he did. They also lost some respect for him as a result.

I felt that a good intervention for Dan at this point, to shake up this old pattern of focusing on others, would be to focus him on what he could control in his life: himself. Maybe this would break up the old pattern and give Dan a feeling of more control in his life. I knew it was not the end result we wanted, but he needed some success in his life right now and some attention. It worked in the way I wanted it to help him. I knew that exercise was one good way to get him out, seeing other people, and feeling better.

 ## The Science

Research demonstrates that the self-reflection required in self-care promotes compassion and care for others as well; furthermore, it shows that it "grows" the brain. In a study, researchers found that long-term meditators had increased the middle prefrontal thickening and enlarged a part of the brain called the right insula (Lazar et al., 2005, p. 1893-1897). Now, to be totally transparent here, I am taking a giant leap and associating writing and dialoguing with a type of meditation. The brain enlarged because of looking inward through meditation, and dialoguing does facilitate self-reflection, although perhaps not at as deep a level as meditation.

In his book *Spark: The Revolutionary New Science of Exercise and the Brain* (2008), John J. Ratey reveals how important exercise is to brain health. His groundbreaking exploration of the connection between the brain's performance and exercise proves that even a short workout can stimulate the mental circuits of the brain. In turn, this will reduce stress and help Dan relax. Ratey shows that exercise can help with human focus and improve the structure of the brain.

Daniel Siegel supports Ratey's research when he writes in his book *Mindsight* (2011b), "Among the keys to neuronal growth are novelty, attention, and aerobic exercise" (p. 110). "Additionally, time spent relaxing and in a playful mood is beneficial to brain growth and neuronal and synaptic expansion," says psychologist Daniel Goleman, author of many books, including *Emotional Intelligence* (1995). But better still, a sense of playfulness creates charisma, and in laboratory settings it has been shown that the "lab rats" are drawn to spend more time with the "playful rats." You see why it is important for Dan to get out and enjoy himself more. His tenseness and down mood would not show up well in a job interview, even on the phone. His stress would decrease when he got out, relaxed, and played some golf.

We live in a hologram

The assertion that we have unlimited power in the form of a Divine Intelligence is so audacious that it would be dismissed out of hand were it not for the scientists who dare to look beyond what we currently think is true. David Bohm moved closer to what Einstein had yearned for but what his Theory of Relativity did not provide: A Unity Field Theory. Bohm was one of the first to show how this could be explained. How does he explain it?

Bohm maintains that the information of the entire Universe is contained in each of its parts. Certain quantum physicists now say that each part of the Universe contains all the information present in the entire cosmos itself.

He says we, as well as everything in the world—including the universal mind, is a hologram. In a hologram, any piece of it provides an image of the entire hologram. For example, since I am a hologram myself, then any cell in me contains the exact energy and information that my entire body carries. The information of the whole is contained in each part, and we as humans here on Earth are the parts of the Universe. (Consider the acorn example given in the Preface.) We are potentially as great as the Universe itself. Bohm concludes that the world is an indivisible whole making everything connected.

Significant research has supported Bohm's conclusions. In 1982, Alain Aspect, Jean Dalibard, and Gerard Roger of Institute of Optics at University of Paris, showed in their research that the connection between the two photons were, indeed, nonlocal, giving new evidence to Bohm's theory that the Universe is one, connected whole (Davies, 1985, p. 48).

At the same time in the sixties when Bohm was working on his theoretical idea that the world is a hologram, Karl Pribram, a neurophysiologist at Stanford and author of *Languages and the Brain (1971)*, known for his pioneering work on the limbic system of the brain, proposed the brain itself was a hologram. He showed that there was a holographic nature to our memories and perceptions because memories were distributed throughout the brain.

He had been inspired by the earlier work in 1946 of Karl Lashley, a biologist at the Yerkes Laboratory of Primate Biology who, while working with rats, surgically removed radical parts of a rat's brain and found no matter what portion he removed, he could not eradicate their memories. Pribram applied his findings to the human brain and realized that patients who had had portions of their brains removed for medical reasons had never suffered the loss of specific memories. He published his model of the human brain being holographic in nature in 1966.

Changing our Bodies by Changing our Beliefs

Can we change our DNA though by changing our mindset? Science says: yes. Studies show (Blackburn & Epel, 2012; Stetka, 2014) that exercise, a positive outlook on life, living in happiness and gratitude, being in service, and experiencing love, especially self-love, promote a long and healthy life. One study showed that environment, not genes, dictates human immune variation (Goldman, 2015). In the old question of nature versus nurture, another study found that environment trumps genes in shaping our immune system (Preidt, 2015).

Even though the brain's sense of survival serves us well when we are under duress and releases more energy through additional adrenaline, this energy comes at a cost to our cognitive brain. Bruce Lipton, in his book *The Biology of Belief,* asserts, "When you are frightened, you're dumber" (p. 151) and cites research (p. 150) supporting the claim (Takamatsu, et al, 2003; Arnsten & Goldman-Rakic 1998, et.al. 1996).

Stress could be defined as too much adrenaline in your system. Too much stress creates physical problems. Most major sickness has been linked in the research to chronic stress (Segerstrom & Miller, 2004; Kopp & Rethelyi ,2004; McEwen & Lasky, 2002; McEwen & Seeman, 1999, p. 152). Lipton quotes research stating that between 75-90 percent of primary-care doctor visits list stress as a major factor (Atkinson, 2000).

Lipton's insights created the basis for what is now called an epigenetic revolution, laying the foundation for a consciousness-based understanding of biology. Our mindset is our body. The ideas in his book give credibility to the idea we have sovereignty over our lives, or what psychologists call internal locus of control. The Divine Intelligence process is setting the stage for Dan to gain that inner control over his thoughts and eventually his life. The downside is how difficult and challenging it is to take full responsibility for himself. We are not victims of our genes; we have unlimited capacity to create a life of prosperity.

Basically, Dan needed to learn how to take care of himself. Taking care of yourself conveys to others that you value and respect yourself, two needs that Dan wanted fulfilled in his life. Dan will be more resilient and more able to handle life's stressors when he is feeling better both physically and spiritually.

Deepak Chopra, in his bestselling book, *Quantum Healing* (2015), emphasizes self-care and starting certain spiritual practices to keep healthy and well, validating the necessity of requiring Dan to begin to focus on his own needs for a change.

Chopra created 10 Keys to Self-Care (p. 35-36):
1. Making happiness a high priority.
2. Making sure your life has purpose and meaning.
3. Living according to a higher vision.
4. Expanding your awareness in every decade of your life.
5. Devoting time and attention to personal growth.
6. Following a sensible regimen of good diet and physical activity.

7. Allowing your brain to reset by introducing down time several times a day.
8. Getting to know your inner world through meditation, contemplation and self-reflection.
9. Practicing gratitude and appreciation.
10. Learning how to love and be loved.

Six Months for the Brain to Change

Creating and sustaining new personal habits will be challenging because of the nature of the brain. Remember from the research cited in the previous chapter that the brain evolves around survival, so our innate tendency is to get things done, not to relax. If we relax, the dinosaurs will get us or another caveman will get to the food first. This means that it is hard work and goes against our natural instincts to change our habits. The brain likes stability and always attempts to maintain the status quo.

Even though I knew Dan would get some immediate relief from this increased self-care, I also knew it took time to create a new habit. How can we be sure that habits will be sustainable? In the future, I knew that for Dan to learn to rewire, he would need to realize that, yes, we *can* rewire the brain, but it takes some time and attention. This would be good practice for eventually rewiring his old beliefs. By encouraging him to set up a new self-care routine, I felt I was preparing him for the tediousness of brain change.

Consider a study conducted at Harvard University by researcher Alvaro Pascual-Leone. Brain scans were taken of blind students learning to read Braille. The subjects studied Braille for one year—five days a week for two hours each day. The section of the brain where the learning took place demonstrably increased in size as the subjects increased the number of words they could read in Braille (Doidge, 2007, p. 198).

The Harvard study uncovered some even more astonishing and interesting information. Changes in brain size were different on Mondays than on Fridays. The Friday motor maps showed rapid and dramatic expansion. Yet by Monday, these sections of the subjects' brains had returned to baseline.

Pascual-Leone continued testing the size of his subjects' brains throughout the yearlong experiment. The Friday maps continued to grow for six months but stubbornly returned to baseline each Monday. Were his subjects smarter at the end of the week than they were at the beginning?

Yet after six months, the results changed. The Friday maps continued to grow larger—but not as much as in the first six months of the experiment. At the same time, the Monday maps began to show a different pattern. After six months of training, during which they showed no change, the Monday maps began to increase slowly and plateaued at ten months.

Though the changes on the Monday maps were never as dramatic as their Friday counterparts, they were more stable. At the end of ten months, the subjects were given two months off to rest. When they returned, their maps were unchanged from the last Monday mapping two months before. The conclusion? Daily training led to dramatic short-term changes in the brain during the week, but more permanent changes were seen on Mondays—after the weekend.

Pascual-Leone found: "The fast Friday changes strengthen existing neuronal connections and unmask buried pathways. The slower, more permanent Monday changes suggest the formation of brand-new structures, probably the sprouting of new neuronal connections and synapses" (p. 199).

This up-and-down effect can help us understand what is required to create new neuronal pathways in the brain. Consider the example of cramming for an exam. While it appears the knowledge base has increased, brain power likely has not grown. Rather, higher performance on the test likely is a result of strengthening the existing synaptic connections. Afterward, the information "crammed" into the brain is easily forgotten, and the neuronal connections are rapidly reversed.

On the flip side, maintaining improvement and making a skill permanent requires the slow, steady work that creates entirely new neuronal pathways and forms new connections. Think of a time when you were trying to learn a new language or complex concept but felt as though you were making no cumulative progress. Did you persist for six months? If so, you likely achieved the "Monday effect," which helped you gain the skill for life.

Lifestyle Choices Affect Brain Chemicals

Brain science is a triad of electrical (brainwaves), architectural (brain structure), and chemical (neurochemicals) components creating a person's state of mind. Lifestyle choices can create a sense of happiness by regulating the chemicals in the brain. By focusing Dan on his lifestyle choices and daily habits, I felt he would improve his chemical brain health. Our body produces hundreds of neurochemicals; only a small fraction has been identified by scientists.

In a 2012 blog post, "The Neurochemicals of Happiness: 7 Brain Molecules That Make You Feel Great," Christopher Bergland offered some ideas about how to raise Dan's Light Frequency to a higher level. This triathlete and Guinness Book world record holder called serotonin "The Confidence Molecule" because we know serotonin helps people feel less rejected and bolsters self-esteem. It can be increased by doing anything with a sense of purpose or by being around people who are likely to accept you. I encouraged Dan to return to his close, inner circle of friends anticipating that they would accept him and offer him support, which they did.

To raise Dan's dopamine level, "The Reward Molecule," I suggested certain goal habits because dopamine is shown to increase when one sets a goal and achieves it. The goals we set were small to encourage success.

Oxytocin is called "The Bonding Molecule," so I challenged Dan to increase his talks and intimacy with his wife and family because when trust and loyalty are felt, oxytocin levels increase. This is seen when people experience more physical touch, which I knew was lacking in his marriage due to both his job loss and his feelings of being unable to provide for his family financially.

Summary of Concepts in Chapter 6

1. We all have needs, and getting them met is critical to our well-being.
2. In the past, the Conditioned Self was created in childhood to meet these needs, albeit in a dysfunctional manner.
3. To develop your Divine Intelligence, you must learn to meet your own needs.
4. When you learn to meet your own needs, you become more attractive to others.
5. It takes six months to create a new neural pathway or to make a habit sustainable.
6. Research suggests that self-reflection can increase the size of the brain.

Look Inward

Conscious Evolution: In this chapter, Dan starts to build new personal habits and begins the tedious process of conscious brain change. In the evolutionary process, any new way of thinking or new way of acting is threatening to the brain, so the brain will resist when we try to install new habits. But we must persevere and continue to make conscious evolutionary changes. The messages of the past have been that taking care of the self is selfish or self-centered, yet to evolve to the next level, we must consciously decide that we are responsible for our own lives and nobody is going to step in and do it for us. To increase our level of Divine Intelligence, we must know that we are the ones to depend on for growth and change.

You can trust that it is okay to depend on yourself when you remember that underneath all the self-doubt and self-criticism, there is a pure, unblocked, joyful nature within you—your ipseity. To return to that state of mind, you must realize it is up to you.

How can you take extraordinary care of yourself?

How will others benefit from you loving yourself more?

7

Universal Spiritual Truth #7:
Hold No Emotional Violence

As long as the root of evil is hidden, it is strong. But if it becomes known, it dissolves. If we ignore it, it takes root in us and brings forth its fruit in the heart. It takes us captive so that we do the things we don't want to do and don't do the things we want to do. It exerts this power because we have not recognized it.
—Gospel of Philip

I could hardly believe my ears when I spoke with Dan again. I was happy to hear that he had just been contacted by a large corporation in the area. "This just feels right, Jayne," he said. "It really does. I'm not letting this one get away." Dan was afraid that he would lose this job opportunity if he did not aggressively pursue it so, unfortunately, he began hounding the company with phone calls and e-mails. To the company, Dan's overzealousness seemed like desperation, and they ended up losing interest in him early on. He was not one of their final candidates.

Dan had seemed to be making so much progress with the ideas we were exploring, his Dialoguing, and his new self-care habits. Yet in one way I was not surprised by the results of his work. The world was giving him back just how he rated himself. I could tell he was still disconnected. I asked him if he would be willing to come back to the office for us to talk. He agreed.

Still thin, but well groomed, Dan arrived at my office on time, his blue eyes somewhat dull and downcast. "Tell me what's going on," I began.

"I don't know," Dan groaned. "I feel like Charlie Brown. Every time I get close to kicking that football, someone snatches it away." He tried a weak grin, but then looked at the ceiling for a few seconds and continued, "Only now I know that it's not someone else snatching it away." He looked at me, "It's me. It's something I'm doing, or…" He paused a minute. "or something my Pleaser is doing."

"What do you think is blocking you?" I asked again.

"My guilt, mostly, almost as if I'm ashamed of myself. I'm ashamed that I can't put all that I've learned about myself into practice and that I can't get a job to provide for my family. I don't know what's wrong with me."

Something else was blocking Dan's progress, and my instinct told me it was something old. My work with others told me that old emotions are often the strongest and the ones that control us the most. At times, Dan seemed so shame-based that I felt we needed to explore the emotion on a deeper level. We'd explored a piece of Dan's past involving his feelings of being second best, but I wondered what else was happening with him. Neuroscience studies show us that limiting beliefs are held in place by emotions, and one of the strongest placeholders is shame.

"Tell me something." I was working on a hunch. Intuitively, I felt shame was a feeling holding Dan back. "When have you ever felt this way before? Like there was something wrong with you?"

Dan sat quietly for a long time, and then I was totally surprised by, and unprepared for, what happened next. Dan leaned over, covered his face with his hands, and began to sob. But the sobs were not what I was used to seeing in my clients because I rarely saw men cry. I realized that when I had seen a man cry, it was totally different from how a woman cried. This man sitting in front of me—his chest began to heave up and down, as if he were exploding with pain. Inhuman, animal-like sounds of deep pain escaped from him. I didn't know what to do, but I knew I was witness to something very powerful at work, as the emotion was so strong. Slowly, Dan pulled himself back together and began to spill out this story that he had kept secret all of his adult life.

"Jayne"—Dan looked up with no concern for the tears running down his face—"this has actually been on my mind lately, though I don't know why, and I don't know what it has to do with anything. I'm not even sure I should talk about it, really. It was all so long ago."

I waited, knowing I was not to be in charge of what happened next. Dan took the sleeve of his shirt and, I swear, blew his nose on it. Then he seemed to come back to the room and looked up at me like a kid who's been caught doing something wrong. I just handed him a box of tissues and played like I didn't notice.

He continued: "When I was nineteen, in college, I met and began dating a girl, Gina, from a nearby university. She was eighteen, a freshman. We fell in love with each other and even talked about getting married once we had both graduated and gotten jobs. She was the first girl I ever had sex with. I really was in love with her. She was pretty and sweet, and she loved me, too. We had a lot in common. We could talk for hours. Then the unthinkable happened. We found out she was pregnant, and everything changed.

"At the time, being pregnant outside marriage was still very much a taboo, and the fact that my girlfriend and I were both attending religious universities made the situation even worse. We were both so scared we didn't know what to do. We looked into abortion, but neither of us could really go through with that. We talked about marriage, but we didn't have any money, any place to live, any way to support a baby. We thought our parents would kill us whatever we did, but eventually, when we were just worn out with worry, we went to my parents for advice.

"My mom and dad were from a very small, conservative town, so they were furious with me for being irresponsible and embarrassing them. My mother told me that the sin I'd committed was completely reprehensible in the eyes of God, and my father accused me of ruining my life and theirs. They told me that the best solution would be for me to remain in college, for us to separate, and for my girlfriend to put the baby up for adoption. They insisted that we call her parents immediately. Her parents agreed that she should have the baby, but they were so upset that they didn't even allow her to come home.

"They made her drop out of school and go live with relatives on the other side of the country. She and I never got a chance to talk about it. These decisions were made in a matter of days. I was sent back to school immediately with instructions not to tell anybody if I didn't want to get kicked out. My dad told me I was lucky he was even willing to send me back to school. He told me that I'd better not let anything like that happen again or he would never have anything else to do with me. I was miserable. I felt that I had ruined Gina's life and lost my parents' love. Again, I had not lived up to the model behavior of my older brother.

"The only time I ever heard from Gina again was the day that she had the baby. She called me at the dorm to tell me that our baby girl was healthy and that Catholic Charities had taken her away and placed her with a nice family. Gina hung up so quickly that I didn't even get to find out what would happen to her now, whether she would be able to go to school, or what she was going to do next. After that, I could hardly concentrate on school myself. I almost flunked out that term.

"Then I made a decision to turn my life around. I decided to become the kind of person my parents would be proud of, the kind of person my daughter would be proud of. I studied like a madman. I made excellent grades and started catching the attention of faculty members, like you, who saw me as a leader. I guess that I started wanting to please others more than ever to feel that I had some value and that I wasn't a total screw-up.

"Despite all of my successes though, I have worried about my daughter every day, but I have not been able to talk about her or find out if she's okay because no one close to me knows she exists. My parents never spoke of her again."

Dan paused. He looked exhausted from relaying the story. Slowly, he began again. "I feel like I should have done more for Gina at the time rather than letting my parents decide what was best for me. I feel horrible about disappointing my father and even worse about committing an unforgivable sin and abandoning a child of my own. When my son Brad was born, I cried for days. Everyone assumed that it was because I was a new father, but I was crying because I felt I didn't deserve him. And I was worried about my daughter and what had happened to her." Even though I couldn't believe Dan could have any more tears inside him, tears again welled in Dan's blue eyes as he spoke, and his cheeks blushed with shame.

"Dan, I am so sorry you had to endure all this embarrassment," I said. "I don't know how you have kept all of this inside you for so long. I understand totally now why you have felt the way you have about losing your job. It has brought more humiliation to your already emotionally packed brain." I knew that being humiliated can be so damaging to the brain development of a young teenager.

"I've just been so ashamed," Dan continued, "too ashamed to talk about it." He wiped his eyes. "Everyone just went on as if nothing had happened. I would have been kicked out of school if the administration had found out, so no one could know there. And when I met Margie, I suddenly knew what true love was all about. I am happy now with her." He hung his head. "I just didn't know how to tell her a story like that. I was afraid she wouldn't want to be with me, and I couldn't lose her, too. Besides, I honestly believed my parents—that it was better to just forget about it."

"This explains a lot. No wonder your energy is so low. How can you possibly maintain high, positive energy while you are carrying this around with you?"

"I've tried. I've really tried." Dan's eyes were swollen and red-rimmed.

"Dan, what your story shows us is that your energy level is being blocked by the specific emotions of shame, guilt, and remorse." I was remembering Dan's results from the testing using the Quantum BioFeedback device. I knew that guilt, shame, and remorse were his highest scores, indicating which emotions were blocking him. His scores on his original testing indicated a baseline of only a 17 percent use of his energy potential. His story confirmed what emotions were blocking him.

I knew that in the next dialogue, Dialogue 6, Dan would learn how to create a set of emotional boxes to eventually empty out the emotional baggage between Dan and his light, which prevented the creation of his goals!

 Coach's Mindset

As I watched Dan cry, I think I witnessed centuries of men's tears come exploding out of Dan. How long have men been told not to cry? Dan had been holding in all those feelings so long that he could hardly contain himself when he started the process of dumping all that emotion out. Dan had been shamed early in his life; as a result, he had wired in many of his limiting beliefs related to expressing his emotions. The buried shame attracted more shameful experiences to him. The thought that a child must be born in a marriage was, at the time, one of society's rules that Dan and his parents accepted without conscious decision, resulting in the thought that he had done something morally wrong. So Dan buried some more shame, and the same deeply ingrained embarrassment about his first child was manifesting itself now as unemployment. His bucket of shame was overflowing, and it had spilled out in my office that day.

Dan today is unaware how his past shame was related to his unemployment. He couldn't really understand how all this buried emotion would keep him from attracting a new job. He had been working long hours, focusing on taking care of his family, and making sure he didn't have time to ponder this past incident of shame. He had been holding back these deeply buried emotions for years. Now, his time off and less-hurried schedule had allowed these feelings to come to the surface.

Dan was indeed stuck in an old emotion, keeping him at a low energy level where he could not focus on positive thoughts. But how could buried emotions impact Dan's search for a job? Let's take a look.

In some ways, Dan had severed the ties between his feeling brain and his thinking brain when he had trained his brain to stop feeling. When important experiences, such as a pregnancy, go unnoticed, are disallowed, not acknowledged, or even forgotten, the result is an incongruency between parts, which compromises the integrity and authenticity of the self. The system is broken into pieces, so to speak.

Little spiritual growth can take place without a connection to our emotions. Becoming aware of his emotions is so important to help Dan uncover enough energy to come across as positive in a job interview. Emotions, like thoughts, affect our energy level. They affect our ability to be who we are.

So you can say that recognizing and expressing emotions is important to Dan's connection to God and his Divine Intelligence. When he shuts down his negative emotions, such as anger or sadness, all of his other emotions are turned off also. If we teach ourselves to not feel anger, our brain begins to store up all intense emotions indiscriminately. Our joy gets warehoused right next to our anger. If we learn to squelch our anger, all our other emotions get pushed down also, and we can no longer find our passion, either. Certainly, after Dan's girlfriend's pregnancy, he shut down and let the Conditioned Self cover him up.

# The Spirituality
Universal Spiritual Truth #7: Hold No Emotional Violence
Self-Compassion

> When we are angry, we have to go back to ourselves and take good care of our anger. We cannot say, "Go away anger, you have to go away. I don't want you." When you have a stomachache, you don't say, "I don't want you stomach, go away." No, you take care of it. In the same way, we have to embrace and take good care of our anger. We recognize it as it is, embrace it, and smile.
>
> —*Thich Nhat Hanh, Nobel Peace Prize nominee*

It is difficult to access your Divine Intelligence if you are still holding a grudge, anger, or resentment toward yourself, as Dan was. As a result, his Light Frequency was low. Buried emotions never die! They just block the light! Just as with the limiting beliefs discussed previously, people are born free of any stored emotions. As we begin to have life experiences, however, our brain recognizes and expresses positive and negative emotions. Babies cry, laugh, and get mad spontaneously. Most of us are taught somewhere along the way, though, that negative feelings are bad, and we're told not to express them. Little girls shouldn't get mad, and little boys shouldn't cry. So we begin to bottle up negative emotions and store them up in our brain. Our universal consciousness has been groomed over the years to think that negative emotions are better kept hidden and not expressed. Repress, suppress, or avoid become the rules.

The idea that energy could be connected to emotional release is not always accepted by those in the West. But many from Eastern traditions believe that our life force (or energy) becomes blocked if we deny our emotions. Hindus refer to this energy as *prana*, and the Chinese refer to energy as *chi*. Further Eastern thought professes that when blocked energy is released through the body, energy begins to flow freely again. Gary Zukav, author of many spiritual books including *The Seat of the Soul* (1989), says it this way: "Following your feelings will lead you to their source. Only through emotions can you encounter the force field of your own soul" (p. 81).

To summarize what is happening to Dan in this chapter: What cannot be faced openly will find its way to the surface in one way or another.

 The Science

The Triune Brain: A Second, Deeper Look

Candace Pert, a research professor in biophysics, believes that this mysterious energy referred to in Eastern thought is "the free flow of information carried by the biochemicals of emotion, what are called the neuropeptides and their receptors. When stored or blocked emotions are released by touch or other physical methods, there is a clearing of our internal pathways, which we experience as energy. One reason we get stuck is because these feelings get retained in the memory, not just the brain, but all the way down to the cellular level" (1997, p. 276). This more holistic concept supports the idea that the body and mind are one. She has shown through her research that each emotion we have is felt throughout our body and not just in the head.

Pert's research updates Paul MacLean's triune brain model, which we discussed in Chapter 2, to show that the model or picture of the brain he designed is present in every cell of our body! Or to put it another way, we have a little brain in each cell of our body. So we can't just say that we are storing up emotions in our brain any more. We must realize that we are storing up these negative emotions in every inch of our body. Looked at in this way, emotions impact our health. For example, we may feel emotions in our gut or our chest. Understanding this new view of how emotions work in the entire body reminds us of our holistic nature and that the different "parts" of our body or ourselves must be understood in relation to the whole.

In Dan's case, I felt he was blocked, and I suspected at this point that he had stored up old, negative emotions from earlier days. As I understood Pert's view of these molecules of emotion, I saw that these emotions were buried inside his body, not just in his limbic brain. To restore his natural energy and Light Frequency, he must address his emotions and release the hold they had on him. Now that we realize every cell of our body has a triune brain in it, we understand more fully why our emotions must be heard. And for our body's natural Divine Intelligence and energy to flow, we must become more aware of our emotions. They are the knowledge we need to be who we are.

Further research has been done to support the idea that we must go back and relive earlier buried emotions to keep them from triggering us and controlling our mind. Much of the research has been with athletes. (See "Approach, not Avoid" in the Endnotes.)

Emotions: The Connection to Our Truth

In our own personal field, our brain is the control center of this electromagnetic energy we call home. Energy is created in the flow of elective current pulsing across a neuron as it connects to other neurons. This energy can be detected as far as three feet from our bodies as it flows out into the Field of the Universe, affecting people and the environment around us.

But it is the heart itself that is the most powerful source of electromagnetic energy in our bodies. This electrical field of the heart is 60 times greater in amplitude than energy generated by any other organ including the brain. It is 100 times greater in strength than the energy generated by the brain (McCraty, 2015, p. 89). Even though the heart produces more energy than the brain, our brain is where we generate the heart's energy, leaving the brain as the one in charge of the whole we are.

As mentioned earlier, emotions are a source of energy. The timing between pulses of the heart's magnetic field is modulated by different emotional states. Information about a person's emotional state is encoded in the heart's magnetic field and is communicated through the body and into the external environment.

Research done by Rollin McCraty, Director of Research at HeartMath Research Center in California and author of *Science of the Heart: Exploring the Role of the Heart in Human Performance* (2015), proposes that we can transmit information emotionally via the electromagnetic field into the environment. This can be detected by others; thus, it shows the human-Earth interconnectivity. Research shows our heart's field changes distinctly as we experience different emotions. Data shows the heart's electromagnetic field becomes more organized during positive emotional – heart-coherent – states (p. 89).

Our heart energy is registered in people's brains around us and can affect cells, water, and DNA studied in vitro. Growing evidence also suggests energetic interactions involving the heart may underlie intuition and important aspects of human consciousness.

Emotions: Energy for the Brain

Our mind is built for divinity. Thanks to new research, we now know the same laws we use to understand how the Universe operates can be utilized in comprehending how our minds work.

In January 2017 in *Physical Review Letters*, physicists show our brains to be more efficient than any known computer we have ever built. They show our neural networks are controlled by the same laws that govern the makings of stars and evolution.

It turns out: Our brains are designed to find the most efficient ways to organize themselves. What the researchers were looking for was how our brains filter out the chaos of information coming at us every minute and decide what to censor and what to save. They discovered that one of the most famous laws of physics, the second law of thermodynamics, works with neurons as well as stars.

When applied to our minds, this law states that the brain will become progressively more disordered unless more energy is put into the system. How do we add more energy to our brains to keep it stabilized and orderly? Add in more emotion! Strong positive emotion decreases the amount of time it takes us to learn. It is the juice we need to evolve.

Our Next Step in Evolutionary Growth: Integrating Our Thoughts and Emotions

Our mind is a system of parts all related and interconnected in its natural state. We have seen that during maturation we divide ourselves into different mental parts, such as a Conditioned Self, and use other coping mechanisms. And in studying the brain, neuroscientists divide the brain into parts to understand how the brain functions. But any system of parts is only as efficient as the communication between the parts. Our feeling brain must communicate with our thinking brain. Just as in personal relationships, such as a marriage, the parts must communicate for the system to run efficiently and harmoniously.

Our evolutionary growth depends on keeping these parts connected and working to the betterment of survival and growth. Inside your brain, your limbic system and neocortex (or your thoughts and feelings) are connected for good reason and are inherent in the structure of your brain. In a famous case from the nineteenth century, a man named Phineas Gage had an iron rod driven through his head in an explosion. Before the accident, he had been a levelheaded man, but after the accident, he was totally unbalanced and unable to maintain focus or be logical. The breaking of the communication between the two centers affected his entire brain (Bohm, 1992, p. 7).

During brain surgery, occasionally doctors have inadvertently severed ties between the patient's limbic system and neocortex, or thinking brain. Such patients then become the subject of serious studies to determine how people behave when cut off from the emotional portion of their brains. The results have been that these patients become indecisive when faced with personal decisions. Why? A lack of strong feelings about one's own life can lead to faulty reasoning. For example, without strong feelings, people make ruinous choices about choosing a spouse, pursuing a career, and other life-changing decisions. In many of these cases, people tend to rely on a combination of "gut" feelings and the emotional wisdom of experience. Remove the connections to this key part of the brain and we become robotic. In fact, the real key to making sound personal decisions is awareness of feelings.

Distractions and Addictions

In this case, Dan's "reactionary personality"—his Pleaser—was trying to block the feelings of shame by keeping Dan busy by doggedly engaging in a job search and persistently pursuing leads, whether they fit his needs or not. His "busyness" was like a distraction for him from the pain he was feeling and, ironically, reproducing another shameful incident: no job.

Old, stored-up, negative energy keeps you from the higher energy state of Divine Intelligence. To move to the next evolutionary step of awareness of his Divine Intelligence, Dan must unload and process any stored-up anger, resentment, sadness, or frustration at himself or others. But before being ready to empty out these emotions, he must step out of his distractions so that his emotions have a chance to surface and be recognized. This is why I had Dan begin to focus on self-care in the previous chapter—so that he could step away from his work addiction. His previous work addiction had now turned into "working to get a job." I knew that as long as he distracted himself by staying in this addiction, he would never have the time to address and become aware of his emotions.

After letting go of these distractions, the next step is to identify what other emotions Dan had stored up in that brain of his. Everyone has this emotional storehouse within, and for some it is more full than for others. When old emotions have not been discharged, they are triggered constantly by current events in our lives. For Dan to create a better life for himself, he had to come to terms with the buried emotions that were left over from his less-fulfilled past.

Let's take a look at more of the science behind Dan's dilemma.

Affective Neuroscience

Affective neuroscience is the study of emotions in the brain. Richard Davidson is considered the father of this field. He has shown in his research that when people are caught up in the throes of distressing emotions, the two brain areas (or parts) most active are the amygdala (part of the limbic system) and the right prefrontal cortex (part of the neocortex). When people get very frightened, upset, angry, or even depressed, the cells in the limbic system start firing wildly and the limbic system becomes overactive. At this time, the neocortex would show in a brain scan to be very quiet. When we are experiencing joy, happiness, or peace, we see a quiet limbic system and an energized neocortex (Schuyler et al., 2014, pp. 176-181). The brain is truly built for divinity!

The prefrontal cortex or neocortex alone is the brain part that facilitates our moods—the right side for negative emotions and the left side for positive emotions (Goleman, 2006, p. 181). But the amygdala plays the key role in emotional expression.

The amygdala is a cluster of interconnected structures perched above the brain stem and near the bottom of the limbic system. These limbic structures do most of the brain's learning and remembering, and they serve as the storehouse for emotions. All passion issues from the amygdala. Just as in the famous case in the nineteenth century, without connection to our emotion, life loses its meaning.

Emotional Hijacking

At times, the amygdala can take control over the neocortex (Goleman, 1995). In neuroscience, this is called an *amygdala hijack*. Think of a time in your life when impulsive thoughts overrode rational thoughts. If you overreact, then you are in an amygdala hijack or Conditioned-Self attack. (See "The Charge Test" in the Endnotes.)

Unlike the other structures of the brain, the amygdala is much closer to being fully formed at birth and matures quickly during infancy. This center of emotional processing is the key to creating new neural pathways that deliver happiness, contentment, and other positive feelings, as well as protection from negative feelings. In fact, it becomes essential that individuals learn to harness the huge amount of energy the amygdala is capable of generating if they wish to retain conscious control of their brains. To gain access to your Divine Intelligence, you must first regain control of your emotional brain and become emotionally nonreactive to old anger triggers. While doing this you must also revitalize the life and energy of your emotional center and then be able to react normally to current life events. As you will see in later chapters, emotions are the energy of God-potential, creative potential. This is the evolutionary step, the shift Dan is taking by going through The Dialogues and working out the emotional charges that have been plaguing him.

Here is a great example of a time when you wired in a new belief during an emotional event. If someone asked you to recall a random day in your life, let's just say May 4, 2007, what could you tell me? What you did? Where you were? How you felt? It is highly unlikely that you would be able to tell me anything about this random day, unless you attached some emotional significance to it, like it being your birthday or when someone you loved died. But what if I asked you to recall September 11, 2001, and asked you to answer the same questions? Where were you that day? What exactly were you doing? How did you feel that day? You would probably immediately experience a flood of memories in exact detail of the terrible events that unfolded on that day. I have asked this question in many seminars and have never had anyone tell me that they could not remember what they did in detail, exactly where they were, or how they felt on that sad day.

We remember incidents laden with emotion when our hearts and minds determine that internalizing the associated emotion would help us in some way. In this instance, fear may somehow alert us to it happening again. The events and emotions of September 11, 2001, caused most of us to rewire our long-held belief—that we are safe in this country and not susceptible to a terrorist attack—to a new belief that we are vulnerable on our home soil. *Hebb's Law*, a neuroscience principle, calls this phenomenon "wiring with fire," suggesting that incidents of intense, fiery emotions are what cause the brain to wire and rewire and thus create memories.

If you could be inside your brain, you would see that the neocortex takes a second or two longer to respond to a stimulus than does the limbic system. In emotional circumstances, it is our heart, not our head, that leads us. For example, if someone says something that hurts you to the core, depending on your evolutionary level of development, you may react very quickly with a smart remark or a protective stance. Or, if you are more mature and have a handle on your amygdala, so to speak, you may think through before you act. You may say to yourself, "That person is in a bad mood" and cut her some slack. So we must become more aware of our feelings and teach ourselves to pause a minute before reacting to move forward in evolutionary growth. Too many stored-up emotions from the past make that impossible.

But we can make our thoughts drive our responses if we do our internal work and release old emotions from our brain. Then we can slowly think through a situation before we react. In most circumstances, we can tell ourselves, "That person didn't mean to hurt me—her intentions were positive," and then we would stop reacting and learn to respond. In this way, our thoughts play the key role in managing our emotions. Once we can take the time to "think through" the circumstance, then a more spiritually mature response can be made. It is definitely a more evolved way of living and thinking; however, it is determined by how full your emotional storehouse is. In Dan's case, his storehouse was brimming over, and he had trouble stopping and thinking before he reacted. If he went on a job interview, he might lose it and say something that would keep him from getting the job. Indeed, he most likely had already done that exact thing in a more subtle way, and this was why he wasn't being hired. It is when we pause and take the time to choose how we react that we are truly evolving into a higher level of living. We can be more in control, monitor our thoughts, then choose the highest ones and live life at a very high level spiritually—or we can stay unconscious and be more robotic in our reactiveness. (See "Emotional Non-Reactivity" in the Endnotes.)

It doesn't take an expert in affective theory to see that emotions and memory are closely connected. Emotions activate neuronal circuits. A greater truth is suggested by the integration of the neuroscience research cited so far. Emotions hold the power to control the brain. In learning to acknowledge and manage our emotions, we have engaged the spiritual power within us. By releasing old emotions, we have restored the free flow of information through the brain and harnessed our brain's spiritual power. This is the turn toward anchoring within and shifting our locus of control from external to internal. By owning this emotional power, we are taking responsibility for our own destiny and activating our Divine Intelligence.

The Teenage Brain

Research now shows that the teenage brain is also as vulnerable as the brain of a two-year-old. Even though we think of the toddler's brain as being especially malleable, the teenage brain goes through a similar stage.

"The brain goes through a rigorous 'pruning' of synapses in early adolescence so that it can rid itself of connections it no longer needs in order to specialize in areas it does need," says Jane C. Hickerson, Ph.D., LCSW, professor at the University of Texas at Arlington. "For example, as children, we play baseball, soccer, tennis, football, et cetera; however as we grow, we limit ourselves to one or two sports, so the brain no longer needs those neuronal patterns that supported other kinds of play. It sheds the patterns it doesn't need and then adds onto and grows more complex patterns in areas that are being used or needed. The result is that during the teen years, the brain is literally shrinking—especially in the prefrontal cortex, which controls self-governance, impulsivity, decision making, the ability to foresee consequences. This means that teens aren't really capable of solving certain complicated problems. Research is now indicating that the brain doesn't fully mature until the twenties, in some cases the mid-twenties" (Hickerson, personal communication, 2011).

This is important to realize to fully understand the dilemma of Gina's pregnancy that she and Dan faced in their teenage years and its effect on Dan's entire life. His brain had been in a vulnerable spot when he had gone through this with his girlfriend. That may explain how powerful this experience was in shaping Dan's brain and thus his limiting belief of his self-worth and value.

Summary of Concepts in Chapter 7

1. When we have been programmed not to feel, the connection between parts breaks down, and communication between the limbic system and the neocortex stops.
2. Memories are created because of emotions.
3. Feelings trump thoughts if we have stored up old emotions from the past.
4. Emotions are our connectors to our truths and our authenticity.
5. Becoming aware of and processing our emotions is key to accessing our Divine Intelligence. Emotions are the energy we use to create.
6. The teenage brain is as vulnerable as the toddler's brain to creating limiting beliefs.

Look Inward

Conscious Evolution: If we don't consciously take control of our emotional development, our thinking brain will take a long time to be able to trump our feeling brain. But if we empty out all our old, stored-up emotions and learn to process our current emotions, we give the thinking brain an edge, a chance to step in and logically help us respond, rather than react, to circumstances. This is the primary goal of conscious brain development.

What unresolved negative emotions are you carrying about others?

What unresolved negative emotions are you carrying about yourself?

8

Universal Spiritual Truth #8:
As Within, So Without

When I set myself straight, I knew the divine child.
—Gnostic saying

Dan had not spoken about his girlfriend or their child in more than twenty-five years. Sitting before me now, he suddenly felt like that confused and scared nineteen-year-old again. Tears flowed down his cheeks as he put his face in his hands and sobbed. He cried for several minutes, overwhelmed by all the old emotions that he had held in for so very long. My silence gave him acceptance.

When he was able to speak again, Dan said, "I can't believe this. I just can't believe that I still have all of these feelings and that they're just as strong as ever. I think I could cry for days." He wiped his eyes on his sleeve. "I never intended to go back to this." He shook his head. "I thought it was all behind me, but like I said, it has tugged at me every single day. I've just ignored it, the significance of it." He looked at me. "I'm not going to be able to ignore it anymore, though." He paused, looking at the wad of tissues in his hands. Softly he said, "In trying to please others, I've neglected one of the most important things in my life." He clenched the tissues in his hands.

"Okay, Jayne, I admit it now. This is about something more than getting a job. I am so hardheaded at times…stubborn…no, obstinate."

We sat in silence for some time. Finally, Dan shrugged. "Now what? I can't just forget about this. I've got to do something. I just don't know what."

"Think about what you want instead of what you think others would want you to do. Move the Pleaser aside for a minute."

"I've got to think about this," Dan replied. "I don't want to screw it up this time. I just need to think."

"And feel?" I asked.

"And feel," Dan agreed. "I don't think I'm going to be able to repack these emotions again. What about Margie and the boys? This will totally blindside them. Margie's bound to feel betrayed. I've lied to her the entire time I've known her. My mother isn't going to take this well, either. She thinks this is over and done with. She'll be humiliated all over again when I bring this up. And what about my daughter? She's out there somewhere, maybe not even thinking anything about her biological parents. Do I dare intrude on her life?"

"What do *you* want, Dan?" I asked, trying to coin the right questions to reveal the answers already there within his mind.

"I'm already thinking about everyone else," Dan conceded, nodding slowly. "Boy, I really am a Pleaser. I've got to keep my head straight here. I've been a good husband and father and son. I have. I've just got to hope that the people closest to me will understand this because I think…I think…I want…to look for my daughter. I think that is what I really want. I want to see her. I want to meet her. I want to get to know her—if she is alive…" Dan shuddered. "It's too late for me to be a father to her, maybe, but at least I can let her know that I care and that I did not willingly give her up. I can do that much." I could feel Dan's energy returning. He left the office that day with much on his mind and heart.

Dan sounded different the next time we talked. I wondered if he had put finding his daughter before finding a job.

"I've had a number of leads in my search to find my daughter," he said, "but so far, nothing has worked out. After all of this, I'm not sure I can find her. Looks like I'm just not going to have any luck in this part of my life either," he sighed. "And maybe it's just as well. I feel like I'm living two lives. I can't bring myself to tell Margie. Instead, I'm sneaking out of bed at night to work at the computer. I don't want to upset her unnecessarily if I can't find my daughter."

Dan did, however, continue his research to find his daughter. He had come upon a book, *The Primal Wound* (1993), by psychologist Nancy Verrier. The book details the pain and rejection that adopted and emotionally-abandoned children can feel because they were rejected by their birth parents in the beginning. At first, the book made Dan uncomfortable. He had spent his entire adult life regretting his decision to give up his daughter, and now that he was finally ready to reach out to her, he was learning about all the damage he had done to her! However, Verrier is an expert on more than just the psychological effects of adoption on children; she also counsels adoptive and birth families and includes information in her book about how birth parents and adopted children can reconnect and build relationships.

The book directed Dan to a few websites that might be able to help him find his daughter. He immediately registered at the sites. He could not search for his daughter directly because he did not know her name, so he submitted her birth mother's name and his daughter's suspected birth date and prayed for results.

In the meantime, Dan was completing Dialogue 7.

Coach's Mindset

In Dan's case, he had admitted his shame but was still keeping a secret from his family. He wasn't able to feel the relief that comes from confession. It was clear from Dan's concern over how his family would react that his Pleaser personality was still in charge. He was still blocked.

Dan had finally fully realized that his journey with me was about far more than simply finding a job; it was about ridding himself of his self-judgment and resulting negative emotions so that he could be free of guilt and shame.

Dan's negative thoughts and focus on "no job" were being mirrored into the Universe and were now coming back to him as "no job." In fact, Dan's patterns and limiting beliefs created the circumstances that led to his layoff. This Universal Spiritual Truth can be summarized with the phrase, "As within, so without." Dan told me once that he had heard me say that phrase so much that he could hear it in his sleep!

Dan was facing a huge amount of internal work that, if not completed, I knew could keep him from finding his daughter, a job, maybe even God.

Dan's belief system had done him a disservice by giving him the message that there was a powerful entity outside himself that he could blame or that would take control and fix things for him. He was like many of us. He believed God was up there, in charge, and he never questioned that theory. Keeping God as some superhuman out there driving the events of his life let Dan off the hook; he didn't have to get into the driver's seat. But if he experiences his own inner power by taking responsibility for his secret, he may also see how to save himself from his predicament of no job and no real understanding for life.

Dan was still holding on to the negative thoughts about himself that were created in the incident with his girlfriend. He felt he had let her down and even had labeled himself as a "bad" person as a result of not taking responsibility for the pregnancy. These unconscious thoughts and feelings about himself had been holding him back. He was continuing to stay in this negative thought pattern by not talking about it to his family.

As soon as he could release this "secret" and tell his family and forgive himself, the quicker he would be able to have positive thoughts about himself and his future life. Everything hinged on increases in his energy level so he could draw the right job to him. The higher his energy level, the higher his Light Frequency and the closer he would get to connecting to that Divine Intelligence, or creative power, within him.

Yet Dan had limiting beliefs that told him not to conflict with others, as it would not please them. Remember, that in his early family life, he had been taught not to talk about his anger or frustration and to bury any negative emotions. This affected his relationships with others and prohibited him from being transparent and showing how he really felt. He needed his family's support right now to overcome his guilt about the pregnancy, but he was too afraid to open up to them. His old beliefs were holding him back from being honest in his relationships.

 # The Spirituality
Universal Spiritual Truth #8: As Within, So Without

In his book *Opening Up* (1990), psychologist James Pennebaker finds that people who are at most risk for illness are those who have experienced trauma and who continue to think about it but do not talk about it. All major world religions, including Hinduism, Judaism, Buddhism, Islam, and Christianity, encourage the disclosure of "sins." Their rules about how to do so may differ, but they all support the idea that it is good to let go of pent-up emotions.

Dying as Transformation

Most religions have this thread of requiring transformation or transcendence into a higher state of being. "There is one truth, not many," says Buddha, "See and know this for yourself." Jesus's inherited religious tradition was Judaism, and Buddha's was Hinduism. Both Buddhism and Christianity are based on older, more historical leanings. Both leaders saw the results of a transformation to be more feelings of compassion, both for ourselves and for others. Buddha and Jesus were spiritual masters inspired by the same source, just appearing in different historical times. Thich Nhat Hanh, a modern spiritual master and Buddhist, in his book *Living Buddha, Living Christ* (1995), says about Hinduism and Christianity, "I touch both of them as my spiritual ancestors" (p. 7). In his book, *Anger: Wisdom for Cooling the Flame*, he concludes: "If we are to be free from our anger, we have to practice, whether we are Christian, Muslim, Buddhist, Hindu, or Jewish. We cannot ask the Buddha, Jesus, God, or Mohammed to take anger out of our hearts for us" (p. 55). Again, it is this personal will, mental force, or Divine Intelligence that most spiritual masters challenge us to activate.

Buddhist "letting go" and the Christian "dying" represent similar surrender concepts of transformation, just different ways of saying the same thing. Dying is the ultimate letting go of the old self, or Conditioned Self, as well as the distractions of the outside world. They both taught a way and path to rebirth. We usually think of Buddha as the enlightened one. Jesus is "the Savior." But maybe Christ's message is different from what has been handed down to us through the ages. It is very limiting to think that Christ must save us. Another way to look at his message is to see his life as a symbol of how we should live ours; moreover, maybe his life is a blueprint or suggests a code as to how to spiritually develop ourselves. One way to view his life is that his birth, death, and resurrection are symbolical acts showing us that transformation involves dying to our own Conditioned Self (or negativity) and resurrecting our Divine Intelligence; the Divine Intelligence Process and this book are structured around those three parts. Maybe being divine is our birthright after all, and we have just ignored the possibility because it also means we must take responsibility for our lives and evolve spiritually, instead of looking to an outside source for the ultimate redemption. But both spiritual leaders—Jesus and Buddha—were encouraging a shift in how we look at ourselves and others. Both are encouraging a change in perception, which, in its own way, is transformative.

 The Science

The brain, as an information processing system, is an amazing entity. Despite its tendency toward negativity, the brain continues to grow and develop; it is always working toward harmony and meaning (Siegel, 1999, p. 139). We are always trying to get back to ipseity, although not always consciously. In everything that comes into your awareness and in every experience, your brain is working hard to appraise the stimuli and create meaning to integrate this new information into your working memory. This is a central function of the brain that occurs with the arousal process of emotions. Incoming information is first rated by the amygdala as to its danger and creates fear if it is thought to be bad for survival. If the information is not dangerous, the brain then seeks to link it back to something similar and begins to integrate it into your value system. Then, if the brain appraises the incident and finds it meaningful, and if similar incidents happen over time, the brain will create a neural network and a mental model or a belief. This process continues to define us as unique individuals. When free from fear, your brain is always working for you toward clarity and meaning. This, of course, is done in split seconds of time!

It takes time to integrate and understand our experiences, but if given the time and safe mental place, the mind will eventually sort things out. The key phrase is "if we take the time." The Dialoguing process Dan is involved in is the space and time necessary for him to process past and present emotions and help his brain get back on target where it can do its job, allow his brain to process old emotions, and take him to a more peaceful and loving mindset. As his emotions are processed, he can then focus the power of his thoughts to create his life. When people fail to take the time to integrate emotional experiences, the result is incoherence in the self-structure (Siegel, 1999, p. 314). We saw in the last chapter how this affects the brain's memory storage. The Dialoguing process leads one toward internal attunement.

Our Inner Voice Begins to Emerge

As Dan continues to dialogue to himself every morning, as well as talk to me, he is able to begin to integrate his past. Spiritual evolution is occurring inside Dan as a result of this process, even though right now he may not realize it. The more he begins to understand himself and the more integrated he becomes in this narrative and storytelling, the more likely an internal voice, or inner guide, will surface. Most people have this inner observer (Siegel, 1999, p. 324). This happens spontaneously to most people as they work the process. Sometimes it remains unconscious, but when people do find this voice, they can then move more toward internal attunement. Sometimes this voice is drowned out by the voice of a particularly authoritarian caregiver; this, of course, is one's Conditioned Self.

It seems our ipseity, our Divine Intelligence, is still in there, always trying to surface and become our real inner guide. I encouraged Dan to tell his stories, as I knew he would work through them and achieve more brain integration, which would result in an inner attunement, and his true inner voice would be heard. When this happened, he would begin to take control of his amygdala and, thus, be in the driver's seat of controlling both his brain and his life.

Our Thoughts Create Our World

So how do our thoughts and emotions act together to create our outside world? Quantum physics has shown that consciousness may affect the reality we observe. Think of our thoughts as the vehicle that we use to get us to the life we want. Our emotions are the fuel we put into the vehicle to make it run. If we have dammed up our system with old emotions, a tune-up is needed before the car will even start. If the fuel is anger, our destiny becomes a negative path of destruction. If we are numbed to our emotions, we become unable to use the emotional fuel, as it is dammed up by the old, unprocessed emotions. Emotions are our energy, our life force, and to evolve and move toward engaging our spiritual energy, we must keep the emotional energy moving and not let it become stagnant.

The amygdala, the seat of the emotional brain, is capable of generating unlimited emotional power to fuel our thoughts if it is unencumbered by old, stored-up emotions. When we become aware of our emotions and release the old ones, we can engage the amygdala consciously, choose positive emotions like excitement and enthusiasm as our fuel, and be more likely to achieve our goals. Our thoughts and emotions weave together to create our destiny. To evolve spiritually, we must take responsibility for clearing out old emotions that are blocking our brain from generating our highest thoughts. These unlimited thoughts can then drive the car down the path to our best life.

Not only have most scientists accepted the fact that our thoughts create, indeed, they found our Universe cannot exist apart from our consciousness. Currently the world of quantum physics demonstrates that our thoughts are the mechanism which changes energy from waves of infinite potential to one exact choice, one concrete piece or particle called matter. So what happened to convince Einstein that we really do create our reality? Nothing. Unfortunately, he died in 1955 shortly before it was proven mathematically that the Observer Effect was real.

How did they discover this truth? Said to be the most important discovery in the history of science, Bell's Theorem substantiates mathematically the Observer Effect as to how the world works.

Specifically, Bell's Theorem points to a profound interaction between our conscious mental activity and the physical world itself. In 1962, physicist John S. Bell first proposed this experiment, but it has been confirmed to be true by many physicists after him. Maybe the reason we have never heard much about this discovery is the difficulty we have in comprehending how it could be true.

The more common name for Bell's Theorem is Quantum Entanglement. Einstein had called this concept "spooky action at a distance." Spooky or not, it is now proven mathematically to be true.

Quantum physicists talk like this: "A change in the spin of one particle in a two-particle system would affect its twin simultaneously, even if the two had been widely separated in space or time." No matter how you say it, Bell's Theorem stands solid and, if we let it, will give us more information about how to create what we want on this planet in this Universe.

The implications are almost unthinkable to real life. First, it forces us to realize the truth: we are 100 percent responsible for what shows up in our lives because we are the Creators of our lives!

The Physics of Consciousness

In 1987, after years of work, physicist Robert G. Jahn and clinical psychologist Brenda Dunne at Princeton accumulated unequivocal evidence that the mind can psychically interact with physical reality through mental concentration by showing that our minds can affect the way certain kinds of machines operate. Combining the idea of the holographic nature of the Universe, it was realized that the brain itself, composed of frequencies of material, can take something non-material which is just a blur of frequencies and make it solid to the touch. Or, as Pribram concluded, our brains construct objects, and Bohm chimed in to say our brains also construct time and space.

Valerie Hunt, a physical therapist and professor of kinesiology at UCLA, provides us with even more information about the power of creating. She has confirmed experimentally the existence of a human energy field outside the brain. Our consciousness is not just contained in the brain but is held in a plasmic energy field surrounding our physical bodies (1990).

Scientists have proven that thoughts are what put this solid world into existence. All our thoughts we have are based on our belief systems, which are built on the personal life experiences of us all. Brian Josephson, winner of the 1973 Nobel Prize in Physics, believed these new ideas might lead to the inclusion of God or Mind within the framework of science.

Consciousness and Light

Current brain research is forcing science to put consciousness, as a fundamental field of study, as important (or more so) than space, time, and matter. Consciousness (or our thoughts) and light are alike in many ways. Both of them occur in the present time. Light does not exist in time and space as we know it, and it is not concrete in the material world. We cannot touch it or hear it. Our thoughts are also invisible, but both may be measured by their intensity or brightness. En*light*ened is a word we often use to say we have become more conscious. "God is Light" is a common phrase. Ipseity is pure consciousness or the light of consciousness. We mention our Inner Light in conversations at times. Two things have always been said by spiritual leaders to be true: the true nature of the self is pure consciousness or the "light" of consciousness and that God is our consciousness. God is present in all things as potential for greatness.

The Power in a Mind Internally Anchored

The research had reassured me that Dan could eliminate the emotional blockages and rewire his limiting beliefs to open up his consciousness to more light. Thoughts are a big part of success. Whatever you think about comes about! I spent a lot of research time examining the power of thought. During my work on my dissertation for my graduate degree requirements, I became interested in a concept called *locus of control*. This concept explains how to be a powerful thinker. Remember that the brain is always working toward meaning and clarity. How can we consciously help it?

In psychology, a person's belief about how much power he has over his own life is known as a locus of control. *Locus* is Latin for "location," so the term *locus of control* literally means where the influence over our lives comes from. Someone who has a high *external* locus of control believes that her life is controlled by fate, chance, and the whims of others. On the other hand, someone who has a high *internal* locus of control believes that his life is the result of his own actions and behaviors. Those with a high internal locus of control are likely to realize they are in charge of what happens to them when they learn to control their thoughts.

The interplay of thoughts and feelings in our creative ability is complex. But the overriding principle is always that we must not let our negative emotions overpower our ability to think positively. The key is to become more and more aware and present-oriented so that we can process our emotions as they arrive, instead of pigeonholing them for later. When we do this, we are more likely to be internally anchored and have the power to create. Dialoguing is one tool we can use to increase our ability to control and manage both our emotions and our thoughts. As we become more and more conscious in this writing, we are able to access our Divine Intelligence.

Summary of Concepts in Chapter 8

1. Our ipseity, our inner potential, our Divine Intelligence can take the form of an inner voice waiting to be discovered in our writing.
2. Narratives and storytelling about our lives help facilitate brain growth and a sense of well-being.
3. When we start to listen to the inner voice through dialoguing, we become more internally located, which means we assume more power and control over our lives.
4. An internal locus of control facilitates Divine Intelligence.
5. Learning to be the conscious narrator of our life will develop our Divine Intelligence and enhance our outer life.

Look Inward

Conscious Evolution: The spiritual truth of "As within, so without" simply means that whatever we think about comes about. Our thinking creates our life! Ernest Holmes, in his first book, *Creative Mind* (1918), was one of the first writers who believed in people's ability to change their lives simply by changing their thoughts. He taught people to change on the outside by changing on the inside. Holmes held a deep belief in the unseen power of the individual who, through the exercise of his thoughts, could radically transform his circumstances. This new kind of thinking is evolutionary! A person can realize untapped powers and resources through mental practice, such as dialoguing. He believed we are all agents of change and that we have a responsibility to reveal, through our thinking, the world in which we wish to live. He believed there was an internal force inside all of us that we could tap into for strength and mastery of our lives.

When we look inward for guidance, we adopt an internal locus of control and accept responsibility for the events that befall us. If thought creates our lives and what happens in our lives, thinking that you have power over your life is the next step in your evolutionary growth in this process and is crucial to creating what you want. Internal attunement is necessary for Divine Intelligence to have a chance to surface. To evolve our view of God means to evolve our view of ourselves and our own power.

What negative things are you attracting to you?

How could you change your thinking to attract positive things to you?

What will your life be like when you take God out of the sky and move it into your heart?

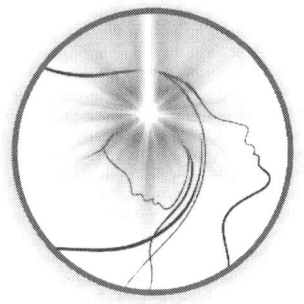

PART 3

Rebirth

It is our responsibility to move away
the stones from the tomb of
our humanness to reveal our own divinity.
Our Resurrection is a rebirth of
the presence of God within us and
a commitment to the Divine Intelligence
within us all.

9

Universal Spiritual Truth #9:
Knowledge of Self Is Knowledge of God

*The greatest of all lessons is to know yourself,
for when a man knows himself he knows God.*
—Clement of Alexandria

Dan's search for his daughter temporarily superseded his spiritual search for himself, yet it was definitely part of his journey. And as in other areas of his life, he was discouraged one minute and filled with hope the next.

"I turn the computer off some nights thinking, 'That's it, I'm through,' but I can't get it out of my head," Dan revealed, "and the next night, there I am, trying something new or retrying a site I've already accessed. It's like I'm obsessed. I'm going to keep looking until I find her. At the rate I'm going, though, we may both be old before I succeed."

"What do you think is blocking your search?" I asked. It seemed to be my favorite question.

"I know what you're thinking," Dan replied wearily. "My discouragement and ambivalence about the search aren't helping, right? I get that part. Really, I do. I just don't know how to change the way I feel about continuing to bang my head against a brick wall."

"What will open up for you when you tell your wife and sons what you're doing?" I asked. I knew that keeping this as a secret could be the block.

Dan shot me a quick look. "No, I haven't told them yet. "No, I haven't. I'm getting closer though. I'm just trying to find the right time, the right way to do it. It isn't going to be easy, you know." He sighed. "But not telling them isn't easy either. I suppose that is a block to my search as well, right? I'm so worried about displeasing them. I can't seem to give myself any peace about this no matter what I do. The Dialoguing helps settle me for short periods of time, but this is just so big.…"

I knew that Dan's relationships were an important part of getting his energy to a higher state. And I knew that he needed to get this old business behind him before he could get back to working on his job situation. I wanted him to commit to move upward to the next step of empowerment. I suggested that he set up a time to go release all these buried emotions and explained what I had in mind.

"A retreat? I think I get what you mean, but honestly, Jayne, I've been on an emotional roller coaster for quite a while now. You want me to go off by myself and get *more* emotional? I don't know how much more I can take. I mean, I've had a hard time holding it together for Margie and Tommy. And, of course, Tommy has pushed my buttons at every turn. If I expressed everything I'm feeling, I think I'd just explode or never get myself back together. I don't know if this is such a good idea. I mean, I'm on the edge, here."

"Perhaps you're on the cusp," I suggested.

"The cusp," Dan said flatly. "Perhaps the truth you are trying to tell me is I need to get unscrewed! My words, Jayne!"

"Well it depends on how ready you are for change…" I explored.

"I'd like for things to be different, of course," he replied thoughtfully. "You know, Jayne, I'm honestly just a little afraid of all this. I think that's really it. I'm afraid of what will happen. I've just gotten a glimpse of my buried emotions, and there sure are a lot there. What if I can't handle it?"

"Dan, this is all so important to you—finding your daughter and ultimately finding a job. It may be hard to convince yourself that this retreat—what I call a Rewire Retreat—is safe, but believe me, the benefits you will get from doing this emotional release will far outweigh the fear you have of facing it. When you finish this, you will have moved something negative out of the way to create a space for something positive to arrive. And you will entertain a new, clear, pure mindset—one that will attract a job to you, a job that is your real calling. Remember how you felt when you were just a kid, still going out to play and not worrying about anything? That is what you will feel like when you finish this work. I can even show you the neuroscience that supports this, if you are interested."

I continued: "You have followed this process so well and have learned a lot about yourself, Dan. Let me explain a little bit about what you will be doing on this retreat. I will have you dialogue yourself back into the original memory of a negative experience you had as a child or teenager. Then when you get back into that same feeling again, I will have you become the adult observer and rewrite the ending so that you have an advocate who took your side, helped you out, and allowed you to process your feelings so they wouldn't be stored up."

"So I can change the ending?" Dan was catching on.

"Yes! At the end of the dialoguing exercise, you will have rewritten your past history. Basically, by dialoguing into the feelings, you will write yourself out of them. Without the heat of the emotion of this memory, you will no longer keep it in your brain. What we know about the brain is that a neural pathway no longer used weakens and degenerates. Then we can rewire or wire in a new empowering belief to replace the limiting one. What do you think?"

"Wow, Margie will agree that I need to be rewired!" Dan laughed at me.

"Well, the hard part is walking back into the old feelings, Dan. No wonder you are hesitating just a little. It is compared to going to the dentist—but just like at the dentist's, you will come out of it feeling better!"

"But, again, Jayne, how will this help me get a job?" Dan asked.

"I don't know, Dan, how will this help?" I was teasing him now with putting it back on him to think through this.

"Well, I guess it is about energy…improving my energy level so I will be more interesting and energized in a job interview." Dan figured it out.

"Holding on to negative energy will keep you from being able to manifest positive outcomes for yourself. It blocks you from the light within you. Or, another way to put it—what you resist, persists. But you will just need to suspend your doubt and take this last leap of faith," I urged him passionately, knowing how much this could change his life. It was so hard to not get more passionate about this than him because I knew of the possible results. I had to hold myself back.

"I know you are right," Dan admitted. "Even with things as crazy as they've been the last year, I'm still afraid of the unknown. But I've made it this far. If I'm going to get to a higher way of living, I have to take the next step. Margie will probably look forward to me being out of the house for a day or two. I'll call my friend Ken. He's got some land and a cabin down in the Hill Country. I know he'll let me borrow it. Anyone who knows my job situation would understand my need to get away. I'll give it a try. Maybe I will find what I am looking for.…"

This time I handed Dan Dialogue 8, asking him not to read it until he arrived at his Rewire Retreat. It contained the instructions on what to do for the time he was away.

 ## Coach's Mindset

Dan deserved a resolution in one form or another, as well as the relief of letting go of all those old stacked-up emotions, before addressing current relationship issues. After he has completed his Rewire Retreat, the relationship issues will resolve themselves. It's important to know, however, that positive thinking alone has not been shown to reprogram the old beliefs. You have to know what to do with the old program as well as how to write a new one.

And Dan would have to go on this retreat by himself. I would give him the steps to write about to accomplish letting go of old emotions, but he would have to do the work himself. I never knew what the outcomes would be.

Letting go of old, built-up emotions is the next step in this transformational process. Symbolically, Dan would be giving up something—the death of the old—and making room inside for his ipseity to have room to grow and develop. This pure, unlimited part of his brain would have a chance to surface and reach its potential. It could be a rebirth.

The Face-Off

Dan had proven time and again that he was open to new ideas, that he understood and was receptive to a process, so I was confident that he was prepared to let go of his old, limiting beliefs and stored-up emotions and regain control of his life. I felt the time was right for Dan to go on a retreat and face off with his Pleaser, but did he? The death of his old self, his Pleaser, would cause a resurrection of his Authentic Self, releasing his Divine Intelligence in this transformational process. I knew 'killing off' the old self would allow new thought to emerge. Transcendence is the resulting effect.

The rules I have created over the years for conducting a Rewire Retreat are specific and delineated by precise steps. Dan would need a safe environment to work with this structured, neurologically-based process. With moving all that emotional energy out, Dan would then have some open space to create something new! Now that Dan was showing the courage to go on this retreat, I was beginning to get a glimpse of that young student who would have done anything in hopes of finding God. He was developing the light energy and eagerness to consciously create.

The Spirituality
Universal Spiritual Truth #9:
Knowledge of Self is Knowledge of God

The more we know about ourselves, the more we can consciously manage our lives. Knowledge and awareness of all parts of ourselves, including our negative self, are necessary to really know ourselves. The

Christian Gnostics said that dying to the old self is to be spiritually reborn. Death of the old and activating Divine Intelligence happen instantaneously when our negative emotions are acknowledged. Since we are to hold no emotional violence, we must acknowledge all our emotions, including the negative ones, to be able to consciously decide on which ones to focus.

There comes a time in all our lives when we are given a choice. "Do we decide to keep using the same old attitudes, defense mechanisms, and coping styles of our old self, or are we willing to shift to something new? Do we hold on to our old, limiting beliefs? Do we dare to let go of the old and activate our Authentic Self and put this new self in charge of our lives?" asked Paul John Roach, senior minister of the Unity Church of Fort Worth in a 2001 sermon expressing the time to surrender.

Killing off our Conditioned Self, our ego, reinstates our wholeness and exposes the layers of ipseity, smoothing out the "broken" places. This is a scary time, as we don't always know, nor can we predict, what will happen with our Divine Intelligence in charge. We are in the middle of making a divine shift to engaging our spiritual power. We are close to turning on the light, but for the moment we are left in the dark, not knowing for sure where the light switch is. The unknown can be very frightening. Buddha would say you must give up the trappings of this world to find yourself. Again and again Christ demonstrated this need to surrender yourself, the human you. Jesus and Buddha, as did most religious leaders, had life-changing experiences in the wilderness, and their wisdom flowed out of those experiences.

The Ability to Forgive Is the Evidence of Transformed Consciousness

The spiritual literature emphasizes the power of forgiveness. The Bible, in Ephesians 4:31, says, "Get rid of all bitterness, rage and anger, harsh words, and slander, as well as all types of malicious behavior. Instead be kind to each other, tenderhearted, forgiving of another, just as God through Christ has forgiven you." Also, according to Luke 17:4, "Even if he wrongs you seven times a day and each time turns again and asks forgiveness, forgive him."

I hear people say they have forgiven people when they are still emotionally charged and are not able to "let go" of the hurt others have caused them. Their head says they should forgive, but their heart is still holding resentment. So until you have gone through an emotional retreat and relived your trauma and changed the ending, until you can own and be responsible for your feelings of anger, organic forgiveness is not really possible. If the people who hurt you are still occupying your thoughts, you have not really forgiven them. In Dan's case, the anger may seem to be more directed at himself; there is a need for forgiveness of the self. However, I felt that on the retreat Dan would need to release and admit anger at others, or his old emotional circuitry would never change. Reliving the events with a different energy level than anger would increase his Light Frequency. The higher the Light Frequency, the greater access to his Divine Intelligence.

The Science

In neuroscience, forgiveness could be equated to a neutral charge in regard to the people who have hurt you. Neuroscience declares that one way to release old emotions is to go back in time to the original incident of shame and rewrite the ending of the incident in a way that is empowering. Then, and only then, is a person capable of true forgiveness and the resulting non-emotionally charged mind. The last task of a retreat is to write out unsent forgiveness letters to those who had harmed you.

Resentment is like taking poison and expecting the other person to die. If we can't let go of the anger, the resentment will eat us up. Resentment is just anger boiled down to a low simmer. Research shows that short bursts of anger, if experienced properly, can catapult people up to a higher energy level. Researcher Margaret Kemeny (1993) says that the release of past anger can enhance well-being if done in short bursts.

The biggest hurdle Dan would face was the resistance to getting angry from the beliefs of his Conditioned Self, the Pleaser. Pleasers believe that conflict and anger are bad and are to be avoided at all costs, and this belief could inhibit his ability to take advantage of that most powerful emotion. But the months of internal work and dialoguing that Dan had done leading up to his retreat had laid the foundation for him to overcome his Pleaser once and for all. I hoped he could get in touch with the original anger and use it to gain inner peace.

Neurologically, you can't be positive if you are stuck in old emotional states, even if the emotions are unconscious to you. Think of it this way: If you have ever had the experience of wallpapering a room, you know that you have to scrape off all the old paper before you can apply the new or it won't stick. Emotions work the same way. Dan needed to let go of his old emotions before he could apply and activate his Divine Intelligence.

As long as he was still holding old negative emotions, he would find it difficult to make this shift to a higher Light Frequency and more difficult to connect to his Divine Intelligence. The old emotions, as well as the limiting beliefs, were acting like a filter, hiding the divine energy and ipseity within Dan. Positive emotions take us as close to God as we can get. Positive emotions like peace, love, and joy *are* God. Divine Intelligence is activated in times of high, positive, emotional charges because of the power of positive emotions. We will see later how science has shown the enormous power of positive emotions.

But at this stage in the process, the goal is to clear out the old emotions. Regaining our natural energy level happens when we own our anger. Anger is the release pin. Again, Kemeny (1993) found that expressing negative emotions has a benefit when you experience them for a number of minutes or maybe a few hours. But when situations, such as losing a loved one, provoke negative emotions over the long term, then you run the risk of unhealthy effects, such as depression. Yet we somehow have the notion that *all* negative events have negative impacts on our bodies. This is not true. It depends considerably on the duration of the experience. In general, research supports the health benefits of removing old, buried emotions.

One of the benefits of writing about negative emotions is increased energy level. Referring to the data from Candace Pert, a neuroscientist and pharmacologist and author of *Molecules of Emotion* (1997), her research shows that energy is the free flow of information carried by the biochemicals of emotion: peptides and their receptors. So when stored or blocked emotions are released by the retreat, there is a clearing of our internal pathways, which we experience as increased energy. This moves us up the emotional ladder to a more positive emotional state of mind.

Many people try to avoid all negative emotions, but in doing so, we lose the ability to hear our inner dialogue and lose touch with ourselves. For example, if you reroute all anger to storage ("I'll think about it later"), you don't even know when you are being hurt by someone. You numb out to avoid feeling. We cut off the pathway to our feelings, and we can't hear what our body is trying to tell us. As we lose our ability to hear our own inner dialogue of our Divine Intelligence, we eventually have to turn to outer authorities for counsel instead of our own inner power. We lose touch with our emotions, we lose touch with ourselves, and we lose touch with our Divine Intelligence. (See "Forgiveness" in the Endnotes.)

Much of the work Dan would do on his Rewire Retreat was based on Dr. David Hawkins's work on enlightenment. His book, *Power vs. Force*, won praise from Saint (Mother) Teresa. His books were preceded by his research on the nature of consciousness and published in his doctoral dissertation, "Qualitative and Quantitative Analysis and Calibration of the Levels of Human Consciousness" (1995). This book brought together for me the basis of the steps of the DI Process because it tied together what seemed at the moment to be the disparate domains of science and spirituality.

At his Rewire Retreat, the instructions would be very specific for Dan to write through the lower levels of emotion up to the higher energy emotions, based on the discovery by Hawkins that they have more power. Dan's negative emotions, which had been bottled up for years, were blocking him from reaching the higher levels of emotions or "states of consciousness" as Hawkins put it. Higher levels of emotional energy would give Dan the ability to attract a job to him, make him feel better overall, and ultimately increase his Light Frequency.

Rewriting Our Histories

In researching the current literature on recovery from trauma, I discovered the groundbreaking work of Judith Lewis Herman, a Harvard psychiatrist (1992). Her findings show what needs to happen in the brain for someone to get over, heal from, and stop the brain from dwelling on past negative events. In short, we needed to know how to clean out Dan's brain and allow it to be restored to wholeness. We needed to re-educate his emotional brain. We needed to unlearn the lesson of helplessness that Dan was recreating in his life over and over again, creating the limiting belief that he could never be number one at anything. The work he would do at the Rewire Retreat could do this. At the moment of getting in touch with the old emotions and letting their truth be known, the brain sees the incident from another view and has the capacity to rewire.

Hebb's Law in neuroscience states that "neurons that fire together wire together." Therefore, to rewire we must also use the fire, or emotion. Returning to the scene of the crime is necessary. After scrubbing off this old anger from the chalkboard of your mind, ipseity (or the resulting clean slate in your brain) will be waiting for you to pick up the chalk and write a new, empowering belief, this time of your own, conscious choice. By having the courage to do his Rewire Retreat, Dan could let go of his old, limiting beliefs and no longer be controlled by them.

Herman, along with many neuroscientists, tells us that to send a new message to the old, emotional circuitry, Dan would need to relive his past negative events and his trauma in a safe environment. The old emotions still brought up shame and anger because the emotional brain was not balanced with the neocortex, or thinking brain, at the time the original event happened. I knew if I could get Dan to go back and remember the memories again, this time experiencing them as an adult who is in control of the situation, he could rid himself of the control the old emotions had over him.

So part of the internal work that he needed to accomplish on his retreat was to go back and re-feel that same fear, sadness, and shame and basically rewrite the ending. This would demonstrate mastery over the emotional brain. In this way, if he could remember details of the old events, such as sensory details, and put words around them, then his memories would be brought more under the control of the neocortex to create a new, more realistic understanding and reaction to the initial event. Soon, in the retelling of the event, the memory starts to transform the limbic system.

This memory retrieval can change the memory for us and make it less traumatic. It can calm down the amygdala and eventually create resonance, balancing the two hemispheres of the brain. When you reflect on a trauma, you can turn it into a teacher in the present and change your patterns. Personal understanding of the memory changes how you make sense of your past, which integrates and modifies the internal structure of the brain.

Our Resistance to Change

Since we know from quantum physics research that thoughts create, then the question arises: If all this scientific proof was provided so many years ago, why is it not mainstream knowledge by now? If a holographic concept suggests we all have access to the unconscious knowledge of the entire human race, why aren't we all able to retrieve it and use it---or at least be aware of it decades after it was discovered? Psychologist Robert M. Anderson, Jr, of the Rensselaer Polytechnic Institute in Troy, New York, says it is because we are only able to tap into information in our own memories. We actually don't remember things we can't believe or that don't support our belief systems. We can't tap into this source of data because we don't believe it is there. We have been taught for too many years that this is not true to change our minds very easily.

Dr. Bernie S. Siegel, author of *Love, Medicine and Miracles* (1986), explains resistance to change is because people are addicted to their belief systems. If we try to change someone's beliefs, they act like addicts, protecting their beliefs with their lives. Before he could rewire, Dan was facing generations of limiting beliefs wired to our general consciousness. Like an addict going into detox, he was facing the fire. His desire and resolve to change his mind would be tested.

Summary of Concepts in Chapter 9

1. Buried emotions never die, but if we dig them up and re-feel them in a safe environment, we can release them.
2. Consciously deciding to go on a Rewire Retreat is activating that inner voice and God within.
3. Facing your Conditioned Self empowers your Authentic Self and kills off the control of the Conditioned Self.
4. The ability to feel organic forgiveness is the litmus test for letting go of old emotions.
5. Organic forgiveness is getting to a neutral charge in regard to old memories.

Look Inward

Conscious Evolution: Willingness, the ability to be open and receptive to doing your own work, is the key to our whole evolutionary movement forward. The resistance to this memory retrieval is like telling the Conditioned Self we are going to change. "Oh no!" it says, "Let's stay safe and not change." If we learn to walk into our own anger, we are taking responsibility for it, and we rise to the next level of spiritual evolution. This is consciously evolving. When we do this, we are learning that we are the Creators, and if we are self-aware enough to own our emotions, we can then own our lives.

If you could create the best life for yourself, what would it be?

10

Universal Spiritual Truth #10:
To Die to Our Human Self Is to Be Reborn

*(I was) very disturbed and (I) turned to myself....
(Having) seen the light that (surrounded) me and the
good that was within me, I became divine.*
—Allogenes, Gnostic philosopher

I had a session with Dan a few days after he returned from his retreat. Of course, I was eager to find out how the Rewire Retreat had worked for him.

"Dan, tell me about where you are now," I said. It was visibly evident that Dan had been impacted by the experience. He looked rested and energetic, really alive in a way that dissolved the lines in his face and made his eyes shine. I eagerly awaited the recounting of his experience.

"I just have so much to say." Dan smiled and went on. "I have to start before I went on my Rewire Retreat. Some things happened that made the retreat, um, well, I'll get to that." Dan sat forward in his chair and put his hands together. "See, even before I left for the cabin, I began to feel that I might be more in control of my life than I'd been in a long time. I didn't always understand the work that you and I were doing, but I can see it now.

"You know, there were times when I have to admit I hated the process's instructions of dialoguing every day. There were times when I thought it was just a futile exercise, but you made me promise to keep at it. And the more I did it—the more I made it a genuine part of my day—the more I was able to open myself up and look at things in a way I never had before. It was as if my brain was sort of expanding and allowing in ideas and options that I had never considered. I didn't always know what to do with this stuff, but on my Rewire, I realized that all the writing I had done in the weeks preceding had actually started the emptying-out process. It's not that the retreat itself was life-changing. The changes were already underway."

Dan looked at me earnestly. "I realized a lot of things while I was writing that 'dissertation' you requested I write with all those questions! But I do know, and I knew at the end of the retreat, that *something* had shifted inside me. I took things that had happened to me and looked at them with a different perspective. It was almost like I was standing back and seeing what was happening as an observer."

He took a deep breath. "I now realize that after I lost my job, I was really wasting so much time frozen in fear and doubt and frustration. And then, I started to dialogue and explore my thoughts. The shift was subtle at first. But then there was this moment where the fear was interrupted, a very small moment when, while writing, I felt a little less stressed. Even though it was over quickly, I could see some hope coming toward me. Then I kept on writing, and I talked more and more with myself, and I began to see some light creep into my situation. The odd thing is—maybe *odd* is the wrong word, it was really just new—I realized that I was the one creating this hope and light through the *discipline* of my dialoguing. I saw for the first time that my feelings, even my attitude, rested on how I was *looking at* the situation. I began to get it—what you have been telling me about the inside creating the outside.

"I'm amazed, I'll admit it—I never thought I could feel this good about myself until I got a job, but you know, I just feel as if I shed a cement overcoat. I can't explain it. The Rewire was one of the toughest things I've ever done. At times, I was scared by the amount of rage I felt, but you know what? This time, I didn't stop myself from feeling it. I just let it happen. At one point, I went outside and just threw rocks at trees. I hurled and hurled the anger out of myself. I had no idea I had such feelings. I raged and cried and cried and raged and wrote and wrote and wrote until there was just nothing left to write.

"After I had emptied out all the anger, I realized the lion's share of my anger was really at myself, for so many things. I saw that I was responsible for a lot of what was wrong with my life; I realized that my lack of awareness had gotten me where I was. I had a lot to be mad about, frankly, including my lack of courage about my daughter."

"You did not plan on being mad at yourself?" I asked. I was pleased at the amount of anger he had discharged because I knew there was a direct correlation between the amount of anger dissolved and the amount of energy recovered.

Dan shook his head. "No. No, I didn't. But there was just so much energy welling up in me that I wrote about all the anger at myself for giving up on my goals, for being so cowardly all my life, and for being afraid to say what I really believed. The last time I remember feeling alive and well was in college before our pregnancy happened. I had escaped the clutches of my parents and had been so happy at school that first year. I was a wild man, full of big ideas, you know? I didn't have to conform to my parents' beliefs anymore. I was free to think for myself. I loved those philosophical discussions you remember. I thought I could create a great life for myself, and I was certain that I was in control of what happened to me to some extent. Yes, and your memory was right, Jayne. I was trying to figure out the God thing...."

"Then, I guess, after the baby, reality hit me, and I knew it was time to grow up. I started worrying about the future and about how I would make a living, so I changed my major to business. I still thought, or maybe hoped, though, that I would use my outside-the-box ideas to run a company and make a difference in people's lives, plus make a lot of money...."

Dan paused again. "Yeah, yeah, I did. Anyway, in those last few hours, I emptied out all the regrets and jammed-up feelings of everything that had happened over the years. There I was sitting on this hill just staring off into space." He looked down and pointed at my water bottle. "As empty as that bottle right there, totally spent.

"Jayne, as I sat there, I felt very empty and void of any feelings, bad or good. And I even felt like there were only a few thoughts floating around in my head. I had cleared out all of the bad stuff I had been feeling about myself. But I let it go. I was able to forgive everyone, including me, and let it move out of my head.

"I took a break at that point and went hiking up a mountain on my friend's place. Well, okay, it was really a hill, but to me it was like a mountain, the mental one I had just climbed." Dan smiled. "So, I got to the top and realized how far I had come. I just knew what I had to do next. I kept on walking, and then I saw a clearing." He paused.

"The same mental clearing that had happened after you let go of all the gunk in your mind?" When Dan had been describing the emptiness that he'd reached in his mind, I, too, had pictured a clearing.

"Yes, just the same," Dan said, but still in his own reverie, not wanting my image of this clearing to influence his recalling of what had happened to him. "It was really a bright sunny day, and I felt the sun on my shoulders. I mean, I could really *feel* it in this moment. I could feel its warmth, and it felt really good.

"But then everything shifted. I could still see this open field, but it became a bright field of light." And then, as if in a different world, Dan started repeating himself. "I got to the top, and since it was not too steep, I arrived at a clearing on the top. And Jayne, as I stood there, it turned into a field of light. I know this is the weird part, but it was like there was light everywhere, and it was very bright...so bright that I felt I had to put my hands over my eyes."

Dan again turned to me to tell me more, and as he did, I could see the light in his eyes. I realized that was what was different when I had first seen him today. From the experience of others, I knew he must have gotten in touch with his inner source of energy. I knew that his Light Frequency was higher than it had been before the retreat.

"Well, this light was everywhere, okay. But then I realized that there was light coming from me as well as toward me. Jayne, I could see and feel this translucent light within me pouring out into the meadow. It was so beautiful. Everything there came alive. I saw—I mean really saw—the flowers growing around my feet like I was a spotlight of brightness allowing me to see things I had not noticed before. I could hear things that I had never heard before, like the noises of bees and birds, and I even think I could hear the butterflies flapping their wings. I know this is so weird, but if I don't tell someone it will go away, you know what I mean?" He looked at me again, but not really for validation, just to let me know he was still aware I was there.

"Okay, keep going. Don't stop now," I told him.

"It really wasn't what I saw that was the most powerful of this experience," Dan said. "It was the feeling I had that was something unbelievable. You know when I told you about that time when my mom had rocked me when I was sick? What you called my Positive Anchor? Well, I have been thinking about that a lot, I guess, because in this beautiful field of light, I felt something sort of like that, but stronger. I felt loved, Jayne. I mean loved in a different way than how Margie loves me or the kids love me. I felt a sense of security within myself—like I loved myself! Yes, that is it, Jayne. I felt loved—maybe for the first time in a long time, at least."

Dan sat back and then immediately regretted what he had said. "Well, you know what I mean...."

"What else?" I didn't want Dan to stop.

"Well, one more thing that happened when I was standing in this intense diamond light in this field. I began to notice other lights around me, and they were bright also. All these lights shining like little Christmas trees together in this field already filled with light. It was so intensely beautiful and full of colors, like in the air, sparkling and dancing at me, and the feeling inside me of a strong force... And no, Jayne, I had not taken any drugs." Dan stopped to come back to the present for a moment. "It was the most beautiful place I had ever seen."

"Tell me more about this...what you call a strong force inside you." I had heard words I knew were important. If we could have measured Dan's Light Frequency with the Quantum BioFeedback device while he was standing in what he described as "intense diamond light," his energy level would be soaring above his original baseline of 17 percent use of his energy potential. I knew he had been in the Field itself where we are sourced in divine energy. He was getting closer to his innate, divine nature, his Divine Intelligence.

"Well," Dan said, "you have talked about an inner anchor to me before, but I never knew what the heck you meant. But now I think I know what it feels like…it's like I felt grounded or…rooted."

He continued: "It was so intense; I think the spell broke, and it all went away! In a split second it was all gone, and I was standing on the top of this hill at Ken's ranch, feeling like a complete fool staring at my hiking boots like they were going to turn into gold or something. And then looking out at the field in which I stood, I could only see the fences that Ken needed to fix and the pile of rocks he had left there last year. And I saw an old campfire we had used last year when we had been hunting on his land.

"It returned to normal, and it was just a hill, nothing unusual at all about it." Dan paused, and his brow began to wrinkle up into a puzzled expression. "I just wanted to tell someone before I forgot it. It reminds me of, you know, when you have this really powerful dream, but you can't remember the details after you've had breakfast?" Dan looked up to see if I knew what he was talking about.

"But Jayne, I think when I sort this all out, I will have experienced a transformation. I don't know for sure, but something happened to me in that short moment in the light."

"So, Dan, where are you at now?" I asked him.

"Well, Jayne, I am right here in this office with you right now," Dan said seriously, and then I saw his mouth twitch a little, and he erupted into laughter. I had to laugh with him, knowing he was making fun of my intensity at following his experience. I knew he needed to make "light" of the situation, and so laughter helped us both. As we settled down again, I rephrased my question.

"So what do you think you did that set this experience up for you?" I asked.

"I know exactly what it was—it was the part of the instructions you gave me that told me to go back and create a different ending to my past memories. After I had written so much I felt like my arm was going to fall off, I realized I had released all the anger at myself and other people. Then the instructions said to basically rewrite my history. In this new version, it was like I was my own advocate in those early days and had someone to stand up for me and protect me," Dan said confidently.

Wanting to see if he had attained a neutral mindset, an emotionally non-reactive state, I asked him how he felt now, a few days after the retreat.

"Before the Rewire, memories of my past upset me, and the thoughts would stay in my head for hours. But now when I think back on my past, I don't feel upset anymore. I don't really feel anything except kind of neutral, I guess. I can still remember the memories of my past clearly, but they no longer make me frustrated and doubtful. Even the anger at my Dad is gone."

"Did that happen immediately during the retreat?"

"No!" Dan's eyes widened, and I could tell he wanted to share something. "I am glad you asked because when I left the retreat I was exhausted, and I have to admit, I had more doubts come up about this darn process of yours. It's like my Pleaser took over for me for a minute. I mean, that one moment on the hill was extraordinary, but it was hard to hang on to. Once again, Jayne, I wondered if you knew what the heck you were doing because I left feeling just tired and empty—but, yes, somewhat relieved—and now that I think about it, much lighter!" Dan was totally transparent about how he felt, and I was glad he could share honestly with me. I had witnessed a similar effect so many times with clients—I usually heard from them that they were tired and spent after all the writing steps had been completed, and it was interesting how the word *lighter* seemed to be the word used to describe their results.

"So, Dan, what happened next? You look so different now." I guessed he had really stepped out of his emotionally charged, reactive state of mind.

"Well, I went home and followed the instructions, and honestly, I didn't talk about it or think about it for three days. Then, when I did start writing again on the fourth day, I realized I was feeling more energized, but still empty. Empty, but peaceful.

"Now, Jayne, there has to be a next step in this process, and I am ready." He raised his eyes and looked up at me as if I had the answer. I had an answer in the form of the next dialogue, Dialogue 9, for him to work.

Coach's Mindset

Dan saw the Field of light because light and energy are the same, and as mentioned in Chapter 1, human beings have light within their bodies. Through the dialoguing and retreat work, Dan managed to clear out the darkness and gain access to his inner light. Light and emotions are both forms of energy, so as he regained his access to the light, his ability to feel positive emotions returned also. *Something* happened to him on this retreat. In a matter of seconds, Dan had arrived at a higher spiritual plane. To get there, he had to relax, to surrender, to "kill off" the old Dan or his Conditioned Self full of limiting beliefs, and risk uncertainty. In short, he had to restore his faith in himself, and when he did this, he created an opening, an empty space where he could rejoin the higher energy and Light Frequency of his own original self.

As he told me later, Dan spent the first hours on his Rewire Retreat absorbed in working on the exercises I gave him. He grieved for his lost girlfriend and child, and he felt guilt over not standing up for himself and others. Eventually, he even allowed himself to feel anger at his father, his mother, and his brother for all the times they had held him back and kept him down. He also felt anger at Margie for not always being the partner he needed, at Tommy for refusing to conform to what Dan wanted, and at himself for allowing the whims and actions of others to influence the course of his life for so long. In the end, the goal he reached was to create an empty space where something new, something conscious, something good could arise out of the void.

After he had discharged the negative emotions, the ending forgiveness exercise put him in a peaceful and contented state of mind, closer to opening up to the God within. I knew that honoring his anger was the most important step in his Rewire process. There are no bad feelings, only stuck ones. The key to his transformation was the fact that he accepted his anger and expressed it. Our feelings are our authenticity, and his anger reunited him with his Authentic Self.

 The Spirituality
Universal Spiritual Truth #10:
To Die to Our Human Self Is to Be Reborn

> We are kept from the experience of Spirit because our inner world is cluttered with past traumas...As we begin to clear away this clutter, the energy of divine light and love begins to flow through our being. *—Father Thomas Keating*

You are here to shine as effortlessly as the sun! As Dan let go of his old negative emotions, his Light Frequency increased until he actually saw and felt it. The moment when he was in the Field of light was an extraordinary moment for Dan. Yes, it may have been only a nanosecond, a short swish into another place for a second, or a tiny glimpse into a vision, but it was enough for Dan to feel the mental force that exists within him. In a way, he had visited "heaven" for a minute, while still alive.

One universal truth accepted by many people, and even one of the popes of the Catholic Church, is that heaven is a state of mind here while we are on Earth. Some people agree that heaven is not a future event but a state of transformed consciousness. Eckhart Tolle, in his book *A New Earth: Awakening to Your Life's Purpose* (2005), said: "'A new heaven' is the emergence of a transformed state of human consciousness, and 'a new earth' is its reflection in the physical realm" (p. 23).

Knowing how the brain works, as well as how the Universe operates, is important to understanding and duplicating Dan's sense of lightness in the clearing. This lightness is the same as the Light Frequency of ipseity. Dan is beginning to see how the brain works *in the Universe*, the power inherent in his self-awareness and authenticity, and how this relates to finding God. He, indeed, did taste heaven here on Earth in his field of light.

 The Science

Light in our Human Energy Field

Science has long said that humans are electromagnetic beings. Valerie Hunt, a physical therapist and professor of kinesiology at UCLA, has developed a way to confirm experimentally the existence of the human energy field. Hunt discovered that there was an electrical presence of the human energy field and she was able to measure the frequency. She discovered that the field was strongest, not in the areas of our heart or brain, but in the area of our chakras. She was convinced that the holographic idea offers another way to understand this energy field (1990).

Electrical Brain Activity

Another one of Hunt's findings was that certain talents and abilities seem to be related to the presence of specific frequencies in a person's energy field. She entered the spiritual realm when she started talking about mystical personalities. She felt that people who measure above a certain frequency are mystical personalities. The question that I asked myself, then, when I was creating the Divine Intelligence Process was: How do we develop a way to raise our frequencies?

As described by Michael Talbot in *The Holographic Universe* (1991), Hunt observed that energy fields changed constantly and that the energy field has an unceasing state of fluctuation. She believes that our energy field is composed of more than just electromagnetic energy. She states, "We have a feeling that it is much more complex and without a doubt composed of an as-yet undiscovered energy" (p. 22). I believe this is where our Divine Intelligence resides.

David Bohm also believed that at a subquantum level beyond the atom there are many subtle energies still unknown to science. As a result of removing the negative energy from his body, Dan in his Rewire Retreat had tapped into his Divine Intelligence and raised his Light Frequency.

But did sending Dan into the wilderness to re-feel all his old emotions actually work? I determined that his Light Frequency was higher, but his readings were still inconsistent, so his Light Frequency had not stabilized at a higher level.

Dan feared going off by himself and spending several days writing about his negative emotions. He even told me he would have rather been whipped. But neuroscience has shown that re-approaching a negative event by writing about it eventually activates a positive feeling in the left hemisphere. Neurologically, walking into or facing your feelings makes them dissipate. Daniel Siegel, in *The Mindful Brain* (2007), said that when it comes to healthy processing of emotions, it is best to approach rather than avoid negative emotions.

Neuroplasticity

Rewiring the brain has always been possible. However, it took until now, with science realizing that our brains have plasticity, for us to understand that we could change our brains, evolving into greater human beings.

A groundbreaking work on brain entrainment, Norman Doidge's *The Brain That Changes Itself* (2007) relates the stories of individuals who changed their ways of thinking. Far from being fixed or hardwired, the brain has remarkable powers to change its own structure and compensate for even the most challenging neurological conditions. Research has shown this through numerous case studies: stroke victims who have learned to move and speak again, older people who have sharpened their memories and children who have raised their IQs and overcome learning disabilities. In other examples, Doidge tells of a man who was blind since birth yet began to see; of another person who was deaf and gained the ability to hear; and of people who had suffered strokes decades earlier (and been declared incurable) who were given neuroplastic treatments and recovered (Doidge, 2007, p. 341).

When the blocked emotions are released, they cause a clearing of internal pathways, and this is the energy that comes after the retreat. Trauma and stress are nothing more than information overload, says Candace Pert, author of *Molecules of Emotion* (1997). She shows that strong emotions not processed thoroughly are stored at the cellular level. If the emotional release is associated with forgiveness, it is especially healing. By learning to bring awareness to past experiences and conditioning those memories stored in your cells, you can release yourself from being stuck and more easily respond to what is happening in the present. Pert, like other researchers, also says that healing can sometimes come from jump-starting the immune system with a burst of long-suppressed anger.

In *The Mindful Therapist*, Siegel names what is happening in Dan's brain during the Rewire Retreat vertical and horizontal integration of his brain. He compares integrating the right and left hemispheres as being like a good marriage. No two partners are alike but find that their whole is greater than the sum of their separate parts. In both instances, honoring differences is important.

Through Dan's autobiographical work of writing down his timeline of memories, talking to me about them, and revisiting his past emotions at the Rewire Retreat, he achieved a vertical and horizontal integration of the brain. Our human brains are quite asymmetrical and, ultimately, integration is about not playing favorites.

In our modern society, we favor the left brain due to its linguistic, linear, and logical nature, yet our right hemisphere contains an integrated map of the whole body and is primarily responsible for the stress response. It is important to understand how data inputs the body to see how important integration is to our health and well-being. Somatic signals or emotions travel through the body starting in the central nervous system. They progress up through the brainstem to the limbic area to the right hemisphere and then to the left hemisphere. This intimate connection of the body and the right hemisphere requires us to also integrate vertically the thinking brain and the feeling brain.

Anyone experiencing trauma or intense stress like Dan's job loss and the long-term loss of his daughter has induced a vertical separation of the thinking and feeling brain. One important factor in enabling a client's brain to integrate is the need for a calm presence in a coach to make it safe enough to talk through past challenges. Most important to rewire is going back into the past and re-feeling the emotions Dan had stored up over the years. These buried emotions were keeping the amygdala stuck in a loop of revisiting the emotions every time something in the environment triggered a past memory. At the retreat, Dan had discharged enough of this past emotion that his brain was no longer controlled by his feeling brain.

As discussed in earlier chapters, past events have been coded into the cells of our bodies through the laying down of synaptic connections. As a result, we develop limiting beliefs as summaries of the experiences to protect us from future pain, and the brain then filters any future input through these limits. Before his retreat, Dan experienced his current job loss crisis through the filter of his past crises and abandonments. For example, the rejection he felt years ago at his parents' refusal to accept his girlfriend's pregnancy is the same response he expects from others because he doesn't have a job. Dan is observing in his mind's eye what he then creates in the future. Our expectations create our reality.

This is where taking the observer mindset as he retells these experiences gives his brain more distance from the events and allows him to revisit the past traumas with a new, more adult viewpoint, increasing the likelihood of brain integration. The observer mindset, or narrative viewpoint, pulls us out of automatic pilot, out of our conditioned brain. Siegel suggests that when you "name" a certain feeling associated with past trauma, you "tame" it and allow the amygdala to relax. This naming calms the mental storms our brain is experiencing. By knowing this and being in a state of reflective awareness as he writes, talks to me about his past, and eventually revisits his past through the eyes of an observer, Dan allows a vertical and horizontal integration to occur.

Siegel states it this way: "Coherence is literally a way of making sense of our life, of feeling fully the sensations of our lived experience, moment by moment, and weaving these with memory and with our visions for a new future" (p. 244).

The Anterior Cingulate Cortex: The Doorway to Our Divine Intelligence

Where is God located in the brain? How do we access God? How do we activate or regulate our ipseity?

Remember, we are dealing with the most complex, sophisticated, living structure in the Universe! The study of the brain in the last twenty years has been greatly enhanced by new brain-imaging technologies. For example, functional magnetic resonance imaging (fMRI) and positron emission tomography (PET) scans can show us the inside of the brain and which part of the brain "lights up" when we are doing or thinking about certain things. This technology has increased our knowledge and understanding of the brain and allowed research to be conducted about the neurobiology of spiritual experiences such as Dan's.

There are many theories about the brain and God. Matthew Alper, author of *The God Part of the Brain (2008)*, believes that people are hardwired by evolution to believe in God for the sake of survival and less anxiety about death. Molecular biologist Dean Hamer presents a "God gene" argument in his book *The God Gene: How Faith Is Hardwired into Our Genes*. Vilayanur Ramachandram, director of the Center for Brain and Cognition at the University of California, San Diego, suggests that there is a "God spot" in the human brain that could substantiate the evolutionary instinct to believe in an outside God. In *The Spiritual Brain*, authors Mario Beauregard and Denyse O'Leary present research that argues that there is a spiritual side to us but, like any faculty, it must be developed before our lives are transformed. But none of these theories really hold up under tight scrutiny.

What really goes on in the brain when a transformation occurs? Physiologically speaking, the *anterior cingulate cortex* (ACC) is located in the neocortex. This part evolved and became an interface between emotion and cognition (Allman et al. 2001). The ACC connects our emotions to our thinking skills, giving us self-control, the ability to make decisions, and the ability to problem-solve; it enables us to decide to be positive rather than negative. It is the key to how we see ourselves in the world. The ACC is the part of the brain that differentiates us from lower animals and makes us human—if not divine.

We activate the ACC when we consciously decide to allow our thinking brain to override our feeling brain. But an important point to remember here is that, until a person has released his old emotions and rewired the brain's emotional circuitry, this is a difficult feat to accomplish. Thus, the Rewire Retreat I sent Dan on was crucial to the ability to put the neocortex in charge over the emotional brain so the ACC could do its job.

After a Rewire Retreat, we are now open to feel our present emotions, express them naturally, and not let them pile up again. We are no longer controlled by our feelings. For example, before the ACC had developed in the human brain during our evolution, we were reactive to the environment with emotions, as if someone "out there" had pushed a button in us, and we were suddenly angry, sad, or guilty. After a Rewire Retreat, we have access to our thinking brain and realize we have something "in here" sitting between our two ears that enables us to choose how we respond, rather than be a victim of circumstance.

The ACC: The CEO of the Brain

The best way to picture the ACC is to see a fulcrum, an imaginary seesaw, that is located right on the boundary between the feeling brain and the thinking brain and acts like a regulator of your thoughts and feelings. When you get too wound up by those old, stored-up emotions, you tip too far over and are out of control. Think of the ACC as action instead of a static part of the brain. Think of it as the energy that is in you that enables you to lead your life and balance your feelings with your more logical thoughts and keeps you from being out of control. So the ACC is not so much a "part" of the brain as it is your spirit. Think of it as Dan's Authentic Self and watch it start appearing in Dan's voice in his conversation with me in the following chapters.

The ACC is where your Divine Intelligence lives. When we decide to live our lives consciously, that little ACC in there is your power on Earth to do whatever you want, an unlimited power available to create whatever you want. With the awareness that this part exists, you also know that you were designed and made to be your own boss. I think of the ACC as being the CEO of your brain, allowing you to shift to a higher mindset. In the evolutionary process, we, as a human race, are beginning to be ready to be our own inner authority and step into our inner power. Indeed, the brain is built for divinity.

So to access the Creator within, we must practice regulating that seesaw in our brain and learn to modulate our emotions with our thoughts. This is much easier after releasing all the buried emotions from the past. After a Rewire Retreat, we have the ability to think through something before we react. The ACC allows us to respond rather than react. Appreciate your ACC and use it consciously—it is your body's tool to express its Divine Intelligence.

Summary of Concepts in Chapter 10

1. Rewiring the brain is possible, as the brain is plastic.
2. The flow of emotional energy is restored when old emotions are discharged.
3. To discharge old emotions, one must approach, not avoid, feeling the emotions.
4. When old emotions are released, it rebalances the relationship between the thinking brain and the feeling brain to a normal, more stable condition.
5. Your anterior cingulate cortex is the connector between your thinking and feeling brain. When you release old emotions, you have restored the ACC's ability to balance the two brains. You can now be more conscious and in control of what you think and feel.
6. In turn, the brain can rewire to a more balanced state.
7. After the retreat, you are now capable of managing your feelings and allowing your thinking brain to override your feeling brain. This in turn activates your Divine Intelligence.
8. Heaven is a state of mind where we are in charge of our emotional energy and choose to live in a positive emotional energy state or Light Frequency; in this state of mind, our Divine Intelligence is at its best.

Look Inward

Conscious Evolution: By going on a Rewire Retreat, Dan took a giant step toward evolution, spinning his world on its axis. He did it by having the courage to step into his emotions. Now remember, we are trained from caveman days and earlier to avoid pain. Dan had to own his anger. He had to take responsibility for his own feelings. When he did this, he opened up a space in him where divine energy could flow, and his very own Light Frequency shone out of him for a moment in time. There was nothing blocking him from his own light. He was real.

Your ACC can be the mental force that can change the physical brain. The movement to ignite this power within is like igniting a spark in your brain, but you must strike the match yourself many times and each time let go of the fear.

How have your emotions controlled you in the past?

If you could rebalance your brain and be more in charge of how you think and feel, what would change in your life?

What could have constituted some moments in which this mental force or Divine Intelligence was activated in you?

11

Universal Spiritual Truth #11:
You Are Your Own Master

> *Whoever achieves gnosis becomes no
> longer a Christian, but a Christ.*
> —Gospel of Philip
>
> *Everyone, when his training is complete,
> will reach his teacher's level.*
> —Luke 6:40

"Jayne, before we go to the next Dialogue step, I do have to share with you some exciting news," Dan said, interrupting my explanation of the next Dialogue he would write.

"The day after I got back from the cabin, I told Margie about the baby—my daughter. She just about went through the roof. Initially she was kind of quiet, but once it sank in, she was furious with me for not telling her before. She accused me of being a liar and of not trusting her with the truth. She just paced the room crying and screaming at me. I thought she was going to throw something at one point. She was so mad, she was shaking. Now normally, I would have tried to avoid conflict. I would have just walked off in an angry huff, but it was so different this time. I just listened to her. I heard her betrayal, her hurt, her surprise...certainly her anger. I just didn't feel any need to defend myself. I've felt guilty and bad about this long enough. She can't make me feel bad about it. I'm not giving her or anyone else that power.

"Jayne, it is like I was standing outside myself observing me. I think this is why I was able to get control of myself and not react like I used to. I feel I have more ability to manage my thoughts and actions, as if from a farther distance away from myself. In the past, I would have immediately tried to smooth things over and apologized and done anything to calm her down.

"Anyway, she finally just stormed out of the room, and we didn't speak for the rest of the day. It was sure a little awkward crawling into bed with her that night. She never looked at me, but I did sleep with one eye open, if you know what I mean." Dan laughed.

"The next day, she told me not to try to find the girl. She started out by demanding. Then she pleaded with me, said it would ruin our family, that the boys would never understand and that I was asking her to take a perfect stranger into the very heart of our family. I know that she's right about the upheaval this will cause, but I need this, and for the first time ever in our marriage, I'm putting my need to do this ahead of her need to squelch it. I told her calmly, but very firmly, that I was searching for my daughter and that I would tell the boys. She just stared at me in amazement and said that I was being incredibly selfish.

"For days, every time we spoke, she told me that she couldn't believe I'd been so dishonest. She asked me a million questions about my former girlfriend, Gina. She even asked if finding my daughter was my way of trying to get back with Gina. I guess that's when I realized why this was so threatening to her. Finally, I just took her in my arms and held her for a minute. You know, I guess I am threatening our family in her point of view. I've done everything I know to do, said everything I can think of to reassure her that my search isn't in any way intended to hurt her or the boys. And she'll eventually realize that not doing this search would hurt me.

"She seems to have accepted it now, or at least she quit fighting it so hard. She knows that I am continuing the search, and she's given up trying to stop me. I don't think she'll ever be totally happy with it, but she has asked a couple of times whether I've heard anything on the websites. I know that your interpretation of all this is that 'As within, so without' spiritual insight of yours. I guess I can't argue with you since whatever is going on seems successful. I do feel more and more empowered by the search. There was a time when Margie could have easily stopped me, but not now...not anymore."

"Have you told your sons?" I asked.

"I'm waiting to tell Brad and Daniel until they come home next weekend, but when I talked to Tommy, did I get a surprise there! He and I haven't had a civil exchange in months, so naturally, I expected him to turn this on me in some way. I was bracing for that, but you know what he said? He said, 'Hey, Dad, I think you're doing a real stand-up thing trying to find her. Way to go, dude.' Then he gave me a fist bump. It brought tears to my eyes. And I realized something right at that moment. I realized that I've been trying to get Tommy to be a Pleaser, and he's not. He's following his own heart, not mine. You know, it's not the end of the world if he doesn't go to college. Why not go to Colorado and have some fun, take some time to grow up a little before picking a career and getting married, having a family? Maybe the kid has his head on straight after all, and I just couldn't see it...couldn't see past my own desires for him to conform. He's really okay. In fact, he's better than that. I'm proud of him for following a dream. I'm going to encourage him to do that all of his life."

Dan's newly found, confident presence was at work, this time inspiring respect in his children rather than rebellion. In our next session, Dan explained that Brad and Daniel, though caught off-guard by the news, were also supportive. Of course, they were protective of their mom and wanted to know her reaction. But after a lot of questions, they seemed to see Dan's resolve. Eventually each boy hugged him and reassured him that if he found his daughter they would welcome her as their sister. This support bolstered Dan as he drove to his mother's home to tell her.

"Telling Margie was hard, but I really dreaded telling Mom," Dan said slowly. "I even considered not telling her right away, not getting her all upset in case I can't find my daughter. We had not spoken about this since they dropped me off at school so many years ago. I wasn't even sure if Mom knew that the baby was a girl. I never told her that I knew. So things went as you would expect. Her first words were, 'Now, Dan, what do you want to go and dig that up for? What's done is done. I don't know why you're even thinking about that. Let it go.' Then she got up from the table and went into the kitchen. I had to follow her to continue the conversation. You know, I felt for her a little bit. I know that I could embarrass her by digging this up. I don't intend to keep my daughter a secret, so the whole family will eventually find out. I knew, though, that it was important not to let my mother shame me anymore. And you know, that was actually hard not to do.

"When she saw my resolve, she, too, accused me of being selfish. Then she pointed out that I would be disrupting this girl's life. Then she cried a little. Finally, I just told her, 'I'm doing this. I'd love your support. I want you to meet your granddaughter, if I can find her. But if you can't support me, that's okay, too, because I'm going forward with this.' And you know? Once she saw my determination, she went to the living room and sat in her favorite chair. She thought for a minute and then said, 'Tell me what you know about this child. If I'm going to meet her, I'd like to know something about her.' That was a huge leap for my mom—huge. I almost couldn't believe it. I told her what little I know, and then we just sat there in the living room in silence for a while. I know that this is hard for her to understand and that she'd rather I not do this, but when I left, she kissed me on the cheek and wished me luck in the search. She wished me luck. She actually said, 'Good luck, Dan. Find my granddaughter and bring her home.' I almost fell off the porch."

"How things have changed for you! What have you changed inside that would allow relationships in your life to be straightening out?" I asked Dan.

"Well, I think I'm in a better state of mind since my retreat. It feels like I'm less trigger-happy with my emotions—like I have more control over how I react. You know, Jayne, I know when I am mad now, and I am okay with it."

"Well, it's time to move on to the next Dialogue now, Dan. Are you ready?" I was moving him back into the process, as his work was not complete yet. He had emptied out a lot of toxic waste, but now, what new beliefs would he want to install in that space?

"Yes, back to the emptiness. I know I want to start at the beginning and design my own belief system this time around. I can see how the emotional release gives me that clear space in which to put new thoughts." Dan was right on target for the next step.

"Do you remember the list of limiting beliefs you uncovered in the second Dialogue? Well, I want you to take that list and use it as a basis for rewriting your belief system. You don't have to necessarily rewrite every one of them, but take some time to decide what you do believe and want to be the foundation for your thinking. Then you and I will create a plan on how to install them."

"Okay, Jayne, I will work on that quickly, as I am also ready to go find my daughter!" Dan looked better than I had seen him since I started coaching him, and I hoped he wouldn't stop right in the middle of the process.

Dan sent me an e-mail the next day with a list of new, more empowering beliefs he wanted to wire into his brain. He was on his way to creating a new inner life for himself. This time it was a conscious, carefully chosen belief system. Dan knew that he was also ready to take the next step to see if he could find his daughter.

Dan's new belief system:

Old Belief	New Belief
I am second best.	I am worth something to my family and this world.
I must not express negative emotions.	I am aware of my anger and respect it.
I must not conflict with others.	It is okay to tell people how I feel.
I must base my opinion of myself on the feedback I receive from others.	I believe in myself.
I must work hard to attain success.	I plan on getting a great job any minute.
I must always worry about the future.	I am happy in the moment.
I must please others or risk being rejected.	I am a good father and husband.
I must never make mistakes.	I learn from my mistakes.
I do not have the power to create my world—my world has power over me.	Life is good for me.
I am not important.	I am important.
I am powerless to the God outside of me.	I am a powerful and conscious Creator.

Encouraged by the support he had received from his family and strengthened by the peace he had found within himself, Dan knew that he was finally truly ready to meet his child. He posted new inquiries on each of the websites Dr. Verrier's books had suggested, determined to finally connect with the daughter he never knew. In doing this, Dan was sending an exceedingly powerful message to the Universe; not only was he projecting strong powerful thoughts and emotions about his intention to find his daughter, but he was also supporting those emotions with resolute action. This message could not be misinterpreted and would undoubtedly elicit a positive reflection right back at him.

It didn't take months, weeks, or even days for Dan to hear back about his inquiry. Physicists say that communication between us travels at the speed of light. Dan had cleared the obstacles allowing him to be reconnected with the Field of light around him. This time, it was only a matter of minutes before Dan received an e-mail from an individual (aptly called a "search angel" within the community) who had seen his post and knew of a possible match. The angel provided Dan with a woman's e-mail address and bid him good luck in his search.

Before Dan began drafting the e-mail, however, he called Margie and Tommy together to share the potentially life-changing news with them. They told Dan not to waste any time reaching out to her. The suspense, they told him, was almost palpable!

Emboldened and assured, Dan began to thoughtfully craft the e-mail to his potential match. He included all the details he knew about his daughter—her mother's name, where he believed she was born, her approximate date of birth, and the name of the charity that had handled the adoption proceedings—and clicked Send.

Later that evening while the rest of his household was sleeping, Dan felt compelled to check his e-mail one last time before going to bed himself. He opened his e-mail and there, in his inbox, was a reply from his potential match.

The woman said that the information Dan had sent about his daughter's history matched hers exactly. Attached to the e-mail were two photos: one of the woman as a baby and one of her as the young adult she is today. Dan was so excited to view those first pictures of his daughter that he roused Margie and Tommy and called them in to experience the moment with him.

As soon as Dan opened the current photo of the woman, the three of them were astonished. The woman smiling at them on the screen looked just like Dan! She had Dan's crystal clear blue eyes, the same chin, even the same way of cocking her head! Dan's eyes welled up with tears as he studied the face of the child he had longed to meet. Seeing the young woman's face seemed to move something in Margie. She and Tommy embraced him and reassured him that she would be accepted into their hearts and their family.

Once he regained his composure, Dan responded to the e-mail with a photo of himself and his phone number, and he requested that she call him as soon as she felt comfortable doing so. The telephone rang the next day, and almost immediately, Dan and his daughter, Lindsey, were making plans to meet face to face.

Dan could hardly contain his anticipation as his plane touched down in Utah a few weeks later. As the plane taxied toward the terminal, Dan thought about the last time he'd flown for a job interview and was amused at the difference between the emotions he'd felt then and the ones he was feeling now. What an incredible difference clearing out all those negative emotions and limiting beliefs had made!

When Dan stepped off the plane and saw his daughter waiting for him, the happiness he felt was overwhelming. Seeing her was just like looking in a mirror, and their interactions were just as natural as if they'd known each other their whole lives.

Dan told me later, "You know, I'll never have that wondrous moment of holding her in my arms as a tiny newborn, but seeing her for the first time was indeed comparable to that. It really was. What a miracle, Jayne."

"Dan, I know I am always asking you this question, but what have you done that has allowed this miracle to happen?" I asked him this question because I wanted him to begin to take some responsibility for the good things that were happening. Just as I had held his feet to the fire with his job loss and the fact that he had created that negative in his life—now I wanted him to know he had also created this positive. But why? He must understand this process or he wouldn't be able to use it in the future—to get the job he wanted.

"Well, Jayne, I think it was just 'out of the blue,'" he said, wide-eyed. When I paused, he smiled and the dots began to connect.

"Hm...you really think that holding on to all those old emotions blocked me from finding my daughter? I guess I was so bitter and angry that no one would want to find me." Dan was silent, as was I.

"I know, you are going to say, 'What do you think, Dan?'" Dan smiled at me again.

"Dare I say again: As within, so without?" I reminded him.

"Jayne, so much is changing right now for me. I mean, inside me—it seems like everything is shifting around after that release of emotions at the retreat. I think I am a little scared of what will happen now." Dan lifted his face to meet my gaze, and his eyes were big, as if he were a child wondering what will come next.

"Dan, it is now up to you to consciously choose what you believe. Give it some thought in your morning writing. If you could fill up your mind with the perfect thoughts and feelings, what would they be? This time around, you have the power to create your own belief system. Are you ready to design your own, inner architecture?" I knew from the light still shining in his eyes since the retreat that he was eager to tackle this next step.

Dan left the office that day pleased with the results of his retreat and eager to write the next Dialogue, Dialogue 10, and fill in his empty space with his own conscious choice, his own belief system this time.

Coach's Mindset

Now that the emotions and old, limiting beliefs that had been clouding Dan's strong mental force were gone, this inner power was attracting good things to him. The more he affirmed it within himself, the stronger his ability to create would become.

Dan's release of negative emotions at his Rewire Retreat had a great impact on his relationships. The emotional neutrality he found at his retreat made it possible for him to react differently now because he was more in control than when he was burdened by all of his repressed emotions from the past. His mind was clear. He had achieved Emotional Non-Reactivity, and his inner light was bright enough that people began to respect and admire him again.

The next step for Dan would be installing his new, empowering beliefs. Research shows that the brain can be rewired (Schwartz, 2002), so Dan now has the opportunity to choose what he wants to wire into that brain of his. The first time his brain was wired, he was not a conscious participant. Now he was in charge. What beliefs did he feel he wanted to own? I suggested that Dan make a list of his old, limiting beliefs and rewrite them into powerful, generative new beliefs—beliefs that he knew would make him feel good.

I gave Dan some specific rules to consider about how the brain wires itself. Some of these rules came from the seminal book on visualization called *Creative Visualization* (1978) by Shakti Gawain.

- First, the brain wires in accordance with emotion, so it is important for Dan to be in a positive emotional state during the installation. In the past, beliefs were wired in with negative emotions; this time, Dan will want to wire them in while in a positive state of mind.
- Second, the brain wires by repetition, so Dan will need to repeat these new beliefs to the brain many times to sustain change.
- Third, a twenty-one-day focus is a good start to getting new neural pathways going in the brain, even though it will take six months of repetition for sustainable brain change, or neural redesign.

In this case, Dan needed to plant his new belief system deep in his head with repetition and then not doubt or dig it up again until it gained enough strength to grow new life into his brain. It would be a matter of discipline as to how quickly he could wire in this new set of beliefs.

I recorded all of Dan's new beliefs; I asked him to listen to the new beliefs three times a day for twenty-one days. This is easily done on most smartphones.

The Spirituality

Universal Spiritual Truth #11: You Are Your Own Master

> Why should I be pleased when people praise me?
> Others there will be who scorn and criticize.
> And why despondent when I'm blamed.
> Since there'll be others who think well of me?
>
> —Buddha (Shantideva 1997)

Like Dan, we are always quick to assume that we cannot possibly realize we have the Creator inside us, much less demonstrate power and influence comparable to that of Buddha or Christ. Most people do not recognize this spiritual energy in their lives as "the source of all." Gnostic teacher Simon Magus said, "God is an 'indivisible point' you will find in yourself" (Pagels, 1979, p. 134). Many people, like Dan did, believe that the divine is something outside, a man sitting up in the sky, or a supernatural being. Alvin Boyd Kuhn, a philosopher and writer in the early twentieth century, put it this way: "Beneath the superficial consciousness, wrapped up with the concerns of ordinary existence in each mortal, there slumbers the un-awakened energy of a divine nature" (Harpur, 2004, p.203). All spiritual evolution is the result of an action of letting go of that trapped divine energy at the core of us all. The divine is hidden within the human.

The Spiritual Law of Circulation

When Dan surrendered his old emotions, he used the spiritual law of circulation. When we give up something, something else fills up its place. The Universe abhors a vacuum, so when we create an empty space, by the laws of science, something is going to replace it. Dan took advantage of this law and began to consciously put what he wanted in the place of the old, negative beliefs and emotions. This is neural redesign.

The Science

Neural Redesign

It sounds like science fiction to think we can now reshape our brain. Installing new beliefs is the point where a person activates her Divine Intelligence. As I explained to Dan, one must consider the following rules about how the brain wires itself, however, as described in the book *Creative Visualization*. They are best used when creating new empowering beliefs to ensure that the brain will accept them. Creative visualization is currently being used in many fields such as medicine, sports, and business, showing that it is a dynamic tool for meaningful change.

1. Never choose a belief that will make you unsafe, as your brain will override it.
2. Use present tense.
3. Use "I am" if possible. For instance, "I am strong."
4. Check out the belief with someone to make sure it is positive, not negative.
5. Always feel the positive results of the goal when you are repeating it to yourself.
6. Choose wording that feels right for you.
7. Suspend your doubts.

Repetition is necessary to wire the new beliefs into the brain. The Hindu people knew this and used chants prescribed by a spiritual master to purify a person's field of consciousness and neutralize the effect of bad karma. The Hindus use a rosary of 108 beads and make a promise to repeat a mantra hundreds, thousands or even millions of times! They don't let their mind wander during the practice, which is called *japa*. To them it is a form of sacrificing your own personal time to spend with God. Neuroscience also supports repetition as one of the best ways to train the brain. According to Alvaro Pascual-Leone, repetition and practice for those first twenty-one days will be crucial to Dan's success in installing a new belief system.

This may be the most challenging part of the Divine Intelligence Process, as it demands so much personal discipline and practice. Dan could have lost the high Light Frequency he had achieved in the Field of light if he had not begun his installation of new empowering beliefs immediately upon return from the retreat. His Conditioned Self was "waiting at the gate" to minimize the power of his Divine Intelligence that he had felt for those few seconds. His brain was eventually going to tell him that the experience was just a happenstance, an occurrence "out of the blue." That is how his Conditioned Self could have sabotaged all his insight from the Rewire Retreat.

Remember that the brain favors negativity and is not open to new thought, at least under stress, yet, if given a sense of safety, it will move us toward meaning and purpose. Dan's meeting with the God inside him—that field of light—illustrates what we must do once we experience God. We must keep in touch with that energy long enough to develop new neural pathways in our brain and reconnect with our Divine Intelligence. You can see why we have been slow to make this evolutionary mental shift of pulling God out of the sky and taking it into our hearts before now. It is challenging and difficult, but worthwhile—and is the next step in our evolutionary growth as a species. Sometimes steps like this take millions of years and many generations, so it is time we get started!

Activate Your Divine Intelligence
In this chapter, you have seen Dan connect with the power of his Divine Intelligence. He has not yet created what he wants; however, he knows now what the energy looks like and the mindset feels like, so he can use this to create. We have known for a while that it is possible to consciously create what we want and that this power lies within us all, but now Dan connected with it!

In 2002, Dr. Jeffrey Schwartz published a book, *The Mind and The Brain,* that would change our view of human willpower or whether we can control our brain. He had conducted studies with patients who had OCD (obsessive-compulsive disorder). People with OCD are some of the most challenging people to help. They experience such life-altering challenges as being unable to stop washing their hands or performing other persistent behaviors that cause problems in their lives. Thus, helping them change their thoughts could be a good test for helping anyone change. Schwartz discovered more than just how to help these people; he made a remarkable discovery. In his studies, he provided evidence for the power of the mind over the actual physical brain. This showed that the mind is not just a mere appendage of the brain, that there really is a spirit in us that we can activate to be in charge of what we think! He called this spirit "mental force" or the "volitional brain" (Schwartz, 2002). In this book, I call it your Divine Intelligence. Science upholds the evidence that our Divine Intelligence exists and is waiting to be activated.

Mental Shifting

Schwartz even uses the term *false brain messages* to describe to his patients with OCD what these symptoms are like. These faulty brain messages can be changed by first becoming aware of the falseness of them (Conditioned-Self thinking) and then choosing to use your brain power to focus on a replacement, thus remodeling the brain's circuits to be more productive. He supports this process when he says that the first skill he had to teach his patients was how to "not" focus on something and then to shift to a new focus. As we learn to be more aware of our limited beliefs, we can then choose to shift focus to a new way of thinking. But we must stop thinking falsely. We must learn to shift our thinking to something different and more positive. Instead of washing their hands, his patients learned to work outside in their garden, go for a walk with their dog, or pursue some other creative endeavor. As Dan develops that ability to shift into more positive thoughts and build a new belief system, he will be more likely to achieve success.

Mastering the Electrical Energy in our Brain

Physicists have proven that the physical world is one large sea of energy with our brain living right in the midst of this energy. How do we harness all that energy to change our brain, or mentally shift our thinking?

As mentioned in Chapter 6, brain science is a triad of electrical (brainwaves), architectural (brain structure), and chemical (neurochemicals) components creating a person's state of mind. Neuroscience itself mostly focuses on the chemical part of your brain. But in this chapter, we explore the electrical component of our mind. Research has shown that we can train our brains through voluntary control over the brain's electrical rhythms for the benefit of changing our thoughts.

Scientists argue over whether our brain's energy is more chemical than electrical, but in truth it is a mixture of several factors. Neurons are actual power sources of both chemistry and electricity. They build up electrical charges by chemical means, continually acting on each other back and forth, increasing energy output potential. As the potential energy builds, it goes into the axon, or the arm of the neuron, which then reaches out to the next neuron. As the energy increases and connects with more and more neurons, the brain completes task after task, keeping the body running smoothly. But the more a cell builds up this charge, the more the frequency of the brain's electrical rhythms increases into what scientists call our cortical rhythm.

Electricity is found throughout the human body. The flow of charged ions causes your heart to beat and your muscles to contract. But nowhere in the body is electrical activity better documented than the brain, which contains roughly a hundred billion electrically conductive, biological wires. The billions of brain cells called neurons use electricity to communicate with each other. The combination of millions of neurons sending signals at once produces electrical activity in the brain, which can be detected using sensitive medical equipment (such as an EEG), measuring electricity levels over areas of the scalp. Since the discovery of such equipment, we have created ways to harness the electrical energy of the brain.

What are Brainwaves?

The combination of electrical activity of the brain is commonly called a brainwave pattern because of its cyclic, "wave-like" nature. This is how energy and thought move throughout the brain.

With the discovery of brainwaves came the discovery that electrical activity in the brain will change depending on what the person is doing. For instance, the brainwaves of a sleeping person are vastly different than the brainwaves of someone wide awake. Over the years, more sensitive equipment has brought us closer to figuring out exactly what brainwaves represent and what they mean about a person's health and state of mind.

Brainwaves are comprised of electromagnetic energy—just like light. Thoughts and feelings create an actual electromagnetic field within the body. The culmination of this electrical energy is called a brainwave pattern, and there are five brainwave patterns. Depending on what we are doing or feeling, our brainwaves change. Brainwave speed is measured in Hertz (Hz). Neuroscientists have identified five brainwave types; the following chart delineates these types of brainwaves, their frequencies, and their accompanying mental states on the spectrum of consciousness.

Brainwave	Frequency	Mental State / Spectrum of Consciousness
Gamma	30 Hz – 100 Hz	Expanded consciousness; awake and actively applying your Divine Intelligence, the results that show up in the material world when your Divine Intelligence and the Field's have merged; being in the flow; performing miraculous feats
Beta	12 Hz – 38 Hz	Wide-awake and alert; a strongly engaged mind; normal waking consciousness
Alpha	8 Hz – 12 Hz	Awake but deeply relaxed and not processing any information; daydreaming; somewhat receptive to suggestion
Theta	3 Hz – 8 Hz	Light sleep, extreme relaxation, deep meditation; hyper-suggestible to the realm of the Zero Point Field—where you meditate and merge your Divine Intelligence with the Field; where you change thoughts into matter
Delta	0.2 Hz – 3 Hz	Deep, dreamless sleep

The Power of Your Brainwaves

A person's brainwave pattern can tell us a lot about their mental state. For example, a person who is anxious will have high beta waves, while people with ADHD will produce too many slow brainwaves. More intentional thoughts create a higher Light Frequency. The brainwave state we are in affects how suggestible we are to new beliefs. The slower the brainwave we are in, the deeper we can go into our subconscious mind. Although ambitious, my objective was to create a meditation to take Dan to a theta brainwave, the most suggestible state of mind.

Opposite of theta brainwaves, gamma waves are your brain at peak performance. In this state of mind, you are fully awake and acting out your Divine Intelligence. This frequency is compared to the ultimate spiritual experience state of mind. It is a state of super-awareness, which reflects a heightened state of consciousness. It is sometimes the result of practicing meditation over years of work, in which you have almost disconnected from brain activity and are close to using zero brain power. You don't have to think about what you are doing—it just happens. It could be compared to being "in the gap" as experienced meditators have achieved. Athletes call it "in the flow" or "in the zone." Spiritual people call it God. I call it "the Creator." Physicists call it being in the Zero Point Field. It is a state of no thoughts or being in the space between your thoughts.

Another way to look at theta brainwave state is that it returns us to ipseity, before we had wired our brains at all. Some researchers believe that in this state you become less of a Conditioned Self and more of your Authentic Self in a transcended way, moving into the universal or expanded perspective. I surmise that Dan was in this state of mind when he found himself in the light of the Field during his Rewire Retreat. When he has practiced being in the theta brainwave and installed his new beliefs, he will be able to create while in the more active brainwave of gamma.

Changing your Brainwaves Using Meditation

A compelling study was done at the University of Wisconsin by neuroscientist Richard J. Davidson, who created one of the most famous studies about meditation to date when he attempted to bridge the chasm between the ancient traditions of Tibetan Buddhism and modern science. Published in 2004 in the Proceedings of the National Academy of Sciences, the study investigated the brainwave patterns of eight Tibetan monks. The monks had spent between 10,000 to 50,000 hours in meditation practice. They were hooked up to EEGs and meditated on "unconditional compassion" as the object of their attention. Then they had MRI brain scans to study what happened in their brain during meditation. The 14th Dalai Lama supported Davidson in the study and became intrigued with the science behind meditation as a result. The control group consisted of 10 students who had no experience with meditation.

Davidson found that the brainwaves of the monks were actually stronger waves associated with problem solving, consciousness and perception. Their brains were more coordinated and exhibited more organized patterns; their brains were more integrated both vertically and horizontally. The monks' brains could keep the gamma signal in their brains alive even after the meditations were over. He showed that mental training in a meditation practice can deliver changes in the interior workings and circuitry of the brain in the area that is thought to control focus, memory, learning patterns, and our perception of consciousness. Basically, this study showed us that meditation creates higher mental activity in our brains as a result of the time spent in meditation, but best of all, meditation is shown to calm the amygdala (pp. 106-224).

Neuroplasticity is being scientifically observed in the brains of those just starting to meditate. Current research by Dr. David Creswell, associate professor of psychology at Carnegie Mellon University, focuses on understanding how meditation makes the brain more resilient for people under stress. Instead of using monks as test cases, he used 35 unemployed, job-seeking, stressed-out adults, much like Dan. His findings, published in *Biological Psychiatry,* showed that meditation fundamentally alters the brain network's functional connectivity patterns very quickly, reducing stress and the inflammation it causes through the body (Creswell, et. al., 2016).

My Work with Dan Using Brainwaves

I knew brainwaves can be changed by introducing sound waves (like music) because, eventually, the brain begins to mimic the sound wave that is introduced. Brainwaves can be retrained to mimic particular wavelengths and pathways. Science calls the concept "brainwave entrainment." It is based on the premise that the human brain has a tendency to change its dominant frequency toward the frequency of a dominant external stimulus such as music or sound.

Since we knew from the above studies that meditation produced higher brainwave frequency, I created a meditation where I took Dan to a theta brainwave, back to the Zero Point Field. While in that empty space of thoughtlessness and quietness, his brain aligned with the corresponding brainwave of the Field. When he was in that unlimited possibilities state of mind, or "wave" instead of "particle" state of mind, he visualized what he wanted: In this case, the details of the exact job he wanted. Visualization was accompanied by a high energy emotional state like excitement, bliss, or gratitude for attracting the right job as if it had already been created and he was living it. Feelings of joy or gratitude would be felt at the same time he was in the state of mind of the Field. At that point, he is the Creator since he is in the mind of God, or what is called the field of unlimited possibilities. With enough practice and repetition, Dan could do what scientists call collapsing a wave into a particle or changing thought into matter.

Dan's subjective consciousness would need to merge with the objective consciousness of the Field, that potent spot beyond time and space, for long periods of time. He found that "sweet spot" of merging with the ZPF, or God, the Creator. In this state of mind, he entered a mindset of observation, or what quantum physicists call the Observer Effect (discussed in Chapters 2 and 8). He was totally in his inner world, unaware of the outside world.

Practice was the key along with discipline, suspension of his doubt, and belief in the process. I created a series of meditations with background music with a dominant theta brainwave to stimulate a lower brainwave in Dan's brain. Zero Point Field, here we come! I knew when you meditate that you are focusing on something, and when you focus like that, the electrical patterns in your brain slow down automatically and relax, and the amplitude of your brainwaves generally stabilize into the theta brainwave range. He would be getting close to theta just by the act of meditation. Through practice and increasing relaxation, he would eventually arrive in the theta brainwave, perfect to allow him to then visualize his ideal job and how it felt to have his dream come true. His brain really had to believe he already had the perfect job.

The type of sound frequencies that are typically used in brainwave entrainment are called "binaural" beats. Two tones close in frequency generate a beat frequency at the difference of the two frequencies introduced. To do this, it was necessary for Dan to use a headset to listen to the recording I created, allowing one sound frequency to come in one ear and another to enter the opposite ear. Thus, the two introduced sounds created a middle of the theta brainwave range.

It was an ambitious project for us both. The plan was for Dan to experience his ideal job enough in the present moment in meditation that the possibility out in the quantum field could actually materialize. Since the Zero Point Field has unlimited possibilities of outcomes, it was the meditation's goal to get Dan to a brainwave low enough in frequency to match the Field where no specific thoughts are found, only possibilities. He had to be in the gap between thoughts where no real thoughts happened. Then, while there, focus enough attention on his dream to feel like it was really happening. Gratitude was the key, for he had to know it was true and then feel how grateful he was for his goal being met. Adding to his writing practice in the morning, Dan's spiritual practice included meditation using these ideas based on electronic brain stimulation. (See Endnotes for more on Electrical Brain Activity.)

Summary of Concepts in Chapter 11

1. In the empty space created by the release of negative emotions, one can consciously choose what new beliefs to install.
2. Installing new beliefs takes six months to be sustainable, but a great beginning is a twenty-one-day focus.
3. Repetition and discipline are key to installing new beliefs.
4. We become luminous and attractive when we activate and feel the God within us.
5. Our new beliefs represent the basis for our Divine Intelligence.

Look Inward

Conscious Evolution: Dan's story may make it seem as if activating one's Divine Intelligence is easier to accomplish than it actually was. He was disciplined in his daily writing, and when it came to putting his new belief system in, he was dedicated and persistent. He knew that it would take time and be repetitive, but he did it anyway. For us to evolve more quickly than our ancestors, we will have to work hard at our internal development; and it is not a practice for the weak. Our Divine Intelligence must be anchored in the boring self-discipline of everyday light or it will never be developed in any of us. As the Zen saying puts it: "Before Enlightenment, chop wood and carry water; after Enlightenment, chop wood and carry water." It is important to admire Dan as he makes his spiritual practice part of his path to enlightenment.

What new beliefs about yourself do you wish to adopt?

If you could change your brain, how would you rewire it?

12

Universal Spiritual Truth #12:
We Are the Creators

If ye have faith as a grain of mustard seed, ye shall say unto this mountain: Remove hence to yonder place; and it shall remove; and nothing shall be impossible unto you.
—Matthew 17:20

The very next day, Dan called with some exciting news: "I have heard from three companies! And they all seemed like they might be able to offer me some wonderful opportunities!" Dan was elated by this turn of events.

"After my Rewire Retreat and ever since I found my daughter, I've felt like a heavy burden has been lifted off my back. For the first time in many years, I feel like I can breathe freely again."

It seemed that finding his daughter had given Dan full faith in his ability to manifest, and now he was creating all sorts of positive changes and possibilities for himself. Nevertheless, he was still challenged, at times, by his family's financial situation. The bills were still there and would start to pile up again soon, and Dan had been out of work for so long that his 401(k) was down to zero. I knew it was a challenging time for Dan to hold on to the new level of positive energy he had felt when he left his retreat. I also knew that if Dan could maintain his positive mindset, even in the face of no money at all, he would have turned the corner on being anchored from within. His own happiness and well-being would be from a source inside him instead of based on his possessions and wealth—a difficult challenge for all of us.

"You know, Jayne, one of these jobs is awfully tempting. It sort of comes through a former colleague of mine. I really think it's mine for the taking. The position isn't exactly what I want, but it could solve a lot of my problems, or at least bring in some much-needed income. The catch is that they want an answer right away. The other possibilities may hold more promise, but it will take time to farm them, if you know what I mean. I'm looking at a 'bird in the hand' situation here."

"Do you believe this is the right job for you?" I replied.

"I knew you'd ask me that question! I've been hearing a voice in my head questioning me on this decision. At first, I wanted to just jump at this job. Margie is still pushing me in that direction. But I've really thought about it. I've tried to truly 'go within,' and my gut is telling me to hold out for that CEO position. I don't have to settle. I don't have to take this job. In fact, I can see problems ahead with this job. It's for a lot less money than I was making, and it has some of the same constraints. My Pleaser is definitely on Margie's side here. Take the money and run. But I want something different. I want something that fits me, the new me. Think I'm going to pass. One of the others really holds some attraction for me."

"How does this decision feel to you, Dan?" I asked. Dan's gut, his Divine Intelligence, was talking to him, and I was glad he was listening.

"Well, scary, to tell you the truth. Two months ago, I wouldn't have passed up anything, much less a nice offer like this one. It's not right for me. I'm going to call my friend tomorrow and decline. I'm going to wait for what I know is a better opportunity. And you know what? Even as I tell you this, I feel my energy going up. For a while there, I was close to returning to something that would have drained my energy rather than generated it. Now in this moment, talking to you, I can feel my energy level going up."

Dan had just experienced his Divine Intelligence talking to him—the unlimited possibilities that God represents, even though he may not have been aware of it. "Now you realize how important it is to honor and respect yourself, Dan," I commented.

"Jayne, just last night, I thought of something I wanted to talk to you about. You know, night is the time you have always been taught as a child to pray. Well, last night I was thinking of the job offers and wanted to fall on my knees and beg God to give me the right job. That is what I have always done when I want something to happen. Ask God, I thought to myself, but who and where is God?"

"What do you do when you pray, Dan?" I asked.

"Well, to tell you the truth, I either beg God to give me what I want, or I ask him to zap someone who is doing something I don't like!" Dan said.

I couldn't help my reaction. "Dan, are you serious?" I asked, very un-coachlike, as I looked up to see Dan laughing at me.

"No, Jayne. However, I do remember praying like that as a child, thinking of God as the big judge up in the sky who would determine who lived and who died." Dan laughed at his childlike image of God.

"Well, so how do you want to define prayer now?" I asked Dan.

"Maybe just talking to God," Dan said.

"I remember when I was in school I read about a famous philosopher saying that prayer is not about changing God—it is about changing us," I told Dan. "It sounds like we need to look at prayer in a different way because you could use a good prayer right now."

"Well, actually I think I do need a new way to look at God, Jayne. When I was telling you my childlike way of viewing God a second ago, I realized I have never grown up beyond that view, even after going through the Rewire. I need another way to think of God; I agree with you. I just can no longer buy the big Father up in the sky sitting on the throne. I haven't believed that since I was a kid. But the thing is, I haven't been able to replace it," Dan said.

"So what is coming to you about your view of God, Dan?" I really wanted to know.

"Jayne, I think what I am thinking is nobody knows what lies out there in space, but I am beginning to realize that God may be a frame of mind or a moment of joy or...a feeling." Dan's eyes were still looking far away, like he was conjuring up a new view of God for himself. "I guess the only thing I am sure of is that people have God in them or the power of God in them—but they don't even know it. I knew it up on the mountaintop when I saw the light in me. I think it was a sign, Jayne, that God is everywhere, even in little ole me."

"I remember you told me you are thinking of doing some research on how people have viewed God through the ages. How can you keep true to yourself and not allow other people's views of God impact yours, Dan?" I wanted to keep pure this new, unplanted ground inside of him.

"Yes, I know, Jayne. I have started reading up on all the various religions, and I am totally confused, as they all have different ways to view God. Yet I think we all have the same God," Dan said.

"Can I have your permission to go in a different direction here?" I asked him.

"Let me guess. 'Close your eyes, Dan.'" Dan was getting a little too close to reading my mind now.

"Yes, Dan, I want you to close your eyes for a minute." I had been trained in hypnosis, which could facilitate this process, I knew, and giving Dan a picture to see in his head would provide him a new perspective on himself. We were at the stage now in the process where he was to uncover his true nature. I was going to help him fill that clearing he had created.

"Now keep your eyes closed and visualize pulling down a movie screen inside your head. On this movie screen, I want you to watch an action movie, one you create. You will be the main character. The movie will be called *Dan's Ultimate Job*! So, on that movie screen, watch yourself in some future time where you are enjoying a perfect day in your career. You are busy working at a job you absolutely love that takes advantage of all your gifts. Think of a time when you were serving others as a leader. As you watch yourself busy during this day, stop to feel the passion that is there because you are doing and being exactly what you were created to be on this Earth. Just watch the movie for a minute....Okay, open your eyes and share with me that one picture."

Dan opened his eyes, and I could tell from the light shining out of them that he had been there! He had just touched someplace where he wanted to be and should be. "Okay. I was in this place with a team of people who were looking to me for an answer. I was totally connected to the people in the room. I didn't know the answer they wanted, but I felt confident that I could lead them to find it. In fact, I felt so confident that I got excited in the dream, uh, the movie. Jayne, I just realized I was the CEO. I was at a board meeting of many people excited about carrying forth a vision but looking to me to lead it! And in the movie, I was leading! I was doing something very important that would impact the world, something very significant, something that I was supposed to be doing. And yes, I knew how to accomplish the goal of the company!"

After sitting in silence, I saw his eyes look off into the distance, like he was trying to connect the dots of what he had just visualized. After a second or two, something clicked and Dan's eyes lit up, as I had seen them do before when he was inspired about something.

"Jayne," he said very softly, "I just realized something. What turns me on is helping other people reach their potential—but the thing is… the thing is…I just 'got' that I get my passion from people, not profit margins. I get excited when I can raise people up! Oh my gosh, Jayne, I know this seems so simple to you, but this is such a powerful new perspective of myself."

"Dan, I don't think it is simple at all. I think you just stepped up the spiritual ladder. Monetizing things actually takes the joy out of doing them, doesn't it?" I identified with Dan, and I, too, "got it" on a deeper level just by experiencing his moment of clarity about who he was. Money really was insignificant when it came to what had real meaning in life.

Still the coach, I asked him, "What would it look like right now in your life if you used this insight?"

This time Dan closed his eyes. I could almost see the wheels turning inside his head. "Well, I have been visualizing my perfect job. I have been thinking of where I want it to be, what I would be doing, and, yes, how much money I need to make. So now I am going to visualize me inspiring people, like I love to do! When I think of what I want, it has now taken on a different intention. Now I want to serve others, and I want a bigger purpose to my life."

"Dan, what do you want in a job? I know we have talked about this many times, but I have never heard you define what you really want—without any constraints." I was guiding Dan to see his goal in a picture and not take it down a notch, but push it up to a higher level.

"Okay, I can see that picture and know what I want. I want to make that movie I just saw in my head be real. But the realness I want is not about money or things. I want my significance in life to come from people. And, indeed, it always has—I just hadn't put two and two together," Dan said, clearly and passionately. His eyes were sparkling in a way I had once seen years ago when he was that student standing in the center of a group of students talking intently about deep philosophical ideas. Maybe he was back!

"Dan, you have just started the act of creation, when you activate this passionate, real part of you. Think of the visualization I asked you to see on your movie screen as the beginning sketch an architect might make when starting to visualize a building she wants to create. Now we need to take the visualization process from the drawing board to reality. So make sure the blueprint is correct.…" I urged him to own the feeling he wanted.

"The blueprint is a *feeling*, Jayne…a distinct feeling of being what I am supposed to be on this Earth. I have had moments of intense passion like this before, and now I realize it had nothing to do with money. It is what I live for…more moments of seeing people rise up and give back to others. Oh no! I think I am beginning to sound as touchy-feely as you, Jayne." This time Dan leaned his head back and roared with laughter. I caught the wave of it and joined him until we were both doubled over in a moment of shared mirth.

"Okay, Dan," I said, as I dried my eyes. "Back to the business of creating. To bring that invisible job into a solid manifestation, you will need to outsmart your Conditioned Self. Remember the spiritual truth of 'As within, so without'?"

"Yes, I remember that everything I think about comes about," Dan said.

"Well, how will your Conditioned Self hold you back from this happening? We had better get your negative thoughts out of the darkness into the light. So take your time, and tell me what limiting thoughts you are aware of right now."

Dan hesitated. "I know you are right, but I still think it would be better not to focus on the limits, and to focus instead on the way I want it to be."

"I can understand that way of thinking right now. That if you just sweep it under the rug—or, in this case, into the closet—that it will go away. But how did that work out for you over the years? I seem to remember that you thought of yourself as second best for many years.... How could it have changed your life if you had gotten that unconscious belief out and examined it earlier?" I reminded him with the best example I could think up in the moment. It is never as easy as just focusing on the right intention because our brains are so trained on the negative, that we must continually bring the negative out into the open so we can then shift to the positive.

"Okay, okay, I get it!" Dan's eyes again glazed over for a moment, and he went somewhere else in his mind. Then he blinked and looked up at me. "So my Conditioned Self is saying something here after all. I can hear the dialogue now that I stop to listen: 'It is impossible for anyone but God or Christ to create something. I am not capable of making this job happen. I am not good enough to do it if I do get the job. Money is very important right now, more than this sappy people stuff.'" Dan looked up at me and smiled and then continued. "'I am second best and should just take a second-best job.' Oh, wow, Jayne, that Conditioned Self of mine is still alive and well!" Dan surprised himself with the strength of his negative thinking. "But you are right—it feels good to get it out! You know, I just figured out—I believe God is a voice in me."

"Begin the dialogue, Dan. What exactly do you want to say back to this limited part of you if there is a God part in you to answer that inner dialogue?" I hoped this would open him up to his Divine Intelligence. So far the inner voice had been a monologue; now I wanted it to begin to be a dialogue and activate the Authentic Self voice within him.

"I am ready for that!" Dan said.

I knew that because he had gone back to the scene of the crime and created new endings to his past memories, it would have empowered him to move out of the helplessness of the childlike voice of his Conditioned Self. He had released all the old emotions on his Rewire Retreat. He had then installed his new belief system, which would give him the power words to generate a new way of thinking, a new conversation in his head. With his diligence and practice, he had created brain resilience—the ability to begin to mold the brain. "So let's just step into this, Dan. Think a minute. What do you want to say back to the Conditioned Self in you right now?"

Dan uncrossed his legs and moved forward in his seat. He furrowed his brow. I could tell he was thinking very deeply. If I had been inside his brain, I would have witnessed the creation of a connection to one of those new neural pathways he had been working on—on the spot! He sat up straight and said with authority, "I experienced my power in that moment on the mountain on my Rewire Retreat. I know that I can generate power myself. It is one of my new beliefs." Dan almost had it.

"Okay, okay. It's coming, Jayne. Give me a moment. This is where I use those new beliefs I have been installing, right?" Dan's face showed me he didn't need me to reply. "So, I will tell that unlimited part of me the following: 'I am valuable just as I am. I am connected to an unlimited power within me. I can do anything. I am a positive influence on others. I am a leader by virtue of my internal goodness…and people are more important than profits!'" Dan paused and looked sheepishly up at me.

"Jayne, I feel a little self-conscious to say them out loud in front of someone. Makes me feel a little too conceited or too big for my britches, as my mom used to tell me," Dan said transparently.

"Okay, let's try something that will give you a more solid feeling of who you are. Close your eyes." I could see Dan roll his eyes at me. But he followed my directions and closed his eyes.

I took Dan back into his past again, but this time to find a memory when he had actually been leading a company like in his movie. I just had a hunch that he had been this passionate leader already, and I also wanted to bring him into a past feeling state or mindset that would remind him where he had been before. He had been connected to his Divine Intelligence many times in his life. He had just never realized its power.

"To keep increasing the likelihood that you will keep your mind focused on your new beliefs, I want you to create another one of those Positive Anchors we have talked about. Tell me your best memory about a success in your business life."

As I suspected, Dan could quite easily recall a time when he had been a strong leader. After several moments of holding his eyes tightly closed, he opened them, and I could see the clear intention in his mind's eye.

Dan said that fairly early in his career, he had been asked to take over a branch of his company that had been struggling: "I had instructions to essentially close down the failing branch and fire all of the employees who worked there. But when I arrived, I began to feel the pressure of laying people off—especially once I met them and realized they had families, just like I did."

"What did you do?" I urged Dan to talk more and create a picture with details in his mind's eye.

"Well,"—Dan continued with his story, and I could feel his energy rising—"I realized that laying people off was not my only option. The town in which the branch was located was not large, but it was close-knit. I decided that if I could persuade the community to support my company, the business the locals generated could be enough to save the branch! So I presented this notion to my superiors and pleaded with them to give me just a few months and enough manpower to implement my idea. They were skeptical, but eventually they granted me two months to carry it out.

"Immediately, I rallied the branch employees together and made a radical suggestion: They would each spend thirty hours of every workweek doing their everyday tasks for the company, and they would dedicate the remaining ten hours to volunteering in the community. The idea meant pay cuts, but it could also save everyone their jobs. To my great relief, all the employees enthusiastically approved of my plan, and within days, they were out and about serving their community. They tackled every task the city council suggested—they built parks, planted trees, painted homes and public buildings, cleaned up trash, all in the name of our company that they worked for.

"At the end of two months, the company was a fixture in the community, and the locals were sending us so much business that the branch actually began outperforming some of the others!"

"So, Dan, help me understand. You've already saved other people from losing their jobs? How did you do that?" I smiled at him.

"This was a defining moment in my professional life!" Dan said proudly. "Not only did I make my company untold sums of money, but I also helped my coworkers keep their jobs and better the community! Wow, Jayne, I can really feel my emotions rising! I feel the same passion now that I did then! I am definitely going to keep this story in my memory."

"Okay, one last step, Dan. Close your eyes again, and pull down the movie screen inside your head. Make this story you just told me into a movie. Watch your movie screen come to life, and see Dan as a leader. Signal me by raising your right hand when you can see the movie."

I could see Dan's eyelids moving around watching something, and I wasn't surprised when he raised his hand. "Now go to the moment in the movie where you were the dynamic leader, and when you get there in your movie, again, let me know by raising your right hand." I was making sure he had the highest moment of leadership in his mind's eye.

"Now, I want you to freeze-frame that one moment in time where you were the dynamic leader. Stop the movie and see one still shot with you in the middle of the screen. I want you to experience this moment on a feeling level now, Dan. Get into the moment so deeply that you can feel what it felt like to be that passionate leader. Now put a black frame around that one still shot, and hold it in your mind a moment, as if seeing this picture saved in your computer." I wanted to give him time to memorize this moment. I knew if he could learn to recreate this high and then confirm that feeling with the repetition of saying his new beliefs, Divine Intelligence would be his.

"Now open your eyes and come back into the room," I instructed. "How was that for you?"

"I felt like a leader again when I was in that movie," Dan admitted.

"You need to feel this new job where you are the dynamic leader as if it has already happened. So I want you to use this past feeling of success, and think about it every time you visualize your new job. When you are practicing your new beliefs, feel the way you felt in that movie—in fact, every second of the day. How could this relate to prayer for you, Dan?" I asked.

"This will be *my* type of prayer. I think, Jayne, prayer is just discipline! I will be conscious enough, or pray enough, to not let others (or even the world of bills and stresses) out there pull me out of the exciting feeling I just created. And I will keep talking back to that Conditioned Self inside me that says I am too big for my britches. I think I have just invented a new way to pray."

I was challenging Dan. I wanted this good feeling, this peace and passion he now possessed, never to disappear into the ethers of daily stresses or to be snuffed out by that old, inner recording of doom. But he had to be the one to do it.

"Hmm. I get it, Jayne. I am getting closer to God, right?" Dan didn't really want an answer, but I could see he was getting closer to uncovering the divine in him.

"Well, Dan," I questioned him, "how is this kind of prayer different?"

Dan paused to consider this. "I am not the victim asking for help anymore. I am taking charge of my own life and not thinking I have to depend on some God out there to help me. I guess I would like to think my inner energy has God power."

I knew Dan was ready for Dialogue 11, where he would learn how to pray in a scientific way. In this type of prayer, instead of asking or pleading with God to change things for him, he would be changing his own brain, allowing more good to manifest for him.

 Coach's Mindset

I encouraged Dan to keep this story and the positive emotions he associated with it at the forefront of his mind and his heart. This mental work would be needed for him to effectively "pray" and "create." Every time he noticed a challenge to his mindset, Dan was to think about his framed picture of being a leader and then to recall his Positive Anchor (the story he told me about his success). I knew that if he called on these positive thoughts and the positive emotions they brought up, he would shift from a low-frequency mindset to a high one. He would channel his spiritual energy to create a job miracle. Brain shifts were keeping him constantly turning within for a more positive thought. By practicing this mental shifting, Dan's brain was gaining resilience, the ability to bounce back when caught with a negative thought or feeling.

But another part to his focus was important, too. If Dan starts focusing on one particular job and feels he must have it, he will narrow the number of possibilities and limit his options. He needs to stay open to all possibilities until he manifests just the perfect one. I had helped take his focus off thinking he had to have an exact job description, and now I had him focused on a certain feeling that the new job would create. This mindset positioned him to pull in exactly the right fit for him.

He needs to be resilient enough in his thinking to ponder one promising opportunity, while always keeping in mind that there are infinite possibilities. If he falls into Conditioned Self, limited thinking, he loses contact with his Divine Intelligence. If he lets his Conditioned Self take over, he will be trying to create in a very human way and not accepting the help of God. *Let Go and Let God.* But this time he was not letting go to an outside force more powerful than himself—he was letting go to accept his own powerful mental force.

My ultimate goal for him was to help him learn to stay in this Divine Intelligence state of mind. I wanted him to always have access to this divine part of himself through awareness, activation, and resilience. His new belief system would eventually be wired in, and he would begin to believe he could do anything, which then empowers his followers. Until Dan could maintain this unlimited mindset, I would continue to remind him that he was the ghost in the machine, that he must be the activator. Engaging this Divine Intelligence could change his old thinking, pulling his mind out of those old layers of experiences inside his head. He would need to catch his Conditioned Self red-handed and pull himself back onto the plane of unlimited possibilities. You might say God lives on this plane.

The Spirituality

Universal Spiritual Truth #12: We Are the Creators

Can We Really Be a Creator?

Does this all mean that our Divine Intelligence alone creates the Universe? John Wheeler, a University of Texas physicist, cautions us that even though our consciousness is the agent that allows subatomic particles to pop into existence, we should not think we create alone. Creation is too complicated a matter to be reduced to such a simple explanation.

Our Divine Intelligence must combine and interact with the greater divine mind of which we are a part to make creation possible. However, it is becoming increasingly obvious that we are the initiator of this creation. The Field is out there for our use; however, until we think, there is no Field. To consciously co-create with the Universe, we must lift the veil of our limiting beliefs and walk into the other side of intelligence where the divine exists. It must feel like Peter felt when Jesus asked him to walk on water. In short, we must realize our own innate powerfulness and change our belief system to match what science is now showing us to be true. Accepting our Divine Intelligence allows us to stay open to learn more and more about this mysterious Universe we live in. Or as Wheeler put it so beautifully:

> Behind it all
> Is surely an idea so simple
> So beautiful
> So compelling that when –
> In a decade, or a century
> Or a millennium
> We grasp it
> We will all say to each other,
> How could it have been otherwise?
> How could we have been so stupid?
> For so long?
>
> John Wheeler, theoretical physicist, mentee of Niels Bohr

Could the one simple idea be: We are God. We are the divine. We are the quantum?

Ernest Holmes, in the first issues of his magazine *Religious Science* in 1927, told us all how to learn to create through visualization: "Think of yourself as you would like to be and calmly state that you are now in the position that you care to be in; that you are now doing the things you would like to be doing; that you now possess the things you care to possess. Look at the picture as you would view a landscape (The Observer Effect); mentally dwell on this picture, trying to find the reality; then leave the entire picture for the Law to work at for you, returning to your everyday affairs with perfect confidence that something is really taking place on the invisible side of your life, and that you will experience, in outward form, all of your inner aspirations."

Scientific Prayer: Use Prayer in a New Way

The type of visualization used by Holmes to be creative is a form of mental practice, like prayer. Instead of praying "to" God, pray "from" the ideal part, the God part, within you. You have the ability to shift from a limited, Conditioned Self mindset to access your Divine Intelligence. This is the way you activate the Creator within you to have the power to create what you wish. This kind of scientific prayer is one method of training your brain to be in a divine mindset. *"That is why you must choose to hear one of the two voices within you. One you made yourself, and that one is not of God. But the other is given you by God. It is possible even in this world to hear only that Voice and no other. It takes effort and great willingness to learn"* (*Course in Miracles*, chap. 5).

Your mind and body are connected as all parts, all in a holistic fashion. We just break down the body and brain into parts so we can better understand them, like scientists do with the natural world. As we practice this mental shifting, the part of the Conditioned Self begins to fade into the background, and we become more unified. As American author Neale Donald Walsch put it in his book *Conversations with God* (1995), "You are, have always been, and will always be, a divine part of the divine whole, a member of the body. That is why the act of rejoining the whole, of returning to God, is called Remembrance. You actually choose to remember Who You Really Are, or to join together with various parts of you to experience the all of you—which is to say, the all of me" (p. 28).

 The Science

To be able to create something positive, we must be able to sustain high levels of positive thought and positive emotion. Our outside world will naturally send us negative information during each day. To be able to create, we must learn to control our focus by shifting our brain back to positivity when we hear something negative. The ability to evolve our brains to a higher level takes what scientists call *resilience*. Resilience is the brain's ability to bounce back from negative thoughts and shift into more positive ones. It promotes the growth of integrative fibers in the middle prefrontal areas (Siegel, 2007, p. 291). Yes, this spiritual practice actually grows the brain! Brain resilience comes from a deep form of internal attunement in which we become our own best friend and are more available to ourselves and thus more likely to have long-lasting relationships with others. We become known to ourselves. This is one of the benefits of the dialoguing and spiritual practice Dan was doing—he took the time to get to know who he was, so his Divine Intelligence began to emerge. (See "Resiliency" in the Endnotes.)

Fool the Brain

How does this mental shifting work? From a neuroscience point of view, imagining and doing are not that different inside the brain. The same parts of the brain are activated in both instances. This is why top athletes use visualization to improve their performance. I was instructing Dan to begin to visualize and "see" the exact job he wanted right now. But more important, the feelings of his Positive Anchor of success, worthiness, and value had now wrapped themselves around his visualization for just the right job. The power of these feelings was sure to help him manifest just the right position.

William James, a nineteenth-century philosopher, said, "The only willful choice one has is the quality of attention one gives to a thought at any moment" (Schwartz, 2002, p. 319). Visualization is to the brain as the real, live event would be. Mental imagery activates the same regions of the brain that actual perception does (Schwartz, 2002).

Visualization Creates New Neuronal Pathways

As discussed in Chapter 6, Alvaro Pascual-Leone's work with students of Braille showed that mental practice could change the brain. But, he wondered, could thoughts alone change the material structure of the brain? He chose piano lessons as the setting for his next study to test whether mental practice and imagination could lead to physical changes.

First, Pascual-Leone taught people who had never studied piano a sequence of notes. He showed them which fingers to move and let them hear the notes. He then divided the students into two groups. The "mental practice" group sat in front of an electric piano keyboard two hours a day for five days. They imagined both playing the sequence and hearing it played. A second group, called the "physical practice" group, actually played the music two hours a day for five days. He mapped the brains of both groups before, during, and after the experiment each day. Both groups were then asked to play the series of notes, and a computer measured the accuracy of their performances.

Both groups learned to play the sequence and showed similar brain map changes. "Remarkably, mental practice alone produced the same physical changes in the motor system as actually playing the piece" (Doidge, 207, p. 201) Also, the imagining players were as accurate as the actual players were on their third day.

Shift to a Higher Energy

Dan can create! If Dan was in touch with this mindset, he had awakened the Creator within him. I knew, without a doubt, he could create whatever he wanted. When Dan mentioned that he could generate a feeling of positive energy when he thought about turning down the job offered and not settling for anything less, he had experienced the ability to activate his Divine Intelligence. Also, whenever he is shifting to a higher-energy mindset, he is using his Divine Intelligence. He is consciously choosing how he wants to be, and this is praying, although he may not at the time recognize the power of this type of prayer.

This is the part of the process that gets scary to some people. Do we really have the power of God within us? And can we awaken this Creator? Absolutely! But one must silence the Conditioned Self to "be on the same wavelength" as the Creator within. The release of emotions at the Rewire Retreat sets the stage, but the Conditioned Self has been around for a long time, and those neural pathways are dug deeply into our brain in our early days. It is no small chore to keep reminding your brain to change its mind, nor is the job ever completely finished.

Recall

There is a way to rattle your Conditioned Self's cage to help you change. You have been connected to your Divine Intelligence many times during your life already, so a good practice is to remind your brain of this. Your body remembers how it felt to be connected to your Divine Intelligence from times in the past. Accomplished athletes call it being "in the flow" or "in the zone" and know how to access this part of themselves. They realize that after practicing an athletic skill for several months, the body stores the skill in muscle memory. For example, if you work out with weights for some time and build up your muscles, you can then stop for several months. When you go back to the weights, your body remembers and quickly rebuilds the muscle tone. Using a Positive Anchor is the same principle.

A Positive Anchor

This same principle acts in relation to remembering times when you activated this higher intelligence in you. This principle is why I had Dan think of a past success. He had been there before. He could have recalled any number of times because your body and your mind remember times when you excelled, just as they remember stressful times. Remember, emotion is what wires in memories, so you wire in a memory any time you have a positive experience, just as you do with a negative experience. Like learning to type or ride a bicycle, you do not have to relearn, just sharpen up a little.

When Dan did our "movie time," he could remember a time when he had already been in touch with his divine nature. When he took charge of his brain and had the intention of focusing on the positive things about himself, it was a Positive Anchor. From experience, I know that going back to a successful time in the past creates positive emotion. This is just the ingredient necessary to create new brain pathways. Positive emotion is more powerful than negative emotion, which I will explain in the next chapter. If you can focus the brain on this positive experience enough times in practice, you can eventually create a new neural pathway in your brain that you can call on when you need confidence. I wanted Dan to have this Positive Anchor as a tool for the future in his job interviews.

Growing the Brain

Learning to shift your brain from your Conditioned Self to your Divine Intelligence eventually changes your brain for that moment. That is what a mental shift is all about: changing what you are thinking about to a higher level of Light Frequency. Research shows over and over that the brain can be changed. When I was studying the mind in the early seventies, the general trend was that the personality, or brain wiring, was shaped by the time a child was five years old, and little could be done to change it.

Over the last thirty years or so, physicians and scientists have used brain-imaging machines to view and study the electrical activity across the surface of the brain, which has provided new insight into the workings of the mind. Today fMRIs provide definitive answers. Even though our beliefs are wired in at a very deep level, with enough practice and motivation, we can change our mental models. Despite the hardwiring in the brain, the brain remains a plastic organ that can be shaped and changed. Yogis can appear to be dead and adjust their own heartbeats through their practice of meditation. I know people who can walk on hot burning coals without pain or injury to their body. These inspiring examples show us how we, too, can similarly change our minds with specific rewiring techniques.

The ability to control the movement of energy and information through your brain is your Divine Intelligence. Even if you are not aware of it, it is acting for you. In the Divine Intelligence Process, we want to become more aware of this agency within that can be in charge of this movement. We can then channel this energy and focus it to form what we want. This is Creation, something Dan is learning.

Summary of Concepts in Chapter 12

1. Shifting is the action we take when we move our thoughts away from a Conditioned-Self mindset to our divine mind, capable of doing anything. This is Divine Intelligence in action.
2. A Positive Anchor is a memory of a former success, reminding us what being in our Divine Intelligence is like.
3. The brain wires with positive emotions as well as negative ones.
4. Prayer, as defined in this chapter, means mentally talking to yourself—keeping your brain in a positive mindset and expecting your good to come to you.
5. There is a mental force within us all, an agency to activate our Divine intelligence, and we can awaken it by shifting our brain to a more positive place.

Look Inward

Conscious Evolution: The fact that we now know from science that we have an agency within us that we can call on to change our minds is evolutionary! The evolutionary step to take is to practice shifting from a negative mindset to a positive one and thus use the Divine Intelligence inside you. Resiliency is the ability we have to change our minds and allows us to overcome negative mindsets and bad moods.

As children, most of us have felt unlimited, and with this free thinking, we believed we could do anything. When in your life, either as a child or as an adult, have you felt "limitless"—like you could do anything?

When in your life have you been at your very best?

13

Universal Spiritual Truth #13:
Nothing Is Impossible to You!

*Knock on yourself as upon a door and walk upon yourself
as a straight road. For if you walk on the road,
it is impossible for you to go astray....
Open the door for yourself that you may know what is...
Whatever you will open for yourself, you will open.*
--Silvanus, *Dialogue of the Savior*

Dan's mood was high when I saw him next, yet he shared with me that it was still up and down. "When I am on my way to talk to you, I am high as a kite, but when I am sitting at my computer and still seeing no answer to my job search, my Light Frequency, as you say, drops to the bottom."

"How are you doing with taking control of your brain and focusing on your Positive Anchor?" I prompted him.

"Yes! I have been doing that every day, Jayne," Dan said.

I knew that practice was the key to maintaining the new neural pathways he had started creating with his new beliefs. I answered Dan with certainty: "I know you can do this. You have already created a miracle in finding your daughter! Your own personal job miracle is just over the horizon. If you look really hard, you can see it!"

"Well, Jayne, I can sense your confidence, and I hang on to it with all my might," Dan replied.

"Dan, today is the day we need to do an exercise—" I started.

"Jayne, I am getting that feeling that we are about to do something really touchy-feely right now," Dan interrupted.

"I know I have entertained you in the past few months with everything from weird conversations with your Pleaser to asking you to travel to a farm and yell at yourself—no wait, I remember now you threw rocks at trees!" I told him. "But would you indulge me again with another conversation? This time I would like to talk to your Authentic Self, not your Pleaser."

"Oh, I will never forget that weird conversation we had that day. But I have to tell you something: That conversation shifted something in me, and I have been a different person ever since," Dan admitted.

"Okay, so could I just do a similar interview, but this time with your Authentic Self?" I asked.

"Sure! Well, since I am more in my Authentic Self than my Conditioned Self most of the time, I figure I don't even have to change chairs right now." Dan grinned.

"You are so right! So, first question to your Authentic Self: What happened that day we talked to your Pleaser?" I followed up on his earlier point.

"Well, the best thing that could have changed. For some reason, now that I think about it, I realized that the part of me that had made all those mistakes in life, my Pleaser, well, I got to the point where I realized that the Pleaser was not me! I know it sounds too simple, but it was so relieving to know that it was not me who did those things, that it was really some false part of me trying to be somebody else." Dan was leaning forward now, really into the interview.

"Why do you think that made you feel better?" I asked.

"Because if I looked at myself from another view, I could see the good in me. Remember, when I said all I wanted out of this process—really, out of life, now that I think about it—I just wanted to know I was a good person," Dan started explaining.

"Yes, Dan, I do remember you saying that. It was almost like a plea or a prayer," I told him.

"Well, now I have realized that the Pleaser is not me. I can see myself as a good person now." Dan pursed his lips in the realization.

"You know, when I started to realize this was on the retreat," Dan continued. "All that forgiveness stuff I did out on the farm—I think it prepared me for understanding myself better. And here is where I got to—we are all good people, Jayne, including me. We certainly start out that way. So I decided I don't have to 'do' anything to be good—I just am, and so is everybody else," Dan said.

"Well, at the risk of sounding touchy-feely, what does that feel like?" I asked.

We laughed, and then Dan said, "It's okay, Jayne, that is just the real you coming out!" We really laughed together then. "Well, relieved and happy. That is how I feel. I mean, I know you would say I feel love, but that is just not me. The best word I keep thinking of is *good*. I have just always wanted to be a good man, and now I know I am—at least most of the time." He smiled.

"So how is that for you, living with the idea that you are good and that—I think I am connecting that life is good for you too?" I asked.

"Absolutely, Jayne; I am so happy now. I mean, I know I will get a job, but it is not just about that. There is something more—I think that knowing and accepting that I am good, I can see the good in others better now. Like you have told me over and over again, they are just a reflection of you and how you feel about yourself in that moment…I think you called it a mirror; well, I can see the good in my mirror now," Dan told me.

"So, Dan, one more question," I pushed. "What about real life out there? Bad things are happening all the time and, unfortunately, will continue to happen, and sad things will happen to you in the future. How will you stay in that mindset you mentioned, of being happy?" I wanted him to connect all this to the real world.

"Well, I really don't know, Jayne. I feel I am just starting to figure out things. I don't really think I have any answers, but in the writing you have insisted I do, I have come to a few conclusions, some ideas that my job is just to see the good in life and in others. That is all I can do," he said. Then he paused and continued: "When I was out on the farm that day at the retreat, I told you I just sat there for hours watching the sunset, and then in the darkness, well, that is when I figured out that I am good and that I can trust life to be good. I began to feel safe and peaceful again, just trusting and having this kind of faith."

"Tell me a little more," I said.

"When I first came to see you, my life was…terrifying. I was truly in my own hell on earth. Knowing that I am good doesn't mean I don't have to work at keeping my Conditioned Self at bay, but I know now that as simple as it seems, I am a good person and everything is okay." Dan looked up, obviously finished.

I realized that Dan had found what the Bible calls "the peace that surpasses all understanding."

"Okay, Dan, now before we quit for today, let's do something fun with this new Authentic Self mindset of yours. Let's test your Light Frequency level and see how well you are maintaining a high level of emotional energy." I knew that he needed to maintain a high mental frequency level to manifest the right job. Quantum BioFeedback would give me a score of how well he was doing with his Light Frequency; I wanted to test his Light Frequency on a regular basis for several days.

"Fire it at me—I am ready for the next step! Jayne, I do think my inner work and the release of old emotions is what helped me find my daughter, so I want to stay with this process of self-discovery." Dan was trusting of the process now. I knew that would make it go faster.

"But don't forget I'm bleeding money here," Dan admitted, and I could see that he had automatically lowered his frequency just thinking about money and regressed into his Conditioned Self. My eyes got big, and Dan saw my reaction to his change in mood. He got it too! "But, Jayne, I just caught myself! The old Pleaser came rushing back in to make sure no one is upset at me about not being able to give them money. Don't worry. I can shift back to being positive. There, done!" He gave me a big smile.

"Dan, one of the highest, most powerful mindsets you could have right now would be feeling a sense of gratitude. The French have a proverb that states what I am trying to say: 'Gratitude is the heart's memory.' One of the highest levels of spirituality is to feel grateful for everything that comes to you: the good, the bad, and the ugly. If you could get there authentically and really feel grateful right now, it would bump your power level up to where you would have a better chance of attracting the right job. Your Light Frequency would be very bright. See what I mean?"

"No, explain more, Jayne. How can I feel grateful before I get a job?" Dan frowned at me.

"Follow me here, because you almost have it. You understand that whatever you think and feel comes about. So if you could feel faith in yourself and how you have control over your mindset—even without a job—then you might feel grateful that you had worked so hard to get to the point where you are actually happy and peaceful—without a job," I said to him.

"Whoa, Jayne, I couldn't go that far," he told me. "I do need a job to be happy."

"Yes, I know, this is tricky business, but you must admit that there have been times in the last few weeks that you have been happy and fulfilled," I reminded him.

"Okay, I get it. If I depend on a job making me happy, then I am still coming from no control over life. But if I really believe I create my own life with my thoughts, I can always change my thoughts and get something else. I am the one in charge, so to speak." Dan looked up, amazed at his own insight. He wanted my approval.

"I don't know, Dan—it is certainly up to you what you believe. But are you beginning to get it—that you are a creator?"

"Yeah, yeah, Jayne, but back to the idea of gratitude. I could be grateful for all I have learned and also have faith in myself that I am capable of creating the right job for myself. This would mean letting go of the fear and doubt—which I am ready to download. Life is good...." Dan was thinking out loud.

"I know this is a big challenge, Dan."

"No, I now know when you are influencing me and that I don't have to be under anyone's influence anymore. So I will consider what you are saying and weigh it against how it feels to me. Hm, so my job is to begin to feel grateful. I don't know if this will up my frequency, but it does feel like a lot of good things have happened, too—things that wouldn't have happened without the job loss. I mean, look at the last couple of months. My whole life is different. I have a daughter. I understand Tommy now. I feel different about who I am. I no longer feel abandoned. I feel energized. I feel connected to myself. I can't measure it in dollars and cents, for sure, but I can look at this as an opportunity. If I really think about it, I think I *can* be grateful, which is one of the highest mindsets that French guy you quoted mentioned. I certainly can't begrudge all that's happened."

I then asked Dan an even more challenging question—whether he could be grateful for his life, right now, in the present moment. I knew that the mindset that would match the ideal job for Dan was a spiritual mental state of high energy and Light Frequency. After wisdom has been gained from the mental shifts that Dan underwent, the brainwaves are in a higher frequency, a result of the underlying dynamics of the way energy and consciousness function.

He paused for a moment and thought before responding slowly. "I think I do feel in a higher state of mind, but it is fleeting, I have to admit. Knowing that I am good comes and goes, but mostly stays if I work on it. I can feel that gratitude, until I get into real life and have to pay my bills or listen to Margie's fears….Some people will think I'm crazy for letting the job go, you know, but in my heart, I know it is the right thing to do. Jayne, I am getting closer, but I am not quite sure how it all comes together." Dan was thoughtful as we ended our time together.

"Dan, can you remember what it felt like standing in that field of light on your retreat?" I prompted him.

Dan's eyes automatically closed, and he was quiet for a minute. "Almost," he said.

"Well, let's try this. I have an exercise that may help you connect the dots. Are you ready to try it?" I knew that the answer always was more mental practice of staying in a positive state of mind—without it actually happening in the outside world.

Dan was progressing nicely through the ascending steps of this process. He was learning to dialogue to himself, letting both his Conditioned Self and then his Authentic Self express themselves. It is important to still allow the Conditioned Self to express the negativity…to bring it out into the open so you can dispute it. I asked him to rate his average Light Frequency for each day on a scale of one to ten, with ten being an ideal mindset in feeling and thought. I wanted him to see what a high Light Frequency could achieve for him in the outside world. He had to connect the dots of the spiritual truth, "As within, so without." First you must change the inside of your mind to be positive, and then the outside world will reflect that change. High energy inside equals a high level of creative power.

Because the inside and the outside worlds aren't necessarily separate, if one has a thought, it either already has shown up or will show up as an event in the world. Of course, Dan has already seen, when he experienced a dramatic job loss, that there had to be a corresponding idea that had brought the event to him, which may have been his limiting belief of "I am not good enough." Either way, one's thoughts determine one's experience.

I explained to him that we would keep up with Inside Wins, or mental shifts to more positive thoughts, and see how they affected his outside world, specifically to attract the right job. I wanted to make sure he connected to the power of his thoughts. So Inside Wins, changes in thought, produce Outside Wins, or changes in circumstances. The Outside Wins were the answers to his prayers, so to speak, or a result of his difficult mental work. He had to make the association of Inside Wins to Outside Wins to motivate himself to use this spiritual practice of shifting in his future life.

Dan must be very careful right now to keep his thoughts positive and unlimited as much of the time as possible or he will have little power to attract the right job to him.

After mental practicing for one week, Dan presented me with the following chart tracing his Inside Wins and how they created his Outside Wins. At the same time, I was measuring his potential Light Frequency every day remotely with the Quantum BioFeedback device.

DAY 1 INSIDE WIN	OUTSIDE WIN	FREQUENCY
• Caught myself worrying about the job market. Shifted the negative thoughts to "Unlimited possibilities are out there for me." Saw my framed picture of my visualization. • Had to practice shifting from this negative thought several times during the day. • Remembered my Positive Anchor.	• Received a call from an old friend who was wondering how I was doing.	60
DAY 2 INSIDE WIN	OUTSIDE WIN	FREQUENCY
• Started the day encouraging myself, reading inspiring works, and vowing to find the positive in every negative story or event. Visualization practice. • Had four negative experiences and shifted all of them with the gratitude tool.	• Received a call from one of my recruiters! He didn't have great news, but at least it was an update.	81
DAY 3 INSIDE WIN	OUTSIDE WIN	FREQUENCY
• Had a coaching session. Discussed and let go of some fears and was even able to change my thinking about some of them during the hour-long session! Left feeling confident—not necessarily about getting a job, but about my ability to raise my frequency, be in control of my mind, and bring the good in the world my way. • Continued to catch and shift my negative thoughts using my Positive Anchor.	• Two friends called with leads. • A relative called with support. • Wife cooked a wonderful dinner for me!	65

DAY 4	INSIDE WIN	OUTSIDE WIN	FREQUENCY
	• Felt my frequency start off around a 5—higher than it had been since I found my daughter, Lindsey! • Remembered to reward myself with verbal praise every time I contacted a lead. • Laughed at myself when I realized I might miss being off work once I got a new job. Prayer gratitude. • Read a business article about how most companies are cutting back and going "lean," but caught the fear and turned it around (although it took a couple of hours to regain the frequency score I had at the beginning of the day).	• Received an e-mail from a company in Dallas asking for a résumé.	78

DAY 5	INSIDE WIN	OUTSIDE WIN	FREQUENCY
	• Felt worried about how I would continue to pay bills. Could feel the desperation and anxiety rising. Began to focus on things I have no control over, like when companies will call. Acknowledged these feelings and recited, "I bring great value to the business world." Did more prayer work.	• No Outside Win except a refund check in the mail I wasn't expecting. I was grateful.	79

DAY 6	INSIDE WIN	OUTSIDE WIN	FREQUENCY
	• Wrote in my journal all morning to build myself back up. Did not look at my e-mails until I'd raised my frequency score back up to a 5. • Followed up with contacts. • Turned around negative thoughts that did arise within a few minutes using Positive Anchor. Prayed. • Felt very confident that I could keep raising my mood higher.	• Received three e-mails from companies with possible jobs, including the one that I liked! • Received two leads from friends.	90

DAY 7	INSIDE WIN	OUTSIDE WIN	FREQUENCY
	• Woke up with high energy, felt like everything I was doing was helping me keep my internal focus. • Shifted from negative assaults in less than one minute! Fast prayer work. • Managed to maintain focus on what I have control over—my mind. Held the positive visualization for longer than usual. Disciplined prayer work.	• Received three more inquiries from interested companies, including one for a position only ten minutes from my house. More gratitude.	98

The resulting scores from the Quantum BioFeedback device mirrored Dan's rise and fall of energy as he calculated his Outside Wins on the chart above. They showed a consistent rise in his Light Frequency Score which measured Dan's use of his energy potential. He was now able to access an average of 79 percent of his energy potential in the seven days instead of his original 17 percent, his score when he started this process! He had the capacity now to consciously focus his energy on his goal.

Coach's Mindset

Dan had raised his Light Frequency by two points with his awareness! He was closer now to the amount of strength it would take to materialize a job. The mystics had called this ability to move your mind and create things *transcendence*, meaning going beyond human capabilities. Just as we believe that science will continue producing new discoveries, I believe that the spirit will continually develop if we continue to think it can. And indeed, Dan felt that his spiritual development was a good goal to work toward, so he was willing to devote much of his time to it. Life became easier as a result of his focusing his energy within. "As within, so without."

Once Dan had practiced his ability to shift his mind to be grateful, I encouraged him to continue developing this practice every day by identifying and appreciating the positives of every experience he had. High spiritual maturity requires that we acknowledge and thank ourselves for creating all our Outside Wins. Even if they are negative, we can learn from them for our spiritual growth. There is no such thing as failure, only feedback. With enough practice, I felt Dan would eventually learn to express gratitude spontaneously, which would allow him to build a powerfully generative mindset that could have a real impact on others.

Before Dan came to see me, he had not been aware of God being on the inside of him. As the days went by and Dan's awareness of this inner power continued to improve, I felt that his chances got better for finally getting a job. And I was right! Dan called me and said he now had *seven* interviews, including three that had resulted in callbacks and additional interest. An offer, it seemed, was just around the corner....

# The Spirituality
Universal Spiritual Truth #13: Nothing is Impossible to You!

> A monk who is skilled in concentration
> can cut the Himalayas in two. *—Buddha, Anguttara Nikaya*

How can our brain become more conscious and stay in its Divine Intelligence? To keep the divine mind in Dan activated, he had to continue to practice shifting from a false thought to a true one, from low energy to high energy. The shift does not take place in one instance. It is a practice. The following chart shows some of the basic differences between a divine, or Authentic-Self mindset, and a human, or Conditioned-Self mindset.

Comparing Your Authentic Self and Conditioned Self	
Authentic/Divine Self	**Conditioned/Human Self**
Imaginative	Limited thinking
Positive thinking	Negative thinking
Unconditional love and acceptance	Nonjudgmental of self and others
Creative	Stifled, old, reactionary thinking
Original	Fake, copy, inauthentic
Confident	Doubtful

We are capable of mentally shifting from a human mindset to our original, divine mind, where anything is possible.

We hear a lot about how we use only a small portion of our brain power, but that is simply because we have blocked our ipseity from developing based on all the limiting beliefs we have wired in from our early life experiences. Now that we have discovered that we can literally change our minds, we must learn to develop our limitless, creative potential and not be scared of it.

Because a spiritual experience occurs in our right brain and vocabulary takes place in our left brain, it is not unusual to struggle with the right words to express what has happened and as a result, we may downplay it. In his book, *The Sermon on the Mount: The Key to Success in Life*, Matthew Fox, a metaphysical mystic and New Thought leader, says that a spiritual experience is like "tasting of the Divine" (Fox, 1934, p. 100).

We choose what we think about and create it, just as an architect envisions a structure in his head before he builds it. You can see how, in problem solving, one goes in and out of ipseity or our prime grounding of infinity. We have the flexibility and brain resilience to solve problems, and when we learn to dance between ipseity and creation, we can increase our probability of manifesting exactly what we wish. But, you say, how do we do that?

In coaching we are taught to have a presence of openness, curiosity, and receptivity to help clients gain access to this ipseity, which could give them unlimited choices and ways to move ahead toward their goals. We partner with them and try to brainstorm new ways for them to stay connected to their ipseity and know there are unlimited ways to get there.

Just think, in the last hundred years we have made phenomenal discoveries as a human race. We have created cars to drive us places, learned how to create a replacement for the human heart, and discovered how to harness nuclear energy. We've had many great technological and medical discoveries, but perhaps the most important discovery of all has been, and continues to be, in neuroscience. With the new technology, we can now observe the brain and see changes occurring. This discovery alone, that we have the ability to change our minds, could forever change the human race, as it implies that **the source of all power lies within *us*.**

 **The Science**

Quantum Physics
What all the quantum physics laws have in common is that they seem inconsistent with "common sense," or how we expect the physical world to behave based on everyday experiences and our old, limiting beliefs. This is because quantum effects cannot be detected by our five senses.

We have built our visible, finite world on what we see, hear, taste, smell and touch. Quantum physics is based on the invisible, infinite world.

In 1913, the Danish physicist Niels Bohr introduced the Correspondence Principle. He was the first to say the rules of quantum physics (the invisible world) can be applied to the world of classical physics (the visible world). Classical physics is deterministic; quantum physics is probabilistic. This turned the classical physics world inside out, later filtering down somewhat simplified as the Law of Attraction.

It has taken us over 100 years, but it is beginning to sink in that what happens to us is controlled by us. This doesn't mean we know yet "how" to control our destiny, but it sets the stage for us to be responsible for our thoughts and emotions since they create our reality.

Science shows us that the act of creation is an act of co-creation between an unlimited energy inside of us and the infinite energy of nature, the Zero Point Field, outside of us. It is when we can go to a state of no thoughts and enter into the Field of unlimited possibilities that we can best start from the beginning and create. While we are in that state of nothingness, or all-ness, we are in the Field of unlimited possibilities. We are always creating; however, we are usually not aware of what we are creating, thus leaving our lives out of our control.

Live without Limits or Constraints

Energy is everywhere. If you think of God as energy, then for Dan to get a job, he must learn to use the unlimited energy in him to create. The energy in him is represented by emotions, and his emotional state has a certain intensity or brightness that can be changed by moving into a higher emotional state. For example, anger and blame are low in energy and can be said to be *dark energy*, or the absence of light. If Dan can move up to another level of emotion, then he can engage the unlimited and available energy within him. This energy shows up in Dan through his higher emotional state, and this is something he can control!

A Divine Mindset: Gratitude

> I have noticed that the Universe loves gratitude. The more grateful you are, the more goodies you get. –*Louise Hay*

One of the highest states or mindsets we can ever be in is the state of gratitude. Research shows that people who are in this state are stronger and more resilient to negative forces. People with self-esteem issues become more assertive if they put gratitude to work. Gratitude increases self-confidence, positivity, and success in life; it has even been shown that focusing on one grateful moment can make you more productive (Norville, 2007).

The Power of Gratitude

Dr. Robert Emmons is considered the father of the science of gratitude. Emmons's research documents that gratitude is a transformative practice and increases one's interpersonal, physical, and emotional well-being and happiness.

Gratitude is one of the highest and most productive emotions for the purpose of creating, according to David Hawkins, author of *Power vs. Force* (2002, pp. 68-69), who, as mentioned earlier, was able to measure the power of emotional states of mind. Emotions are the power of God. We can use them to rewire and to change the brain. Different emotions have different degrees of power. Hawkins has shown this concept to be true; from this research, emotions are weighted according to the following list, from a high to low degree of power:

Bliss/peace
Joy
Love
Acceptance
Willingness
Neutrality
Forgiveness
Anger
Fear
Grief
Apathy
Guilt
Shame/blame

The lowest emotions on the energy scale are shame and blame. Anger has more power and is a step above; it can be used as a tool to facilitate moving up the ladder of emotions to a higher one, just as Dan did on his retreat. At the retreat, the goal is to attain Emotional Non-Reactivity, which is the same as neutrality on the preceding list. As you can guess, emotions with high energy include peace, love, harmony, and exuberance. Evolutionary history depends on our working on moving ourselves up the ladder of emotions, trying to stay in the higher emotions for well-being, as you can see that positive emotions are more powerful than negative ones on the scale. One of the goals of the Divine Intelligence Process is to move Dan to a higher level of Light Frequency, to get him closer to getting a job, closer to remembering his ipseity, and closer to God, the Creator. The mental practice is always about shifting to a higher mindset.

Summary of Concepts in Chapter 13

1. Different emotions have different levels of spiritual power.
2. The more positive the emotion, the more powerful the ability to attract your desired outcome.
3. Gratitude is one of the highest emotional frequencies we can have.
4. Outside Wins are created by Inside Wins, and high emotional intensity is the key.
5. When we learn to focus our thoughts and energies more perfectly, we too can create miracles.
6. We create small miracles every day, but we fail to notice them or attribute them to our Inside Wins.
7. When we change our thoughts, we get different results on the outside.

Look Inward

Conscious Evolution: Own your power. When we experience divine moments, sometimes we discount the outside results of our power with expressions such as, "That just happened out of the blue!" We are prone to downplay our strengths and our godlike energy to create. Evolution-wise, we must push our Conditioned Self aside and accept our inner power. As a human race, as we move toward letting go of limiting beliefs, negative emotions and accepting our greatness, the light within our bodies will become more readily available for us to use and enjoy.

What are the challenges to accepting your greatness?

What does it feel like to know you are connected to the infinite power of God?

What does your Conditioned Self say about the possibility of having God within you?

What would happen in your current relationships if you saw only the unlimited potential inside everyone?

14

Universal Spiritual Truth #14:
We Are Capable of Performing Miracles

Truly, truly, I say to you, whoever believes in me will also do the works that I do...I can guarantee this truth: Those who believe in me will do the things that I am doing.
—Jesus, John 14:12

"This time it's different," Dan said. "I can feel it. I'm learning to be more patient with myself and with the process. And I am staying internally focused, Jayne, with all the practice you have given me. I *am* very grateful." Dan leaned forward now to discuss his job situation.

"I have narrowed it down to three positions that I really like. All three of the positions would be good for me, but I'm especially interested in one of them. It's with a startup, and they're doing some great stuff. I've researched them heavily. They have the capital, and they have a solid business plan and vision. Plus, it's a CEO position, what I've always wanted...maybe on a smaller scale, but still very much along the lines of what I've been aiming for. I've met with them twice now.

"The only problem is that I haven't heard back in two weeks, and I'm starting to get antsy. I'm afraid they've lost interest in me, and I'm fighting myself to keep from picking up the phone or e-mailing."

"So, what are you worrying about?" I knew immediately that Dan's worry could preoccupy him, cause him to slip back into his old mental habits, and eventually decrease his Light Frequency and impede his efforts.

"Hm," Dan replied, "I see where you are going with this. I have to be careful, don't I—careful not to lose my internal confidence and focus and get back into a negative or fearful mindset? From what I am learning, that will take away my ability to manifest the right job."

"You're right! Here is the kind of thinking that is messing with you. By focusing on one option rather than being open to unlimited possibilities, you are putting unnecessary pressure on yourself."

Dan said, "So I want to keep my mind unlimited and open to all the possibilities!"

Dan had just defined Divine Intelligence! "Let me help you refocus on a spiritual truth for a minute. Answer me this: How many actual possibilities are out there for you?" I asked.

"Three," Dan answered earnestly.

I asked again: "Think for a moment. *How many* opportunities are out there for you?"

Dan paused to think, and then replied, "Okay. I get where you are going. The opportunities are unlimited. The Universe is open to me—as long as I stay confident on the inside of my value to the world. I don't have to get this specific job or even one of the other two. I can let go of my nervousness and stay confident. There are no limits to what I can create."

"Exactly! And what would that perfect state of mind look like and feel like for you in this moment?" I was pushing to get him to shift away from his human thinking and back into a more unlimited, divine mindset.

Now Dan replied: "If I'm in this high state of mind, I can take my hand off the telephone. If I am open to every possibility, if I stay in the present moment and expect good things to come to me, the right job will become available. There is no urgency. I would get back to my gratitude feeling that all is well.

"But I have to admit, Jayne, that no matter how many times I shift, I can't seem to shake this one doubt that keeps popping up," Dan said.

"Tell me about this doubt that's limiting you, so we can remove it to get you more open and receptive," I responded.

"Well, I can see how being in a good mood, or high frequency as you say, in an interview would make me more attractive, but how does it attract a job opportunity in the long run? I mean, how could the perfect job for me know whether I am feeling confident? Especially when I don't even know what that job is? I just don't understand that at all. I want to believe this works, but some of it still seems like mumbo-jumbo. Remember, Jayne, I like scientific facts, not that woo-woo stuff," he said.

"I know you have been doing a lot of research on spiritual, as well as science, stuff. In any of your readings, have you come across anything that might help us here?" I knew he was interested in the scientific theories out there and that he had been doing a lot of research on his own in the relatively new science of quantum physics.

"Yes, I have read about a physics principle called nonlocality. Even Einstein had trouble accepting that law: he called it 'spooky action at a distance.' But since then, they actually proved that it is real. They have shown that an electron in one part of the world can affect an electron in another part of the Universe," Dan explained very confidently.

"Okay, now apply that thought to your situation." I pushed him to extrapolate.

He paused for a long time. I had to reach up and cover my mouth with my hand to keep from giving him the answer. But finally, the light-bulb went on: "I never put it together before, never could see how it relates to me, but now I get it! Everything and everyone are connected, so when I change my thoughts or feelings, they affect everything. It's kind of freaky, but now that I think about it, science shows it is true! Hm...now that I think about it, I have no doubt that it's true. It's just hard to accept, as it seems unreal."

"Well, how did you know that everything and everybody are connected?" I wanted to know if he was just saying that or if he really believed it.

"Science," he said emphatically, but his eyes were looking far away, and I knew his brain was going eighty miles a minute.

"All this information helps, Jayne. I get it that you think if I keep my mind in the exact same mindset as the one I would have when I get the job—like attracts like; I will attract a job that will give me that same good feeling. But I still need facts here, not some airy-fairy, New-Agey law of attraction you mentioned. I want to know how it really works out there—scientifically." Dan was frowning at me.

"Dan, I would like you to keep investigating on your own how all this works. I know you are doing a lot of research about spirituality and different religions. But could I have your permission to give you my opinion?" I knew that as a coach, to ever give out my opinion about something, I needed to make sure my client identified it as an outside source that could be different from his own thoughts.

Dan nodded his agreement and looked eager to hear what I had to say.

"Here is what I have based this whole dialoguing process on. I know I have probably oversimplified it, Dan, so check it out on your own. But here's what I think you will find: Science has shown that there is light in the human body. This light serves as a kind of a connector field to all the cells of your body, so they can communicate at lightning speed and keep your body running in a balanced healthy state. For example, there are many neurons or cells in our brain, but it is the connector Field of light between these cells that allows the formation of new synapses. In this way, new patterns can be formed and changes can occur in the way we think—so we can be creative and not just automatic in our thoughts. However, this power that the brain has to be creative can be held back by strong emotions, thus, the need for your retreat." I was teaching now, not coaching.

And now Dan joined in as we partnered on figuring out this world we live in: "So all of our emotions, thoughts, and patterns communicate through the Field of light within our own body to stay well. It is really not about the brain cells; it is about the connections and what is between the cells. Is that what you think, Jayne?"

I stopped and realized we had switched roles and loved the equal status we had arrived at.

I could see Dan listening intently, so I continued: "Well, check it out yourself, what do you think?"

Dan quietly said, "I am still trying to figure out who is running the world out there. But the more I read and listen to you, I think it may be me....Oh, wow, now that is a scary thought."

"Well, maybe it is time we took responsibility for our power, Dan. Science has also proven that this Field of light exists everywhere—connecting not only tissues inside our bodies, but outside, connecting people's thoughts and feelings to each other and all the Universe. This Field of light is electromagnetic energy and is unlimited in capacity and amount. *Unlimited*, Dan. And all this energy is available to us at any time. It's like the answer to using our mind to its unlimited capacity. We are connected to a universal energy field that is unlimited! Can you imagine what power we really have in this world?"

I continued: "This Field of light acts like a reflector to our thoughts and feelings. When we think certain thoughts, we send them out into the Field, and it reflects the exact same thoughts and feelings back to us. You have heard the idea that a new invention usually occurs in several parts of the world simultaneously; well, that is the Field at work. So if you reflect out to the Field a certain intention about the kind of job you want, then it will connect with any like-minded thoughts and feelings that are out there. So if there is a job that you want, it will find you—if your mindset is bright enough in energy and intention. Scientists have also shown that what you pay attention to brightens and is more likely to attract than something you have not been thinking about a lot. This is why I have been asking you to not only visualize the job you want but, more important, to *feel* the job you want, because the Light Frequency in your brain when you feel something is where the power to attract lies."

"But why don't I know this? Why didn't I learn this in school if it is true?" Dan was still curious and unbelieving.

"Well, I don't really know why the scientific community doesn't agree about all this and hasn't accepted this proven knowledge—maybe it is just too much to believe! And it goes against everything we have been taught in science so far. Whenever someone comes along with research and experiments that turn the scientific community on its ear, the reaction is usually the same. Change is slow sometimes. But for us, the important thing is to keep our minds and hearts open to unlimited possibilities. Remember, the first spiritual truth, the one that is hardest for me to keep in mind, is that we can't change someone else. 'Everything begins with you—and me!'"

I went on to explain a recent, exciting discovery by scientists in 2012: the discovery of the "God particle." "Dan, it actually explains how matter works. It is technically called the Higgs-Boson particle, after the scientists who discovered its existence. We know that science shows that our inner world, the world of atoms, molecules, and now bosons, is where it all begins. First there is thought—and then there are things resulting from our thoughts. Well, out there in the Universe, first there is light—in the form of waves, as scientists first thought. Then they discovered that light could also be a particle, just as it could be a wave, and when it was a particle, it had mass."

"So out there in the world, who or what turns that wave into a particle?" Dan asked.

"Well," I said, "they believed there is this one particle, smaller than anything known to man, and that when it collides with certain other particles, it creates mass. Yes, like the Big Bang theory, only different," I added, smiling, "and now it's proven to be true. They have isolated this one particle—even though it has been very elusive over the last twenty or so years that they have been studying it."

"So how do we turn waves or undefined and infinite thoughts into things? Using that pure, unlimited part of our brain we are all born with, we can create things like skyscrapers and spaceships. Well, there must be a God particle in us!"

"So, God, or what is running the world out there, is really an unlimited energy source." Dan was thinking with me.

"There has to be something magic and mysterious and godlike inside us—maybe we find it in the light that shines out of our eyes or the smile that brings light to others. Somewhere inside us shines a light that may look like a wave when we haven't figured out exactly what we think, and then sometimes it is a particle when we knock out all the unlimited possibilities of thoughts and choose one thought. This one thought we have creates things—in the form of physical buildings, our bodies, or the families we live in. Now we can say we have the Creator inside us—even if the scientists call it some nondescript name like a Higgs-Boson particle."

"Okay, Jayne, that's pretty cool. But why the retreat? Why was that so important to this ability to get the job I want?" Dan was still trying to put the pieces together, connecting the dots of science to his own life.

"Because negative emotions stored in your body block your inner light—and you can't get to the energy in the Field to create. They have done studies with cancer patients and found that their inner lights were dimming and going out because there were blockages; negative emotions act the same way in the body—toxic to our inner balance," I said.

"So then, after I went on the retreat and emptied out all the obstacles between my thoughts and the connecting field, I would more likely be able to communicate with, with…this Field of light?" Dan's eyes got big. I knew he was really getting it.

"Oh, I get it!!" he continued. "I found my daughter right after I emptied out all my negative emotions, so what I put out into the Field found her!" Dan sat up in his chair and moved forward to where he was sitting on the edge of his seat. His face showed this incredulous look.

"Okay, Dan, I have just broken all the rules of coaching. I gave you my opinions and ideas. What does all this mean to you right now?"

"It means that staying in a confident mood affects my chances of attracting the right job. If my negative emotions don't get in the way of my thoughts, then they have the power to create. I got it! I just have to keep my Light Frequency high, and everything will work out! If I do my inner work of focusing my thoughts on what I want, the outer work will take care of itself. I'm so glad that I figured this out! And I am definitely going to read up on that physics principle. I am pumped!"

"I'm thrilled that your professional life is back on track, Dan. But just out of curiosity, how's your search for God going? And how do you think it relates right now to your job search?"

Dan thought a minute, then burst out: "I think God is the Field of light! That is the only explanation for me finding my daughter—it had to be the connecting light that found her. It was a miracle—yet it was partly created by me, when I eliminated all the blame and guilt and negative emotions I had accumulated over the years. Incredible! These were blocking us from each other!"

"But you said 'partly created by me'?" I was pushing Dan to figure this God thing out in his own way.

"Well, partly, because I have to have the Field to create—don't I? But then that also means I have light within me—God within me, so to speak. God is light and is in me! God is in me! So God and I, we co-created that miracle together—and we can co-create this perfect job if I do my part and keep the doubt and uncertainty out of my mind so it won't block the Field sending me the right job!

"Just now, I felt that feeling again—the way I felt when I was standing in that Field of light on my retreat! I mean, it is gone already, but it was there for a second." Dan was almost yelling.

Dan's voice rose and his excitement was evident. I could almost see the neurons lighting up and connecting in his brain and the light between those neurons getting brighter. "When you started describing this Field of light, Jayne, all I could think about was my experience on my retreat. Do you remember that I told you I stood in a field of light for a few moments? Well, I think it was God, Jayne. God is something that is so grand and unlimited that we have a hard time imagining its greatness."

I noted with a smile that Dan had changed his reference to God from *him* to *it*. But I wanted to know more about where he was with finding God. "Well, so tell me more about what you are figuring out about God." I wanted him to voice what he had been thinking to make it more real.

Dan replied without hesitation, "Jayne, I know right now, in this moment, what God is all about. It is an energy, a light, a feeling inside me, and I am always connected whether I know it or not. When I am in negative space, God and I create something negative, and when I am in a highly positive state of mind, we create something good. It is my choice because I am always existing in the mind of God. Let's put it this way: God provides the energy, and I give the energy direction through my thinking. Co-Creation at its best, right Jayne?

"Since I figured out that I am good and that life is good, I am now very powerful to create. But what I am learning is that I have to work at keeping myself clear and aware or else I can't experience God like I now know it to be. I must become *aware* of the good. So as long as I keep that state of mind, I will keep myself headed toward my true destiny. I really think I had a spiritual rebirth at my Rewire Retreat. Maybe our job here on Earth is to develop our minds to the point that we could all be Christ-like. I guess Christ saw the good in everyone, and that is how he did those miracles." A mischievous smile appeared on Dan's face as he said this.

"Ever since the Rewire Retreat, all these great memories have been flooding back to me. And you know what?" Dan laughed. "I just realized that this isn't the first time I've wanted to be Christ-like."

"What do you mean?" I asked.

"Once when I was really young and I knew there wasn't really a Santa Claus, I still tried to believe in Santa Claus *and* Superman." Dan paused briefly. "And, yes, I lumped Jesus in there with the superheroes.

"One day, my brother suggested that we see if we could turn water into wine—you know, like the miracle Jesus pulled off at some party. Well, it was easy enough to accomplish. We just found the water hose, filled up a bucket with water, and got a huge bottle of ketchup from our mother's pantry. We made the water look red by adding the ketchup and voilà! We had ourselves some wine. We drank it all and pretended we were drunk like some of the adults we saw." Dan found this very amusing.

"Dan, maybe the reason you remember this story is that you wish you could create a miracle right now, in your job situation." I paused.

"Well, I do wish I had that mind back—that five-year-old mind that still believed anything was possible and had not yet been tainted with limiting beliefs. Now that I think about it, I was in a state of pure awareness in those childhood days, that ipseity thing you talk about. I never doubted that I was good and that life would turn out all right," Dan mused.

"Maybe the reason Jesus said in the Bible that you should come to him like little children is because a child's mind is in the form of theta brainwaves most of the time. That means they are much more open and receptive to new ideas, and it also means they can be easily influenced," I added.

"But, Jayne, I really am starting to believe that we have the same kind of mind that all these great spiritual leaders do. I just don't know how to develop myself to become as powerful as some of them…," he said.

"Well, you have been working on your positive mindset. What else would your mind look like if it were spiritually strong?"

"I think my mind should be giving, compassionate, and especially nonjudgmental, reflecting the good that I feel is everywhere. This will be challenging for me, but since I've smoothed things over with Tommy, found my daughter, and accomplished so much else, I feel like I can do anything now. All these things seem like miracles to me when I stop and think about it. Now I understand that miracles just relate to spiritual truths." Dan's mindset was incredibly high now as he began to appreciate himself and everything he had created so far.

"No matter what happens with my job, I will continue to work on developing the God—or maybe a better word is the Good—within me as best I can. That is all I can expect of myself. And just working on my own mind, Jayne, will keep me plenty busy in the future! This mind of mine could still use a lot of work!"

"So, Dan, just for my sake—humor me—where are you on the search for God?" I tried to get Dan to synthesize all he was learning into his new view of God.

"Well, I know one thing for sure: Religion has nothing to do with this! This is about me, finding the best me there is." Dan stated.

Dan picked up his Dialogue workbook that he had brought with him to his session. He held it up for me to see. I didn't understand what he wanted because the contents are always very private, and I didn't intend to ever read his private journal.

"See this workbook, Jayne?" I nodded, wondering where he was going with this. "Well, do you see how it glows? Can you see the light coming out of it?" Dan was in a light, happy mood. "Well," he said, "this morning in my dialoguing, God started writing to me. I brought it in because I was confused about why I thought God was writing to me, as I really don't think of God as outside me. So I just figured it out—by God I mean the highest part of me. And this morning in my dialoguing, God, the mind of God, came out and started talking to me. I know it was God, Jayne—I knew it at the time! At least it was my new way of looking at God. I mean, I wasn't hearing voices or anything. It was really me talking to myself. God, Jayne, is a voice inside me reminding me of the good!

"Jayne, I have found God, and he—no, *it*—is inside me. Well, I know God is everywhere, but the only God I can really believe in is the God in me, my highest, ideal self. I wish that everyone knew this! That God is everywhere, including inside all of us—waiting to be developed and acknowledged." Dan looked at me and laughed again—looking lighter and more at ease than I had ever seen him. Well, maybe not; he reminded me of the younger Dan I had watched lead scores of students in discussions about the meaning of life.

"Jayne, I am standing in a different place now about God. Somehow I had gotten the message to seek God through the rituals of the church, but now I am beginning to see that the path to God not only leads outward, but inward to my own heart. At least, for me, I connected with God through getting to know the real me.

"You know that is our work on this Earth, don't you, Jayne?" Dan looked at me and tilted his head back and laughed, a huge belly laugh. "Of course, you do! That is what this whole thing—all these Dialogues—has been about, hasn't it?" Dan's eyes narrowed, and he returned my smile.

Dan got up to leave, knowing there was still more work to be done. I handed him the final dialogue, Dialogue 12; the requirement for graduation from the Divine Intelligence Process was contained in this Dialogue. Dan would be required, in writing, to expand his view of God and then to apply it to his present life. I could tell he was ready to take complete responsibility for his life and, thus, complete this process.

He was as excited as I had ever seen him. I agreed with him. There was always work to be done.

I don't know why I thought about the time as Dan left my office—perhaps I was caught up in the moment, knowing that Dan had found God, the initial goal he had set with me. He was now in this moment in his Divine Intelligence. Whatever the reason, I looked down at my watch and jotted down the exact time he left—11:32—in my journal alongside the rest of the notes I had taken about our session. I felt it was in that one moment that God was alive and well inside Dan and that he knew it. There is an invisible point of balance when people become consciously aware of their inner divinity, and Dan was experiencing the ability to push back on his human self with his divine self and merge the two to become one with God.

This moment with Dan was the culmination of six months of intense work for him. During that time, Dan had integrated complex spiritual concepts into a view of God that he would carry with him for the rest of his life.

I was so proud of Dan's resilience, self-awareness, and internal focus. It was all there, and the sky was the limit about what kind of job he would pull to him. I had no doubt the right job would come to him. I just had no idea how quickly it would come!

Dan had been gone only a few minutes when my phone began to ring. When I answered, I was surprised to hear Dan's voice again so soon after he left the coaching session.

"Jayne, you're not going to believe this! I just opened my e-mail and found a message from the company I interviewed with weeks ago, the one for the CEO position I told you about that I wanted so badly. They want me to come to Chicago to meet with their board. I think they're going to make me an offer! I'd almost completely let this one go, with our talk about there being so many possibilities out there for me—even though I really wanted it. I can't believe this! I had let it go! And it must be the right fit, as it came back to me. And here, out of the blue, I get this e-mail. No, I guess it is not out of the blue, is it, Jayne? It seems they've been interested in me all along. It's a miracle—that I created, by the way!"

On a hunch, I asked Dan what time the offer came in. He said, "Hold on a minute and let me check my e-mail again to see what time is on it.…The e-mail was sent at eleven thirty-two, to be exact," he said.

I looked down at my notes until I found what I was looking for—that moment just a minute ago in the office when I had felt so sure that Dan had found that sweet spot of invisible, inner power. I finally found where I had made the time notation in my notes. Dan had shifted to his higher mindset at 11:32. I was reminded that an internally sourced mind attracts at the speed of light, what Einstein called "spooky action at a distance."

Dan asked me to give him a quick emergency coaching session to help him prepare for the meeting with the board in a few days. I was pleased that he was remembering to remain diligent in his inner work. Just as he found out who he was, he also knew exactly what he wanted to do. I asked him what he felt was important to him.

"Jayne," he said, "I've been waiting for this moment for months, but I am aware that my life is about something so much bigger than a job now that I have found what I was looking for—me, the real me.

"I realize that what I think about impacts the world! I am not just a number out there who will live and die with no one ever really knowing I lived. I mean, I know my children will remember me, but I now think I am here for a purpose. Right now, keeping my Light Frequency high, even when the odds are against me, is very important to me. I will not risk giving up this feeling of having the presence of God within me that I have now. It's more important to me than making money or being a leader. So I've decided to approach this interview with a different mindset than usual."

"Tell me more about your plans!" I could feel his high energy and couldn't wait to hear what he had to say.

"I plan to be so self-aware that nothing could happen in the meeting that would shake my positive and powerful mindset. I am what I am, and they can take me or leave me—I will not change myself to please them. And…I plan to share this journey with them!"

"What do you mean, Dan?" I asked.

"Well, I'm going to talk to them about my recent Dialogue training—I have a feeling they will be receptive—and I'm going to lay out a plan to teach each one of them how to keep this kind of mindset. But mostly I feel that I must begin to be able to talk about what I think God is. I mean, I know it is not businesslike, but they tell me they are a spiritual company. The more I talk with them, I think they are about some spiritual mission that I am not aware of yet," Dan said.

"But, Jayne, no matter what kind of company they are, can you imagine a corporation where individuals are engaged and flourishing with this kind of unlimited thinking? Their productivity would have to be higher. I need to be around people like me, Jayne. I want to work with people who want to be the best they can be, in addition to running a great business. This will be a good test to see if I am with like-minded people in this position. I will never again risk losing myself to gain money or outside approval. Never!"

I was beaming now listening to him, but I wanted to keep him focused. So I asked, "How do you think this slightly unorthodox plan for the employees will affect your chances at nailing down this offer?" I hoped I knew the answer he would give me. He reminded me, again, in that moment, of the young Dan I had first observed in discussions of spirituality and God. I think it was the real Dan then, and he had returned.

"Honestly, I'm not worried about it. If they don't want me as I am, then I'll know they're not the right fit for me, and I'll just keep looking. But I know that this new company they are creating can only benefit from this kind of mind training. Just think what we can create if we all put our minds to it!"

 ## Coach's Mindset

Now Dan was feeling unshakable. He had learned how to use his Divine Intelligence. He had literally created new pathways in his brain. This new way of thinking then allows for more fulfilling relationships with his family. He had reason to believe that he would soon get just the job he had always wanted. His Inside Wins were creating Outside Wins.

He was becoming internally anchored and less controlled by external circumstances. He was living the rewards of the spiritual life.

Interestingly, one of Dan's biggest Outside Wins was the change that occurred in his mother as a result of Dan's insistence on finding his daughter. After Lindsey came to visit the family and met his mother, Dan's mom began to check in with him daily. Her phone calls were supportive and loving. Suddenly Dan felt something from his parent that he had never felt before: total unconditional acceptance. Of course, this was a result of Dan's newfound love for himself. He had tasted this at the Rewire Retreat. I reminded Dan of the spiritual principle defined by David Bohm…that the invisible world of your thoughts controls the visible world of things. "As within, so without."

When Dan decided he wanted to be the best person he could be, he tapped into the attributes, or a couple of the Power Potentials, that makes humans unique: inner self-awareness and brain resilience. No other species aspires to further itself, much less recognize its shortcomings. Because we possess this special ability to modify ourselves, we have the power to turn a shortcoming into a strength and to turn human into divine.

Because I was Dan's coach, it was my job to see the divinity in him and to hold the light on until he was strong enough to shine without my help. And he was close.

Before Dan completed the DI Process, he was prone to allow others to influence his opinions; therefore, he never had the strength of mind to make his own choice about what he felt about God. He is not alone; many people accept the version of God that was given them as children and don't ask too many questions. Without really thinking about what he might want for his children or about the teachings of the Church, Dan had simply agreed to raise his children in a religion he did not even understand. He just followed the rituals without engaging his mind or his heart. Now, however, I knew that Dan had the confidence and self-awareness necessary to form his own conclusions about God. He had lived all his life on borrowed beliefs. Now he believed that God was within him as a source of wisdom, comfort, and joy. He knew the importance of developing his Divine Intelligence.

When Dan came to me for coaching after losing his job, his mindset had been negative, hopeless, darkened by negative emotions and memories, and in no condition to serve as his connection to unlimited possibilities. But Dan was able to adopt a mindset that supported the properties of a higher, godlike consciousness. In short, his slate had been cleaned off, and his divinity stood imprinted on the blackboard of his mind in all its bright, shining glory.

Once he had come to terms with God's existence inside him and adopted a divine mindset, Dan's brain had become profoundly godlike, demonstrating acute intuition, moral purity in thoughts, resonance with others, creativity, and presence. Dan's thinking when he was shifted into his God Consciousness, was clear, principled, and inspired, and he would use this power to influence and inspire others.

Divine Intelligence is everywhere, all around us, and even, according to many religions, really inside us. We are all capable of engaging it, as long as we are willing and able to challenge our human selves and put our divine selves in charge. Now that Dan had forged a connection with the divine, he was finally prepared to achieve his ultimate goals.

Divine Intelligence is the awareness of the power of the inner divine source inside you and others. You don't have to believe in God so much as to believe in yourself. When recognized and activated, Divine Intelligence flows and shines outward to touch everyone and everything.

It is important to note that Dan is not theorizing that he is God. All humans have the potential to develop their minds so that they can use the laws of nature to create. Some spiritual leaders have obviously developed their minds to the ultimate and are able to use their divine ability in wonderful ways to help others. The closer we get to that state of mind and being, the closer we are to the Creator within. When we learn to focus our thoughts, we too can direct light.

 **The Spirituality**

Universal Spiritual Truth #14:
We Are Capable of Performing Miracles

Modern Miracles

> Miracles happen, not in opposition to Nature,
> but in opposition to what we know of Nature. –*St. Augustine*

Psychologist Abraham Maslow said, in reference to spiritual experiences by leaders in past civilizations and religions, "It is very likely, indeed almost certain, that these older reports [of mystical experiences], phrased in terms of supernatural revelation, were, in fact, perfectly natural, human peak-experiences of the kind that can easily be examined today" (Maslow, 1994, p. 20). "These experiences are a sign of mental health," he said. He believed that these experiences were commonly associated with an enhanced sense of connection to the world and others. So Dan's experience may not be so unusual, but rather not acknowledged by people who don't want to seem "weird." *Course in Miracles* (2011) defines a miracle as any change in perception. (See "Modern Miracles" in the Endnotes.)

I imagined someone like Leonardo da Vinci coming back to life to find the world the way it is today. He would consider most of what we have created—computers, electric lights, indoor plumbing, heart transplants—to be miracles. If some of the world's greatest inventors, such as the Wright brothers or Alexander Graham Bell or Thomas Edison, had buried their inner divinity, their ipseity, under negative thoughts, they might never have contributed their miracles to society. They had somehow stepped out of their False Selves.

And what if people such as Gandhi, Martin Luther King Jr., or Saint (Mother) Teresa had not been dedicated to seeing ordinary people in their highest selves? Would the world be the same today? All these human people learned to use God's natural laws to change the world, and indeed, most of them could be called miracle workers. Eric Butterworth, a metaphysical minister, said, "God can do no more for you than He can do through you" (Butterworth, 1968, p. 183). Jesus put it this way: "It is your Father's good pleasure to give you the kingdom" (Luke 12:32).

To Hindus, Inside Wins are realities, and they are not ever thought of as superstitions or anything other than miracles. The study and scientific exploration of inner thoughts and emotions seem as valid as studying math or sending a person to the moon to Hindus. They naturally blend spiritual truths with science. Most of us think of miracles only as something that happened in Palestine two thousand years ago. But in India, every generation has its saints and yogis who perform miracles. What seem like superhuman feats are considered everyday occurrences to Hindus.

 The Science

How did Dan communicate with the Field? In research mentioned earlier conducted at HeartMath, as well as the research from David Hawkins, who proved that different emotions have different power levels, positive emotions are shown to impact humans and the Earth and to have a greater impression than the weaker, more negative emotions.

After my encouragement to not get hung up on trying to convince this one company to hire him but rather to stay receptive to the unlimited opportunities of the Universe, Dan was able to shift to higher emotional, or Light Frequency. This may have been felt by the board members of the organization with whom he had interviewed and attracted them to him, even if they were not conscious of the pull. Within seconds, they had decided to call him with an offer. I was teaching Dan to align with the source of energy of the Earth, solar system and, indeed, the Field for energy instead of reacting to other people's energy.

Mirror Neurons

Just as there is light in our body between our cells acting as the medium to carry messages to different parts of our body, this Zero Point Field serves as a channel of communication between each of our brains helping us stay connected (Fells, 2009). Daniel Goleman, author of *Social Intelligence* (2006), coined the term *mirror neurons*. Neuroscientists have discovered that our brains are affected by what we see others do with their brains. For example, if I watch you eat an ice cream cone, I can taste that ice cream cone myself. Or if I am married to you and you are upset, I realize it immediately when I first see you. The implications for relationships are major, as this shows that we affect others with our thoughts and feelings. Therefore, if we keep our thoughts positive, not only do we model that state of mind for others, but others will feel that in their brains and become what we are feeling.

Thus, mirror neurons are neurons within our brains that mimic (or "mirror") the behavior of neurons in others. So if one person is feeling high in energy, her neurons will operate at a high frequency, which others' neurons will perceive and imitate. Whether they realize it or not, most great leaders take advantage of mirror neurons to achieve their position; people who project positive energy and glowing light attract and inspire light in others. People enjoy the high and the positive feelings associated with the light; therefore, they remain loyal to the source that attracts them.

Of course, we do not need neuroscientists or high-tech medical equipment to help us recognize each other's inner light; we need only to interact with one another. At some point in our lives, we have all been in the presence of an individual whom we have described as "glowing," "radiant," or maybe just "inspiring." We have famous examples, as well: Gandhi, the Dalai Lama, and even Princess Diana have exhibited an ineffable radiance that attracted others to them. Not surprisingly, you will discover that your energy and emotional state can expand and contract almost instantly depending on another individual's emotional state.

This research also showed that the amount of power you have in a relationship is impacted by how much your brain would change someone else's brain. For example, parents have more power than their children in relationships. As parents, if we are in a bad mood, our children will most likely mirror us and be in a bad mood. The same thing applies to business relationships: Your boss's mood will likely impact yours. If a business leader walks into a meeting in a great expansive mood, he will influence his team in a positive way. Mirror neurons just prove how important it is to keep our mood and thoughts high in our Authentic Self mentality to make relationships much easier for us.

As we embrace these universal laws, we accept that the world is governed by thought. We can no longer defer to superstition or luck for causing our hardships when we know we are internally sourced. The spiritual truth of "As within, so without," or as Dan puts it, "Whatever you think about comes about," is as real as other laws we do not doubt, such as laws of gravity, electricity, or mathematics. This means that all of our thoughts and feelings yield all the experiences and relationships that affect our day-to-day existence. Until recently, the implications associated with this theory had been too tremendous for human beings to handle. After all, if we create everything in our world, that must mean that we are responsible for every unpleasant scenario—a divorce, an illness, a job loss. While this interpretation is correct, it is also somewhat one-sided, as it fails to recognize the power that comes with being a creator. After all, if we can create negative experiences, we must also be capable of creating the positive experiences we really want. As we evolve, we will continue to be more and more internally sourced and capable of creating in a positive way.

Because of Bell's law of nonlocality, described in Chapter 8, Dan has the power of thought and is responsible for the life he creates. This power within him creates his life, even though he is not conscious of it. During our initial conversations, it was clear that Dan's anxiety, uncertainty, and spiritual struggles seemed insurmountable to him. He could not see how his struggles were just creating more struggles. As he became the initiator of his own life, he connected to his own internal energy, and he connected to the energy of the Creator that is invisible to him. He could connect to the divine potential inside himself (inside all of us) to craft his life as he wanted it.

What Dan was discovering was that the electromagnetic field of his brain was part of the Field and playing off the Field, resulting in his current life. The brain is our access point to the Field. We must share responsibility with the collective consciousness for the direction of the world's light. Our mind, our connection point, is made up of cells and neurons, which use energy to communicate with each other.

We all affect each other with our energy levels, our Light Frequency. The Field is the medium through which we all communicate, whether we know it or not. And our thoughts and emotions are what we use to communicate. Now that Dan had rid his mind of energy-inhibiting, limiting thoughts and accepted the Universal Spiritual Truths, he was empowered to use the Field consciously to connect to the power of the Creator.

The Power of Recognition of the Field

Light seems to operate across vast distances instantly. It is nonlocal. Additionally, because everything in the world—humans, animals, ideas, opportunities—is connected within the mind of God (or the Field), everything can potentially be affected by the thoughts that we project into the Field. Therefore, the outcomes that befall us are all the direct result of our mental interactions with the Field. When we choose to activate the mental force inside us, we have an unlimited amount of power to create our physical world. Our own Divine Intelligence is just a small fragment in the bigger infinite mind of the Creator.

Divine Intelligence: A Powerful Presence

Michael Talbot, in his book *The Holographic Universe* (1991) calls our inner light "the Human Energy Field" (p. 165). He reminds us that ancient traditions have talked about this energy field surrounding the body for thousands of years. For example, in India, writings that date back five thousand years call it *prana*; Jewish mystics called it *nefish* and said that each body had an egg-shaped bubble of light around it; in China, since before Christ, it has been called *chi*. He states that there are at least ninety-seven different names for this energy in different cultures.

Many religions and cultures think that if a spiritual leader is especially gifted, the energy field of light surrounding his or her body may be visible to everyone. Of course, we see in pictures that saints have halos around their heads. Talbot states that the great Sufi mystic Hazrat Inayat Khan gave off so much light "that people could actually read by it!" (p. 165).

Our greatness. Our inner divinity. Our unlimited ability to create. These words may strike fear into us because they put a huge responsibility on us to live our best lives and to do our internal work and spiritual practice to develop who we are.

When you are internally sourced, you have quicker access to your Divine Intelligence. People who are internally located are self-responsible and accountable; they accept and admit errors and are able to move past them. Their light is brighter. They are aware of their own needs and are prepared to meet them so they can give back to others without resentment. They are creative, consciously manifesting and creating their lives. They are resilient, which means they can maintain high levels of mental and emotional positivity and well-being in the face of adversity. Internally- sourced people can reframe and shift back to depend on their source within for answers rather than rely on the beliefs of outside sources.

Internally-sourced people are also self-aware. They are observant and they carefully consider events; they do not simply react to them. They are Emotionally Non-Reactive, which means they do not allow old emotions or beliefs to control them or cloud their judgment. Usually present-oriented, they are actively engaged in the here and now rather than dwelling on the past or worrying about the future. They respond rather than react.

In studying Christ's life in the Bible, his sayings in the Gospel of Thomas, and in studying writings about how Buddha created a divine consciousness (as well as examining many other religious texts and scientific research), I uncovered twelve attributes of the Divine Intelligence. These Power Potentials, as I call them, allow us to maintain a connection to the Creator within and be more likely to create the outcomes we desire. The following list describes some of the potentials of our Divine Intelligence.

Divine Intelligence: The Twelve Power Potentials

1. **Self-responsible:** Is self-disciplined enough to be accountable, accepts and admits errors, and can move past them.
2. **Self-aware:** Is observant, carefully considers events; does not simply react to them. Can be an observer to one's own life. Is transparent in communicating to others.
3. **Open and receptive to all possibilities:** Is assured that the highest energy source within is capable of giving us all that we need. Is unhindered by negative, limiting beliefs and emotions.
4. **Nonjudgmental:** Gives unconditional, positive regard and shows love to all.

5. **Luminous:** Exhibits brilliance through the energy of positive emotions. Able to attain the highest Light Frequency; has high emotional energies—love, compassion, forgiveness, empathy, tolerance, and gratitude.
6. **Internally attuned:** Is aware of one's own needs and prepared to meet them. Uses one's internal guidance system to make decisions.
7. **Emotionally Non-Reactive:** Does not allow emotions or limiting beliefs to cloud one's judgment.
8. **Consciously creative:** Consciously manifests and creates one's life. Uses the following Universal Spiritual Truth: "As within, so without." Takes 100 percent responsibility for keeping the highest mindset regardless of events in one's life.
9. **Resilient:** Maintains high levels of mental and emotional positivity and well-being in the face of adversity. Able to reframe and shift from negative to positive. Can recognize when one is in one's Conditioned Self and shift.
10. **Capable of a powerful presence:** Exhibits influential leadership; emanates the highest mindset and Light Frequency.
11. **Authentic:** Is able to stay in an Authentic-Self mindset.
12. **Mindful:** Stays in the present moment and observes inside thoughts as well as outside happenings.

The result of knowing, developing, and cultivating the twelve Power Potentials is high Divine Intelligence, and it shows up in the outside world as a powerful Divine Intelligence.

Summary of Concepts for Chapter 14

1. Inside each of us is an energy field. Our ability to create something important in our lives depends on the strength of this energy field or what I call our Light Frequency.

2. When you are internally sourced, you have more power to use this Light Frequency or inner energy field.

3. We attract and communicate to others through the strength of this energy field. Science says we keep in touch with each other by mirror neurons.

4. When activated by us, we are connected to our Divine Intelligence, which consists of twelve sources of potential power.

5. With access to our Divine Intelligence, we have a powerful divinity and the ability to attract what we want in life.

Look Inward

Conscious Evolution: We can do what Buddha or Christ did—just as modern miracle workers such as Gandhi, Saint (Mother) Teresa, and Martin Luther King Jr. have done. If we learn the Universal Spiritual Truths and practice using them, we will see our own miracles transpire. It is all in how we think and how we use the power of our emotions. It may take us many generations or even thousands of years to learn to be as powerful as such spiritual leaders, but we must begin to think we can. We can retrain our brain. Eventually, we will hit the tipping point in evolutionary history, and we will all know our greatness. When the world's light radiance increases, we will all be happier, healthier, and wiser.

When have you felt in touch with this inner energy field?

Which of the twelve potential power sources could you cultivate to connect to your Divine Intelligence?

15

Universal Spiritual Truth #15:
We Are All Connected— One with God

Resurrect in this life!
—Gospel of Philip

When we spoke again after the interview, Dan said, "It was so amazing. As soon as I sat down in the meeting, I felt my energy surge. It was as if everything we've been doing just came together, and I was able to speak easily and sincerely. I didn't feel like I had to please anyone. I knew that I could just be the best me possible. Jayne, I had written all my new empowering beliefs on the palms of my hands!" Dan was laughing. "It just kept them in the forefront of my mind while I was interviewing." And I knew that meant that he was using his powerful neocortex to its fullest.

"And the more I talked, the more interested they became. I could see it in their faces. It was like the mirror neurons you talk about. They were reflecting off me, and I was reflecting to them. The energy in the room was incredible. I wish you could have been there. It wasn't an interview, really. It was more of a discussion on how we could work together and incorporate some of the principles that I've learned from this process.

"Just being with them, I could feel their openness and readiness to hear what I had to say about the best way to run the company. You are not going to believe this, Jayne; they said they'd be more than willing to let me implement my newfound spiritual principles within the company! I knew that I had already influenced them to go a certain direction by the end of the interview. Now I know I'm ready to take the helm and be the leader these people need."

The company Dan had interviewed for was a startup and a nonprofit, and like so many new businesses, it was experiencing some growing pains. They had recently lost their original CEO and were looking for a dynamic, new leader to fill the newly created role and get the company off the ground.

"But, Jayne"—Dan smiled as he explained—"you don't even know the best part of this company. You are going to love this! Do you know what they are doing? They are a consulting firm and work with corporations who are visionary enough to want their product. It is not for every company. But then I don't want to be CEO of just any company."

As Dan soon found out, his attraction to the company was no coincidence. The individuals Dan met with explained that the company was headed by a board of directors comprising some of the most influential spiritual leaders of today. They had procured innovative new software capable of measuring the universal consciousness. They were looking for unique methods for helping people access their inner potential and increase their energy levels, or what I was calling their Light Frequency. One of their goals was to teach someone how to have a powerful enough presence to change other people.

Dan explained, "The scientists and spiritual leaders at this company are engaged in exploring the extent to which interdependence occurs at the universal level. It's what Einstein called 'spooky action at a distance,' remember? Jayne, what was so lucky was that, because you have talked about David Bohm's theories, I was able to talk about him as if I had known him personally."

"Dan, this is right down your alley!" I was excited for him.

Dan continued: "They have increasing evidence to show that it does. That is 'all is one,' as Bohm said. For example, this company was started right after 9/11. What inspired them to begin this company was reading about a study showing that random-number generators around the world behaved in highly nonrandom ways on September 11, 2001."

I was so excited. "Yes, I know about these experiments with random-number generators, Dan."

Dan laughed. "Well, actually I had no idea what they were."

I told Dan: "RNGs are computer programs that create numbers that meet statistical conditions for randomness, as required for certain research experimental designs. You can understand how interested the scientists were when they saw what happened on that date, 9/11."

Dan said, "So, what did happen?"

My brain was working hard to drag up the information that I had read about years ago. "Let me see if I can remember this right. It seems hard to understand, but these generators' statistics roughly matched the time frame of the terrorists' activities."

I continued: "I remember now that the probability of these computers all being nonrandom at the same time in the same way proved that it wasn't random, or at least they had to consider that it might be true: that human consciousness—in other words, the combined mindset of all of us that day—impacted the numbers of the generators. So do you see what I mean?"

"I don't understand it all, but it seems clear to me that the implications are staggering. The universal consciousness creates the world! Or at least that is what they told me," Dan said.

"So everyone may have to accept soon that our minds are capable of transforming physical matter? But what is this company's ultimate goal, Dan?" I asked.

"They are able, through the software they have invented, to take the pulse of the world's mindset. Their software can determine the consciousness of people—what you call Light Frequency. They can measure the mental attitude and emotional state of a group of people and come up with a measurement of a universal mindset. They really believe in this stuff!"

The company officials informed Dan that the universal mindset—that is, the combined Light Frequencies of every person on Earth—has considerable influence over international social and political stability. When the universal consciousness is high, the resulting international atmosphere is relatively peaceful and energetic. However, most people on Earth are stuck in very low Light Frequencies, which are characterized by such destructive emotions as aggression, hate, craving, scorn, regret, despair, blame, and humiliation. This prevailing negative universal consciousness yields the social and political unrest and upheaval that are so rampant in the world today. "As within, so without."

"Okay, this is exciting, but what do they think they can do with it? I mean, I heard you say something earlier that sounded like they could have a great impact on the world at large. Change our mindsets to make a better world? Is that their business plan?" I could see how big business at this point was looking for a better answer than the usual solutions. I really hoped this was true.

"They are out to train enough leaders who know how to be in a positive mental mindset or high frequency so that eventually there will be a tipping point, and they can influence the development of this planet! Well, they told me to check out the research of one of the board members. Her name is Lynne McTaggart, and she is actually not a scientist, but a journalist who has done exhaustive work trying to prove there is a field of energy out there, like a secret force we can draw on—like what I think God really is.

"Jayne, they showed me where they could prove that thoughts change ice crystals. I know, pretty crazy! But they believe that thought can change physical matter."

Dan's interviewers told him, furthermore, that positive emotional frequencies are vastly more powerful than negative ones; they cited David Hawkins's research, which suggests that if 15 percent of the world's population were in a state of consciousness above the normal low level, they would have the power to counteract the negativity of the remaining 85 percent (Hawkins, 2002, p. 282). So, the company reasoned, if they could simply help a handful of individuals raise their frequencies, they could offset the negativity and, hopefully, prevent future worldwide disasters. The company made it their mission to use the tools they had developed to monitor the universal consciousness and wanted to help people of all religions and backgrounds.

I was reminded of Dan's original goals of finding a job and finding God. He seemed to have a job now, so I wondered if he had also found God, the other goal he had set with me when he began his coaching. "So, Dan, what about this God thing? I know you feel as if you know how to connect with the Field of energy that you call God. But what are your final conclusions about your beliefs about God? Are you satisfied with where you are?"

Dan smiled and leaned back in his chair. "Well, this time, Jayne, it is you who will be surprised, because I have written my ideas about God all out in a speech." Dan's smile got bigger, and I could tell he was feeling like he had one-upped me and already had the answer to the question about finding God.

"Well, tell me more about what you have figured out about God. I am very interested," I said with all truth. I could just see the Dan from his college years standing up in front of a group and reading out his manifesto about God. I smiled to myself at how his Authentic Self had really emerged.

"Well, before I went on this last interview, I realized that, because of the spiritual nature of this company's mission, I would need to be clear about my view of God. So I drove back out to Ken's ranch that afternoon—to the exact place where I had the Field-of-light experience at my retreat. I wanted to be in that same spot—not that I thought anything would happen; I guess I just felt it was a sacred spot to really gather up all I knew about God and put it all together. You know how much I have been reading and researching spirituality. So I sat down in the bright sunlight and started writing out my opinion about God." Dan pulled out a couple of folded, crumpled-up pages that looked nothing like something important, much less a speech.

"Are you ready to hear this, Jayne? I felt a little scared when I was reciting it to my future employers—I wondered whether they would like it…it's a pretty radical view, and I'm not sure you will agree with it." Dan looked up at me like a child eager for approval.

"But," he stated strongly, "I don't care what anyone thinks about these ideas. They are mine and I own them." Dan's face morphed into a mature and wise man's expression.

"Good catch!" I said.

"Is there a title for this?" I asked, really not knowing why I wanted to know.

"Well, as a matter of fact, yes. I call this speech 'Getting Unscrewed.'" Dan smiled wickedly.

I laughed out loud. "Dan, that is just so you," I said.

"Here, read this and see what you think. It is kind of long, but I had a lot to say." Dan tried to hand me the manifesto.

"Dan, would you read it to me?" I asked.

Dan looked at me and pulled the papers back to himself. I could tell that he was glad I had asked him to read it because he was very proud of his work, like it was his personal philosophy and something important. He got out his reading glasses and stood up. He seemed way too big to be standing right in front of me in my small office, but I didn't want to take away from the formality of his approach.

Dan cleared his throat as if he were a college professor about to begin a lecture. I leaned back and knew I was going to hear a speech from a great spiritual leader. He began reading slowly at first, yet in a strong, steady voice.

> *"It has been said that these are times of great challenge for us as human beings. Will global warming destroy life as we know it? Will some world leader push a button and start a nuclear holocaust? Will cancer and other diseases become so prevalent that we all suffer and die premature deaths? Will hell come to this Earth?*
>
> *"Whoever is now within reach of my voice, put your hands over your ears and close your eyes if you are not ready to evolve through spiritual growth and if you are not willing to see that you have a part of God within you. I want to yell this across the globe or state this truth on a national TV program or make headlines on Time magazine read: 'Humans have finally discovered the secret to life: God is inside them.' All power lies within us. God is in us—every*

one of us. And as soon as we see this divine power within ourselves, we will then see it in others. The question is, are we going to own it, develop it, and nurture it so that we can be great and loving people? Will we choose to evolve a different way than we have in the past?

"The purpose of evolution is to awaken in us the recognition of our shared divinity. The same divine power that is claimed exclusively by religious leaders is within you. It may be that this part of you is currently asleep or has been dormant for years, but it doesn't mean it isn't in you. It has just never been developed. It may be lying dormant within you, but you are connected to this ultimate source of power and can turn it on whenever you decide you are ready.

"The limiting belief that stands in our universal way of finding this unlimited power source within us is the way we define God. For thousands of years, we have been tricked into thinking we were born in sin and that God is a person much bigger and stronger and more powerful than we are. All great religious books are full of wisdom—and all were written by men for men to control men. I no longer accept this old mental model handed to us by our forefathers that we are fallen creatures doomed to have to plead for God's salvation.

"We are born with God inside us. Are we supposed to believe that God is sucked out of us—and if we are good enough we might get it back?

"People down through history have suggested the idea and have known the secret, but they continued to dance around it without really getting the attention of the world. Over the centuries, people have carried the truth with them and refused to believe that we are not divine. Early scientists like Galileo, Copernicus, and Newton espoused the spiritual belief that God is on the inside even though they were forced to hide it by the Vatican. The artists Leonardo da Vinci and Michelangelo kept this truth; the writers and philosophers Dante, Blake, Milton, Goethe, and Hegel carried it up through the years to us. Tolstoy wrote a book called The Kingdom of God Is Within. Psychologists Sigmund Freud and Carl Jung supported the idea of God within. In the late nineteenth century, a *group of New Thought leaders, such as Ernest Holmes, Matthew Fox, and Wallace Wattles, took up the message and began to develop organizations to support new thinking about God. And more currently, quantum physicists Wolfgang Pauli, Werner Heisenberg, and Einstein all talked about the mystery of the force within us. So science and spirituality are blending to give us a way to develop this latent potential within us all.*

"All the major religions of the world have this as their basis, if we just look underneath the interpretations of our forefathers. Christ symbolically represents the divine in man, as do spiritual leaders in other religions. They represent examples, rather than exceptions, showing us the way we can be also. The commonality in all religions is salvation. But salvation is something we do for ourselves. Many ancient texts have a central message of the power of human thought, such as the Vedas, the Zohar, the Bible, and especially the lost Gnostic Gospels. All these religions have the same message… that God is on the inside…but maybe we, as a people, were not strong enough to accept this truth that we can save ourselves…at least not until now…

"The good news is that, when we get straight on the idea that God is part of us, we realize our purpose on Earth is to unveil this inner divine spark, nurse it, and make it grow. We need to evolve our view of God, take God out of the sky, and place it into the hearts of anyone who is willing to take responsibility for his or her unlimited potential. Instead of a Big Man up in the sky, God could be better described as a Big Mind in which we are all a part, and God can only evolve more as each of us evolves our mind.

"We should all be developing the God within us instead of worshipping a God outside us. I just want to comfort people, telling you that if you know who you really are, you will have no fear again. If you discover the God within you, you will always feel connected to the greatest power source in the Universe. Evolve, open yourself up to a revolutionary, new concept of who you are and what life is about.

"I think God should be embraced not as what we seek, but who we are. And I believe people are ready to hear about the real definition of God.

"We need a new way to think of God. For me, the old way doesn't work anymore. I believe that God is an activity within us—a movement of our soul toward our innate goodness. The only spiritual "work" we have to do is to remove our limiting beliefs about ourselves and let the Authentic Self shine out of us. It is what we all have within us, and all we must do is make a mental turn toward reaching up to touch the good. I believe that life is good and that we can trust that the Sun will come up in the morning, that the trees will continue to flourish, and the fields will bring us food. To evolve means to always work toward the ideal, knowing that utopia is possible. Evolution always longs to improve itself and reaches toward being godlike. Evolution is the gradual resolution of our Conditioned and Authentic Selves. Evolution always leads us to an unending state of excellence.

"I think the coming religion will serve us best if it is about spirituality. Each person must do their own thinking about what they believe about God, not simply go with some set of beliefs handed down for thousands of years from our ancestors. I believe spirituality focuses on our ascent upward, rather than our fall into sin. I want to always be working toward being a better person.

"Now it is time to pull back the curtain all the way and expose the truth, allowing all people of the planet Earth to step together out of the darkness, seeing the clear message that we are all born with the light of God within us. As we step out, we take the responsibility on our shoulders to develop the potential of our human spirit. This action has the awesome power to draw all the religions of the world together, ripping away the limiting belief that we must turn to a person outside us for power and rendering powerless the religious divide.

"To know oneself at the deepest level is simultaneously to know God—this is the secret available to us now. Let's begin the journey walking in the right direction.

> *"Instead of being fearful that I will go to hell someday, I want to find heaven right now in this moment on this Earth. Instead of all the creeds and rules, I want to find a lifestyle where I am always becoming more responsible for myself, of learning about how to manage my emotional power, and how to use unlimited thinking to create a great life for myself, my family, and the world. I want to accept the awesome responsibility that the source of all power lies within me.*
>
> *"This is what I call the true definition of God: the unlimited potential within us all,"* Dan concluded.

He sat down heavily and let out a huge sigh of relief. The crumpled pages fell to the floor in front of us. He took his hands and rubbed his eyes and seemed to be totally spent. It had to take a lot of energy to try to raise up humanity, as he was doing, out of centuries of limiting beliefs. He had exposed himself, the core of who he was, and his Divine Intelligence was working. I let him have his alone time, but when he looked up, I saw that light again, that high Light Frequency coming out of his eyes—*I must be seeing the God within him*, I thought. Divine Intelligence at work.

I could only mumble in awe of him: "What courage you have to be able to express yourself like this. You truly represent the Creator within all of us in your message."

Universal Spiritual Truth #15:
We Are All Connected—One with God

As Dan came back into himself, he said: "Jayne, that is the speech I gave at the interview. And afterward, the people interviewing me broke out in spontaneous brainstorming and sharing. Here is a little of what they told me. They seemed to want to give me even more scientific information to support my thesis."

He continued, "Here's the exciting part of what they told me: It has been shown that the power of human thought grows exponentially with the number of minds that share that thought. Plato called it 'gathering God.' The inner light we all have within us is ignited when enough of us become a critical mass and evolve the Mind of God. Then we are able to perform miracles, not just as one person, but as a group of dedicated people out to make a better world."

Dan didn't share the name of the company he was being interviewed by, but I knew of organizations out there such as The Global Coherence Initiative—doing just such research and consciousness training. The GCI conducts research on the mechanisms of how the Earth's fields affect human mental and emotional processes, health outcomes, and collective human behavior and explores how collective human emotions and intentions may be carried by the Earth's electromagnetic and energetic fields. Their mission is to demonstrate that increasing heart connections will lead to intuitive solutions for global challenges and transformation of our world and consciousness.

When they set out to find a new CEO, the company had not been looking for someone with technical prowess to head up the software side of the business, nor were they interested in hiring only a business-minded individual who would look for ways to profit from their resources. They wanted it all: a leader with business savvy and a powerfully influential mindset who would inspire employees to find and use their own Divine Intelligence, trust in their own abilities, create a culture of cooperation and a belief in change, support innovation, and thereby promote their mission—improving mindsets.

When Dan had walked into his interview, the interviewers had been shocked by his transparency and calm presence and stunned by his speech about spirituality and the future of religion. Even though he had been unemployed for months, the light in his eyes and the confidence in his gait were unmistakable and infectious. Dan told them he had been waiting for this one perfect opportunity. Dan's speech and presence had impressed them immediately, and they knew that he was the best man for the job.

Because the company was a nonprofit, Dan's salary would not be as high as the salaries most CEOs would command. In exchange for a lower salary, however, Dan would be made part owner of the company and would be in charge of hiring the team of leaders that he wanted. The position seemed to offer Dan everything he had always wanted, but Dan had known better than to leap at the first opportunity that presented itself to him, even if it was for the CEO spot he had always wanted. His thoughtful mindset told him to consider this position carefully and to remain cognizant of his limitless other options to ensure that the job he ultimately accepted would be the perfect one for him.

"So," I asked Dan, "do you think this is the right position for you?"

Dan smiled slowly, unable to conceal his certainty: "You know, I told you months ago that I wanted to be a better person and help others. I think this is my chance. This is a unique opportunity to work with people who respect where I'm coming from and what I can offer besides just business experience. I think I can help my fellow workers as well as those we serve. My work will really be important to me. This is more than a paycheck. It's a life, a life of growth, change, sharing... I'm actually going to be able to benefit others. The whole idea just fills me with excitement, Jayne. And that's really what life is all about, isn't it? I feel humble and powerful at the same time—and just completely happy. They've given me twenty-four hours to make up my mind, but I don't need that long. Once I talk to Margie, we'll seal the deal. Jayne, I am so happy I can't stand it!"

I left Dan with these parting words: "Dr. Michael Bernard Beckwith once said, 'Joy is evidence of the presence of God.'"

As soon as he'd arrived back home, Dan began calling his family members and sharing the details of the position with them. The old Dan, who was disconnected from God, hung up on his past, and distraught about his future, would have allowed the family to pump him up or pull him down with doubts and help him decide; however, his newfound awareness—this new mindset of God—gave him the ability to carefully consider whether the offer was appropriate for him. Sensing his energy, each of his family members responded enthusiastically and encouraged him to accept. By the end of the afternoon, Dan had an answer for the company: He enthusiastically and unconditionally accepted their offer.

But Dan's new position was not the only result he had gained from the dialoguing process. Now that he had finally replaced many of the negative, limiting beliefs that were undermining his goals and ambitions with positive thoughts and emotions, he had also gained the ability to affect the people in his personal life in ways he wanted. His newfound presence was also felt at home.

"How will you use this ability, this Divine Intelligence, in your personal life? You said in your speech you wanted a lifestyle of being a good person," I asked.

"Well," Dan said, "I want to make sure my relationship with my family will continue to improve as I start this new job—after all, if I don't have them, I don't really have anything. The main message I got from studying the Gnostics was they believe that life is good and that we are born good by nature. I want to always work toward being a kinder, wiser person."

"Before the retreat, my relationship with Margie was at a breaking point. My frustrations with her would just boil over, I'd lose my temper for practically no reason, and we'd get into a huge argument. But now Margie and I are learning to communicate better with each other, so we don't lose it with each other. And Jayne, you are going to love what I did with Margie. I did one of those Positive Anchor deals with her."

"How did you do that, Dan?" I couldn't wait to hear about it.

"Well, I just had her close her eyes to make it really dramatic, like you did with me. Then I asked her to try and remember the first time we met. I asked her to think about what we had on, what we were doing, and especially how she felt about me. Well, okay, Jayne, she shared this great feeling with me, and I just asked her to try to feel that again and again so I would have a chance to be happy again with her—just like we were in the beginning!

"And you know what else? I've come to a new conclusion about what makes a marriage work. It's not about avoiding conflict—I know you might be shocked to hear that from a former Pleaser—but we are both not avoiding conflict anymore. We do argue at times now, but by discussing things in the present, neither of us holds on to negative feelings about each other that would affect our love. The result is more respect in our marriage. And…" Dan seemed to have to think about this a minute before he said it. "And better sex!"

He had me speechless, so I tried to get him to tell me more: "What else is different in your relationship with Margie?" I wanted him to keep talking about all the positive Outside Wins to reinforce the power in them, but honestly, I was just really wanting to avoid the mention of sex.

Dan smiled, knowing exactly what I was doing and enjoying watching me be the avoider and squirm this time. "I continue to practice speaking up about my own opinions with Margie, even though I know it may not please her. And wait till you hear this: She's decided to take a permanent teaching job again! She tells me it makes her feel more confident, valuable, and equal to me. She feels comfortable making joint decisions with me again. She laughingly told me that she no longer assumes that nagging and bickering are her only means of making herself heard. And by getting out of the house and interacting with others on a day-to-day basis, Margie's realized that she actually has more to talk about with her friends, the children, and me.

"And the boys in college have changed, too! They got part-time jobs a few months ago to help pay for their school and living expenses. They know that money is still going to be tight, even though I have a job again, so they've volunteered to continue working because they are enjoying the income and the sense of independence! It seems like they're finally thinking of me as a father and not just a checkbook!"

"So, Dan, do you remember when we first started coaching, I dared to tell you that you had 'created' a job loss for yourself?" I wanted to remind Dan that he was creating all the time, whether he was conscious of it or not.

"Oh yes! If I remember correctly, I was very clear that I didn't think it was my fault or that I had anything to do with losing my job. I guess you knew how that remark pissed me off, Jayne." Dan laughed.

"Well, so why did you create this job loss—even if it was unconscious?" I pressed him.

"Well, I have been thinking about all that, Jayne." Dan had on his serious face all of a sudden. "And I now know exactly why I created a job loss. I wanted so desperately to have a more meaningful job and life that I couldn't think of any other conscious way to get to where I am today! And I guess it worked in the long run." Dan smiled at me.

"Well, only because you chose to do your inner work and figure all this out about what you needed to be to live on purpose, so to speak." I wanted to give him my respect for what he had done.

"So, what else has changed and improved?" I took him back to where he was before I had interrupted his train of thought.

Dan's relationship with his daughter, Lindsey, he admitted, still had quite a bit of growing to do. She had her own life and her own adoptive parents, with whom she was very happy. Dan had to let go of his desire to become the father to her that he wished he could have been. She told him she just needed his support and the knowledge that he was there for her. She did not visit or participate in the family as often as he had once hoped she would, but she did fly to meet her new grandmother, and the two communicated on a regular basis.

But the newfound Dan, the God within him, was far from being finished. His work on developing his mental force, his Divine Intelligence, would last a lifetime.

"There's something else that might surprise you, Jayne," Dan said as our coaching session was drawing to a close. "I know that I'm not finished with this process—in fact, I'm sure it will take a lifetime for me to fully develop my Divine Intelligence. Even though I'm just in the earliest stages of learning, I still feel this new part of myself growing stronger. Well, actually, I feel sort of like I'm growing beyond myself, if that makes any sense."

I knew he was referring to transcendence: moving beyond his human limitations by igniting his Divine Intelligence.

"I'm so pleased that you're continuing to take such an active interest in developing your Divine Intelligence!" I replied.

Of course, Dan realized that if he desired continued success, he would have to do more than simply sit back and enjoy the positive changes; he would have to continually exercise his mindset to ensure that it was characterized by the properties of Divine Intelligence. He would have to remain in the present so that he would be able to communicate effectively with the Field. Any negative blocks would hinder his and his company's mission.

During our short time together, Dan had developed his view of himself, his view of his family, and his view of God. Now that he had accepted the Creator within himself and taken full responsibility for his own salvation, he was reaping the immense benefits, mainly the priceless feelings of contentment and peace of mind. Now, no matter what happened in the future, as long as Dan stayed internally connected, he would always be able to consciously create, using his own personal presence's influence.

Up until this point, I had been a source of strength for Dan. However, after he rewired and found his daughter and the job he wanted, he finally realized that the generative power and strength of God really was inside him. Now that he was immersed in the process and beginning to be sourced from within, it was time for me to take a backseat. Once Dan had become confident of his own Divine Intelligence, he was prepared to work independently of me. Whoever achieves gnosis, or this inner knowledge, becomes "no longer a Christian, but a Christ" (Gospel of Philip 67.26–27, NHL 140).

I knew that Dan no longer needed me, but I also knew that ending our professional relationship was Dan's responsibility. He must have read *my* mirror neurons. He began our next telephone call with an announcement that he was very grateful for the tools I had given him to rediscover his God within.

"Well, Jayne, I can't thank you enough. The wheels are really turning now. I feel I could set the world on fire right now! Margie and I are packing up for Chicago. Believe it or not, the house sold in just a matter of days. In this economy, that's nothing short of a miracle. We'll leave just after Tommy graduates. He can't wait to get to Colorado for the summer. He's even found a job working at a summer camp for kids. Brad and Daniel are staying at school to take a few classes and work, too. Margie is going to teach in the suburb where we will live. I've gained a lot of faith watching this whole process and knowing that none of this success is coming to me 'out of the blue.' I am creating it all, even in this moment."

And with that funny grin I could hear on the phone, he also announced, "I owe so much to you, Jayne, for partnering with me in this process. At one time, I would have said I couldn't do it without you, but I know now that we all have this potential to connect to our real self. I'm just glad that you were there with me to point me in the right direction. I don't think that was any accident either. Even in my worst state, I was able to attract what I needed when I needed it: you. I'm ready now to launch.

"I'll miss our talks," Dan said, "but Jayne, you need to continue your work with others who are still lost in the wilderness. If you don't mind, I'd like to stay in touch occasionally to keep you up with all that's going on. I'm jazzed. I'm the kind of person I've always wanted to be. I'm off to change the world."

I knew that he was right and I knew that he would!

And so it was!

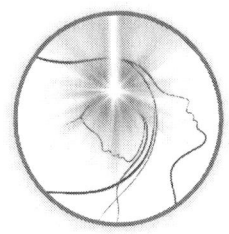

EPILOGUE

Dan had uncovered within himself the secret force of the Universe! He had gone beyond human limitations. His inner changes had profoundly affected the people he was closest to in his personal life, but now, how would Dan's spiritual, emotional and mental changes affect the world in general? In connecting with God, Dan had found a new job position that would empower him to lead. Only developing the mind of God within him could have given him the ability to create his life in this way.

The Next Evolutionary Stage

Because evolution is a gradual process of self-growth leading to the discovery of our own divinity, the final step is to shift from thinking of ourselves as a finite entity to realizing we are part of a bigger mind of God. Enlightenment is really the realization that God is both within and without.

The following poem by Jalalud'din Rumi captures the Sufi experience of union with the divine approximately eight hundred years ago. While the interpretation of poetry is always subjective, the English translation of this beautiful Persian passage speaks to me as the promotion of tolerance for other people's viewpoints. The Field is separate and distinct from the limited mind, which creates barriers that prevent us from knowing God. By working on the mind, we can recognize and commune with our divine Creator.

Rumi eloquently wrote:
Out beyond ideas of wrong doing
And right doing there is a field. I'll meet you there.
When the soul lies down in that grass
The world is too full to talk about.

Being in a Mindset of God Is Eternal and Immortal

If you look at Christ's life symbolically, he dies to his separate self to resurrect to eternal life. "By dying to what we are not, we come to life as what we are" (Freke & Gandy, 1999, p. 183). The Gnostics saw our deepest self as the Self of All; thus, we are connected to our source. Simon Magus, an early Gnostic, says that this process gives the soul "permanent peace" (Freke & Gandy, 2001, p. 176). Spiritually, the God within us is like light. As with all types of energy, the light energy that exists within us, or that inner divinity, cannot be destroyed, not even by death. The flash of light that people see when they witness death is not the destruction of the deceased's light, but rather the transference of her light to another place, the return of her light to the Universe.

We know that a person's inner light is eternal because we see and feel it every time we remember someone who has died. The more positive memories we have of the deceased—the more influential and radiant she was in life—the more brightly her light shines in death. Thus, if we want our light to shine brightly after we have passed, we must ensure that it shines brightly during our time on Earth. It was important that Dan understand this while I was coaching him because I knew it was important to him to leave this legacy for his children.

The Religion of the Future Will Be a Universal Religion

> Behind the secrets of nature remains something subtle, intangible and inexplicable. Veneration for this force beyond anything we can comprehend is my religion. –*Albert Einstein*

In the beginning of this book, the first spiritual secret was that God is light and inside everyone. Now we see that we are all a part of a greater eternal light. In the Gospel of Matthew 5:14, Jesus says it this way: "You are the lights of the cosmos." And when you think about it, the star in the gospel story of Jesus's birth must have been a symbol of the light within Christ and within us all. We can use this light to guide us back to who and where we are supposed to be—in the kingdom of heaven right here on Earth.

The Internalization of God Works with Any Religion

Just as Dan's goal was to be the best person he could be, this is the real goal of all religions. As Saint Teresa, known to the world as Mother Teresa until her canonization in 2016, stated in *A Simple Path*: "I've always said we should help a Hindu become a better Hindu, a Muslim become a better Muslim, and a Catholic become a better Catholic" (p. 31).

Gerald Massy, an expert on religion who died in 1907, wrote about "The Coming Religion" in one of his lectures. He thought that each person must do his own thinking, somewhat like what I have called an internal locus of control. He thought that this new religion for the future must "transcend personal God and avoid dogma and theology. This religion will proclaim man's ascent rather than his fall. It will be a religion of accomplishment rather than worship. Above all, it will be a joyous religion, a cosmic path for all" (Harpur, 2004, p. 203).

THE EVOLUTION OF DIVINE INTELLIGENCE

Historical Timeline

3–4 million years ago: The cerebral cortex layer began to appear in the human brain.

c. 5000 BCE: **The Hindu religion** originated at least this early, if not earlier. The Hindus believed that God was inside every person.

c. 563–483 BCE: Life of **Buddha**. He developed Buddhism based on Hinduism.

c. 469 BCE: **Socrates** was born. He was one of the first to espouse the theory that knowledge comes from divine insight. Philosophy was born! The mystery religions, inner dialogue, and inner voice concepts started with him.

c. 429 BCE: **Plato** was born. He wrote down his own ideas based on the early Socratic Dialogues. He was one of the first to look inside the mind for answers.

c. 399 BCE: **Socrates was executed** for not believing in external "gods of the state," among other reasons.

c. 7–2 BCE: **Jesus of Nazareth was born.** His life symbolized that birth, death, and resurrection can happen to us all. We, too, can become like him and discover the divine within us.

12–30 CE: **Jesus is thought to have studied in the East.** These are known as his lost years, as nothing is mentioned in the Bible about this time in his life, but it was later documented by historian Edward Cohn and others.

33: **Jesus was executed** on charges of sedition against the Roman Empire. It was still a fearful prospect in the world at that time to consider a man discovering his divine powers.

130–60: **The Gospel of Thomas was written.** It is said to be the Secret Sayings of Jesus and to tell us that God is within.

185: **Irenaeus** coined the term *heretic* to describe a person who does not accept that Jesus was the only Divine.

205–270: Philosopher **Plotinus** discovered the existence of what he called the *nous*, known today as Divine Intelligence.

313: **Emperor Constantine**, in a single edict, created his view of Christianity, which we still have today.

325: **The First Council of Nicaea** was held. It created a uniform Christian doctrine, excluding the Gnostic Gospels. With this decision, we took a step backward in negating the belief that we are all divine. This council confirmed that Jesus was divine and excluded anyone else.

1209: First attack against the Cathars, a Gnostic branch in Bezier Languedoc, France. This was the beginning of the **Albigensian Crusade** against the Gnostics.

1244: In the **Fall of Montségur**, 220 Gnostics were burned at the stake. History records this as the end of the Cathar religion, but legend holds that four people escaped, carrying a treasure of sacred texts and beliefs.

1307–1312: **The Knights of the Templar**, an early Christian sect, were imprisoned for heresy.

1321: **The last known execution of Cathar priests** occurred in Languedoc.

1400–1700: Resurgence of interest in Plato's philosophy: **Renaissance** of the divine spirit within.

1473 – 1543: Life of **Copernicus, mathematician and astronomer.** During his lifetime, everyone believed the Earth was still and the stars revolved around it. He suggested the Earth might be moving through space; however, this went against the religious orthodoxy. He remained silent until shortly before his death **with the publication of his book,** *On the Revolutions of the Celestial Spheres.* **His new cosmology** exemplifies the classic paradigm shift as he started **a radical revision of the current scientific worldview.**

1564: **Galileo** validated that Copernicus was right; however, the **Vatican put him under house arrest for the rest of his life for heresy.**

1642: **Newton**, 150 years later, **provided the mathematical equations** of planets orbiting the Sun and proved the new paradigm true.

1648: During the Cossack massacres led by Bogdan Chmielnicki, a spiritual movement called **Hasidism** began within Judaism to encounter God personally.

1828–1910: Life of **Leo Tolstoy**. He wrote *The Kingdom of God Is Within You.*

1842–1910: Life of **William James**, the father of psychology. We began to examine what was inside us.

1869–1948: Life of **Mahatma Gandhi**. He espoused nonviolence, peace, and conflict resolution. When asked what God was, he stated that God is truth and truth is what the voice within tells you. In the final years of Tolstoy's life, he mentored Gandhi; you can see his influence in Gandhi's doctrine of passive resistance and nonviolence.

1875–1961: Life of **Carl Jung**, a modern-day Gnostic and contemporary of Freud. He believed that the spiritual purpose of humankind was to know well-being. Individuation was the journey to meet the self, and at the same time, one would meet the divine.

1894: **Tolstoy's writings were banned** in Germany and Russia.

1896: **Gospel of Mary Magdalene** was discovered by a German collector in an antiquities market in Cairo, Egypt.

1897–1903: Ancient fragments of the Greek versions of the **Gospel of Thomas**, dating back to 130–250 CE, were discovered in Oxyrhynchus, Egypt.

1898: The presentation by Nikola Tesla of High Frequency Oscillation for Electro-Therapeutic and Other Purposes at the American Electro-Therapeutic Association in Buffalo NY, September 15, introducing the Electrical Nature of the Human Body and the therapeutic characteristics of high **Light Frequency.**

1905–1915: Albert Einstein formulates his **Theory of Relativity** (special and general), a pillar of modern physics, superseding Newton's 200-year-old theory, a way to understand the Universe as a whole.

1913: Niels Bohr originally formulates the **Correspondence Principle**.

1918: Max Planck, originator of quantum theory, is awarded the Nobel Prize for his discovery of energy quanta.

1921: Albert Einstein is awarded the Nobel Prize for his evolutionary contributions in quantum theory.

1925–1927: Werner Heisenberg puts forth his famous Uncertainty Principle, one of the cornerstones of quantum physics.

1927: Ernest Holmes (1887-1960) establishes Science of Mind, a New Thought movement that God is within.

1929: Edwin Hubble discovers that **the Universe is expanding**.

1935: Victor Weisskopf popularizes **the Zero Point Field**, makes major contributions to field of quantum theory (1930-1940)

1945: The **Nag Hammadi codices** were found in Egypt. They consisted of thirteen papyrus codices and fifty-two Gnostic treatises dating from the second century or earlier. This discovery substantiated the earlier Greek version found in Egypt in 1897; the reemergence of these documents symbolized that we were ready to receive the message that we, as humans, have Divine Intelligence.

1964: John Stewart Bell originates **Bell's Theorem**, a significant contribution to quantum physics, which verifies Quantum Entanglement. Specifically, Bell's Theorem points to a profound interaction between our conscious mental activity and the physical world itself. Einstein had called this concept "spooky action at a distance."

1966: Many of the leading scholars of Gnosis gathered in Messina, Italy, and created a set of statements defining **Gnosticism**.

1971: Work of Paul C. Lauterbur contributes to the invention of magnetic resonance imaging scanner **(MRI), allowing access to view the human brain.**

1977: **The first known translations** of the Gnostic Gospels were released to the public in English.

1979: Elaine Pagels published *The Gnostic Gospels*, a book that brought the new gospels into public view.

1980: **David Bohm** proves mathematically that **the Universe is a hologram**.

1981: **Fritz-Albert Popp** conducts research that confirms the existence of bio-photons from DNA in human body, **shows all living things emit light.**

1991: Neuroscientist **Karl Pribram** shows the brain is itself a hologram, **the Holographic Brain theory**.

1995: Cistercian monk and Catholic priest **Thomas Keating** creates the concept of contemplative prayer, turning us more inside for understanding of God.

1997: **The International Coach Federation** was born. Its underlying premise is that people have the answers to their problems within their own mind.

1997: Candace Pert proves **energy is free flow of emotions**, publishes *Molecules of Emotions*.

1999: **Pope John Paul II makes headlines** by declaring that "heaven is not up in the clouds nor is Hell a distinct place."

2000: Psychologist **Martin Seligman** changes the climate of psychology and creates a new branch of psychology called Positive Psychology.

2000–2012: **An explosion of popular books and paradigm shifts** occurs to focus more on self-help and looking within for the answers.

2002: David Hawkins proves **emotions have different levels of power.**

2003: **Elaine Pagels** publishes *Beyond Belief*, a book about the Gospel of Thomas or the Secret Sayings of Jesus. With the release of these books, the possibility of Divine Intelligence was made available to the more common reader.

2004: Giacomo Rizzolati discovers **Mirror Neurons**.

2005: Bruce Lipton proves **we are not limited by our biology**.

2007: Antoine Lutz, John Dunne, and Richard Davidson suggest there is a state of mind known as **"ipseity."**

2010: USA Today shows **72 percent of millennials consider themselves more spiritual than religious**.

2012: Discovery of the Higgs Boson **"God particle."**

2013: Dr. Jayne Gardner publishes *Divine Intelligence.*

2013: 2.1 Million adults were practicing **yoga and meditation** outside the traditional religious settings.

2014: Time Magazine declares this to be the year for Mindful Living. **The Mindfulness Revolution** has taken off.

2017: Researchers Stuart Hameroff and Roger Penrose suggest **our soul does not die; it returns to the Universe**.

Today: Another reader has joined the thousands of Creators who have awakened their Divine Intelligence and begun to explore their limitless potential.

ENDNOTES

Chapter 1
Differences between Coaching and Therapy
Memories hold the key to what the brain thought was important and held on to, and most of the time this original belief system is still in operation today. Thus, by looking backward, we may find what is holding a person back from achieving his goals. This illustrates one way coaching and therapy are different. Coaching takes you back into your past, but it does so for one specific reason: to identify your limiting beliefs and patterns. Going backward is quick but necessary in coaching to uncover these limiting beliefs, but we don't tarry long in the past. Therapy is needed if a person being coached has endured intense trauma, as this could mean that the client may get stuck in the past, which could trigger a depression. For safety reasons, I don't allow anyone to undergo this process without the guidance of a trained, professional coach.

Coaches are trained to investigate a person's history before starting this trek back into the past. If much trauma occurred, then the coach will refer the client to a therapist, as well, for more support going through this process. In therapy, the client spends many hours rehashing what happened and lamenting the damage. This is sometimes needed if a person has endured great pain while growing up. Dan was like most of us, however. He had a relatively good childhood with parents who tried very hard to give him love and support. But like all parents, they were unable to give that perfect unconditional love at all times. It is in those times when we create our limiting beliefs. Thus, Dan was a good candidate for coaching and did not require therapy. This also explains why everyone, even someone raised in a stellar family environment, will have limiting beliefs.

In coaching, we work with healthy people, so taking them back into the past is safe if they are guided by a coach who knows what to watch out for in the backward glance. In coaching, we draw upon our memories for a quick self-discovery to uncover these limiting beliefs, using our memories to define them for us.

Chapter 2
Readiness for Change
James Prochaska of the University of Rhode Island and his colleagues (Prochaska et al. 2008) developed the Trans-Theoretical Model (TTM) of change in 1977. They have redefined it over the years and conducted research continually on proof of its stages of change. It has been used by many organizations as a model for change. The TTM labels the stages of change as follows:
1. Precontemplation: Not currently considering change
2. Contemplation: Ambivalent about change
3. Preparation: Some experience with change and trying to change
4. Action: Practicing the change
5. Maintenance: Continued commitment to change
6. Relapse: Falling back into old behaviors and no longer using the change

The further you go into the stages, the brighter your inner light becomes and the stronger your ipseity or Authentic Self's influence on the world. In short, your Divine Intelligence is piqued at the action phase, yet must be monitored through many relapses until the new state of mind becomes an actual part of the brain.

Chapter 3
Quantum BioFeedback Device
I was currently measuring the ability of my Divine Intelligence Process to discover where light was being blocked by emotional sources. I was using a Quantum BioFeedback device to measure my patients' potential for Light Frequency before they began the Divine Intelligence Process and after they completed the process. I would send relevant data about each patient to a colleague who is trained in using this device, who would then run their data on her BioFeedback device. I was

interested in proving a person's thoughts and emotions affected their Light Frequency. I knew these trapped emotions had to be keeping them from accessing their Divine Intelligence. As I took my patients through this process, I had repeatedly observed how certain unexpressed emotions would suppress their energy levels. My purpose was to compile data about the process's impact on my patients' Light Frequency.

Chapter 5
The Conditioned-Self Chart
The following chart provides more information about the common characteristics of each Conditioned Self Personality Profile. I credit a fellow Adlerian, Dr. Roy Kern, for his original Lifestyle Scale which gave me the inspiration for this chart.

CONTROLLER / LEADER:

Controller - Before Rewiring:	Leader - After Rewiring:
Often viewed as "needing charm school." Focuses on other people to change. Has a fix-it mentality. Thinks it knows best what will work for others. Thinks people should become more like him/her. Wants employees to be loyal soldiers, looking to them for the answers. Sometimes wrong, but never in doubt.	Works hard to get things to happen. No matter what the project, "gets it out the door." Does not get distracted at work and takes satisfaction in completing tasks. Seen as a leader who inspires others. Delegates very skillfully, seeing the vision of everyone working in their best suit. Makes a good CEO.
Frequently Heard Saying: "It's for your own good."	
Major Distraction Technique: Anger outbursts – need to control others.	
Possible Limiting Beliefs: • I must always be in charge to get things done. • I must get others to do things my way. • If I control things, everything will turn out right.	**Possible Empowering Beliefs:** • I am a strong leader, inspiring others to greatness. • I trust others to make good decisions and do their jobs well. • Only I change the world I have created.

CRITIC / PROBLEM SOLVER:

Critic - Before Rewiring:	Problem Solver - After Rewiring:
Often sees things as "never good enough." Constantly criticizes inner self. Often the first one to step up and take responsibility, whether or not at fault. Thoughts stay mostly in the past and can always recall regrets – things it wishes it had done differently.	Thinks things through and examines them from all sides. Does not jump to conclusions and relies only on solid evidence to make decisions. Speaks up for what is right even if there is opposition. Acts on own convictions and values. Valued in business meetings for stating things like they really are. An excellent problem solver.
Frequently Heard Saying: "I am so sorry."	
Major Distraction Technique: Gossip.	
Possible Limiting Beliefs: • I must be hard on myself to win. • I am never good enough in what I do. • I must keep pushing myself to get ahead.	**Possible Empowering Beliefs:** • I see solutions to even the most complicated problems. • I am whole and complete. • I am successful in _____.

AVOIDER / WORKER:

Avoider – Before Rewiring:	Worker – After Rewiring:
Often "procrastinates." Avoids difficult situations, uncomfortable feelings and disagreements with others. Believes other people will hurt them; trusts very few people. Does not mind helping others. Avoids confrontation and often a workaholic.	Makes careful choices. Consistently prudent. Disciplined. In control of appetite and emotions. Calm in an emergency and reacts quickly in a good way. Can compartmentalize the day to stay focused to get things done.
Frequently Heard Saying: "Wait until tomorrow."	
Major Distraction Technique: Any major addiction.	
Possible Limiting Beliefs: • I must work harder than most people to get ahead. • If anyone is upset, avoid talking about it to them. • I must avoid feeling anything negative.	**Possible Empowering Beliefs:** • I have boundless energy within me. • I am aware of my feelings and have a choice of how to act on them. • I work hard and play hard.

PERFECTIONIST / TALENTED:

Perfectionist - Before Rewiring:	Talented - After Rewiring:
Often viewed as "out of control." Nothing is ever good enough. Tries to control habits like eating, sleeping, and exercise to the extreme. Achieves and accomplishes only the best. Very competitive. Always has a project.	Completes projects on time, with precision and attention to detail. Punctual and efficient. Dependable, consistent and trustworthy. Learns from own mistakes quickly and increases momentum because of the learning. Loves beauty. Makes a good airline pilot or brain surgeon.
Frequently Heard Saying: "Just one more time."	
Major Distraction Technique: Details.	
Possible Limiting Beliefs: • Everything I do must turn out perfect. • Don't try anything unless you know you can do it perfectly. • No matter what I do, it will never be good enough.	**Possible Empowering Beliefs:** • I am perfect in this moment. • I have everything within me I need at any moment. • I can risk trying new things.

PLEASER / INTUITIVE:

Pleaser - Before Rewiring:	Intuitive - After Rewiring:
Often "over promises but under delivers." Sweet and docile. Changes identity to suit those present – a great mimic. Afraid to be original and never known to express anger (although full of anger!). May be unsuccessful in management positions. May be the "C" personality – prone to "cancer."	Known as kind and generous. Balanced in ability to take care of self and others. Enjoys doing good deeds. Aware of the motives and feelings of others. Knows how to "fit in" in different social situations and how to put others at ease. Thought of as wise. May be a good sales person.
Frequently Heard Saying: "Of course, I have time to do it for you."	
Major Distraction Technique: Figuring out other people.	
Possible Limiting Beliefs: • I must please everybody. • I respond to everyone's needs. • Other people's needs and wants are more important than mine.	**Possible Empowering Beliefs:** • I am living in my own values of what is important. • I can say "no" to protect myself. • I am anchored within for contentment.

DOUBTER / TEAM PLAYER:

Doubter - Before Rewiring:	Team Player - After Rewiring:
Often feels "woe is me" and plays the "victim" to own benefit. Gets people in its service by eliciting sympathy. Feels sorry for self, sabotages self, and is dependent on others. Looks busy, but may not accomplish anything.	Loyal and dedicated team member. Has sense of newfound personal worth; does not allow others to take advantage. Prefers to let their accomplishments speak for themselves. May seem childlike and creative. Expects the best in the future and works to achieve goals.
Frequently Heard Saying: "Help me."	
Major Distraction Technique: Tragedy – the more, the better.	
Possible Limiting Beliefs: • I am always wrong. • Nobody listens to me. • Others know better than me.	**Possible Empowering Beliefs:** • I trust myself to make good decisions. • I am a success within myself. • I like myself just the way I am.

(See Chapter 13 Endnotes for "Levels of Emotional Power.")

Chapter 7

Approach, not Avoid (Siegel, 2007)

Scientists suspect that athletes choke when too many thoughts flood the prefrontal cortex, the thinking brain—or where the brain holds informational memory. The remedy is that athletes should not be focused in that part of the brain during actual competition, as the brain becomes too busy when they worry. At the moment of performance, the athlete wants to be "in the flow"—or in the motor cortex part of the brain, which controls the execution of the body's movements. So scientists found that in experienced athletes doing their best, their attention was not in the prefrontal cortex or the neocortex, but in the motor cortex. When athletes talk about being "in the zone" or "in the flow," their prefrontal cortex is quiet. Later they have little recall of the event and cannot remember the details because they were not in their thinking brain at the time.

Experiments have shown that when top athletes start thinking too much and musing over the details of their performance, instead of letting their muscle memory do the work, they tend to make mistakes. For example, psychologist Robert Gray, a senior lecturer at the University of Birmingham in England, put college baseball players through a hitting simulation—asking them to concentrate on whether the bat was moving up or down—and he found that their performance suffered.

So if this is true, how do we learn to calm the neocortex?

Nobody could be a better example of ipseity developed to its finest than an Olympian athlete. Hap Davis, a psychologist for the 2004 Canadian Olympic swim team, conducted some research in which he asked his swimmers to watch videos of their failures. While they were watching these videos, he had them hooked up to an fMRI machine to measure the blood flow to specific areas of the brain. While they were watching their failures, the fMRI showed high levels of activity in the limbic part of the brain, specifically the amygdala, the emotional center of the brain, as well as low levels in the motor cortex. This may indicate the athletes' emotional state when they choked.

But Davis didn't stop there; he added in a "cognitive intervention" while the athletes were watching these awful moments of past failures. He asked the athletes to share their feelings over and over again as they watched these videos. He also asked them how they could correct their performances. Here is the importance to my process—after the athletes had watched the videos again and worked through their emotions, the fMRI showed that their brains were much healthier for competition; after these rewires, the blood flow was located in the motor areas, and prefrontal cortex activity declined.

Davis believes that the athletes got to a neutral place in their emotional brains. "Watching the failure washed out the negative emotion," he said.

The Canadian swim team watched their mistakes continually as part of their training. "The general practice of addressing failure is absolutely vital," says Steve Portenga, a psychologist for USA Track and Field. Specifically, Dan O'Brien, a former decathlon gold medalist, watched and re-watched his famous choke at the 1992 Olympic trials so much that he became desensitized to it and won Olympic gold that year. This compares to Dan's revisiting his negative memories and writing about them on his retreat so much that he desensitized himself to their power; revisiting that old hurt—facing it and not avoiding it—helped him release it.

The Charge Test
The charge test is a good way to find out the degree of control that buried emotions have over someone. Experiencing and appropriately expressing our feelings is our way back to authenticity. In everyday occurrences, if you express feelings appropriately, there is usually little charge to your expression; that is, the emotion or feeling you are expressing usually lasts *less than seven seconds*. If the feeling lasts longer than seven seconds, the feeling is said to have a *charge*, or a connection back to your past.

When a current event triggers feelings, it becomes difficult to separate the current reaction from all of the past feelings in your emotional closet. The door may be flung wide open, exposing the whole closet crammed full of boxes filled with strong and powerful feelings. For example, if someone pulls out in front of you in traffic, a normal reaction, according to the charge test, would be to experience seven seconds of frustration attached to that everyday experience. If you experience any intense emotions that last longer than seven seconds, you are still stuck in past emotions from earlier experiences.

The emotion with the most lasting hangover effect is shame. Dan was exhibiting shame about his job loss. Other states with emotional charges include guilt/blame, hopelessness, grief, regret, anxiety, and anger. When Dan reacts to his son Tommy's problems, he is most likely reacting to stored-up emotion about his past and then letting it discharge at his son. Just like Dan, we are usually unconscious of our kicking-the-dog mentality.

Emotional Non-Reactivity
The ability to pause before reacting is a part of what Daniel Goleman calls "emotional intelligence." Pauses are important because they give us the opportunity to consider all of our choices in the moment and make better, more informed decisions. Therefore, Emotional Non-Reactivity is the emotional state that results from dealing with past emotional

triggers and living a life in the moment, not controlled by the past. A person who has not discharged those old triggering incidents will continue re-creating those incidents to give herself a chance to change the outcome. Therefore, reaching a state of Emotional Non-Reactivity to her past is one of the goals of this process. For Dan in particular, he needs to clear out anger to be able to have a high Light Frequency and then be able to be congenial in a job interview. He must have access to his thinking brain and not be controlled by the emotional brain. Emotions trump thoughts if we have not discharged our past triggers.

In neuroscience, Emotional Non-Reactivity keeps the emotional brain from trumping the thinking brain. The first message your brain receives always goes to the limbic system first to sort out whether it is dangerous and to alert the proper danger signals to protect you. This is why we sometimes say the feeling brain is more powerful than the thinking brain. Once a signal is reviewed by the limbic system, if you have not processed your old emotions, the brain is more likely to hang on to the message and react with intense feelings, just as it did during a similar time in the past. But if the limbic system is not overloaded with past traumas, it will not reroute into the danger zone and will save a lot of energy. It allows the ipseity to rule over this false personality. Thus, one can make decisions from a cognitive brain and not be controlled by emotions. This may seem such a slight nudge to the brain, but in the evolution of our brain, it is a huge step for humans.

Chapter 9

Forgiveness

A conference on neuroscience at the University of Wisconsin in May 2011 showed that practicing forgiveness is a fast track to good mental health. A research study at the Fetzer Initiative Laboratory by Dr. Richard Davidson at the University of Wisconsin–Madison showed that contemplative practices, such as meditating on compassion and forgiveness, changed the structure of the brain and how it behaved. The study showed that activation of the amygdala is associated with lack of trust and fear, which calms down when a meditator focuses on compassion and forgiveness.

In a research study by Antoine Lutz and colleagues (2004), expert meditators focusing on compassion, a feeling of forgiveness, who did not have a particular target in mind, had the largest amount of gamma rays ever recorded. The outcome is consistent with massive neural synchrony and integration of the brain. Other studies (Gilbert, 2010; Neff, 2009) suggest that compassion promotes better health, better psychological well-being, and enhanced interpersonal relationships. This compassion includes a kindness to self.

Chapter 11
Research on Electrical Brainwave Treatment
Upon reflection later, I realized that much of the success of this project with Dan depended first on my belief that it would work. Below is the summary of the meta studies showing proof of the rewiring. Most of the research is about physical health as this is something scientists can actually measure, where manifesting a job or money would be more difficult.

History of Use of Electrical Brain Activity
Using the brain's electrical properties through the operant conditioning of the brain prove promising to assist in changing the brain to be more receptive to new ideas and beliefs. There are several different types of brainwave treatments such as neurofeedback (biofeedback), brainwave training, and electrical stimulation of the brain (ESB).

In an article in *Cerebrum* (2001), Dr. Lester G. Fehmi and Jim Robbins discuss the use of these kinds of electrical conditioning of the brain to treat an array of different psychological and physical conditions. I summarize some of the findings in the following paragraphs. They begin with a short history of the use of electrical stimulation of the brain to treat medical conditions (55-67).

The first person to discover that the brain generates electricity was British scientist Richard Caton, who in the late 1900s, built a device called a reflecting galvanometer. Wilder Penfield, a neurosurgeon in Montreal, was the first physician to observe electrical brain activity on a live person during one of his surgeries. He later became a legend in brain science.

Experiments with electrical brain activity eventually became a discipline called electrical stimulation of the brain, or ESB. Then something really exciting happened in the middle of the twentieth century when Neal Miller at Yale University proved that we could lower or raise our heart rate by a jolt of electricity. Next came teaching people to recognize and then later reproduce a particular frequency on command. Later in the 1970s, M. Barry Sterman showed that operant conditioning of brain activity is an effective intervention for implanting pacemakers and to treat epilepsy.

In his article, "The Unfinished Science behind the New Wave of Electrical Brain Stimulation" (2014), Greg Miller references a landmark study in 2000 published by two German scientists, Michael Nitsche and Walter Paulus, who showed that electrical therapy may make the brain more plastic and better able to compensate for damaged connections. Their research showed that we could boost brain cognition and treat brain disorders with electrical stimulation successfully.

Success Research Using Brainwave Activity
I found study after study after that initial 2000 landmark study that showed how changing brainwaves can enhance cognitive functioning. Transcranial direct current stimulation (tDCS) sends small amounts of stable electrical current into the scalp. Depending on the region of the brain being stimulated, tDCS can influence neural activity that results in increasing attention, expanding memory, improving visual abilities and mathematical skills and alleviating symptoms of depression (Sanders, 2014).

Even though this type of treatment is considered alternative and ignored by much of the medical community, neuroscientists are conducting new research in this area of vibrational energy therapy. Transcranial magnetic stimulation (TMS) stimulates the brain with magnetic fields. Results show that if used properly, it can ease depression and alter cognition (Sanders, 2014).

Chapter 12

Resiliency

Scientific research in dialoguing has shown that dialoguing and other methods of reflecting on yourself make the brain more flexible and capable of regulating emotions in a more powerful way. Researchers also found that dialoguing enhances the immune system and activates positive effects and mental coherence due to the encoding of the feelings (Petrie et al., 2005).

James Pennebaker also showed that people who use words to describe their internal feelings and thoughts are more flexible and can regulate their emotions in a more adaptive manner. In other words, labeling a nonverbal dimension of the mind with a word is a good thing for the brain (Ochsner et al., 2002). People who are writing or talking about their problems show immediate signs of reduced stress in the form of lower blood pressure and heart rate levels (Pennebaker, 2004). Expressive writing is a method of releasing anger (Pennebaker et al., 1987).

Chapter 13
Levels of Emotional Power

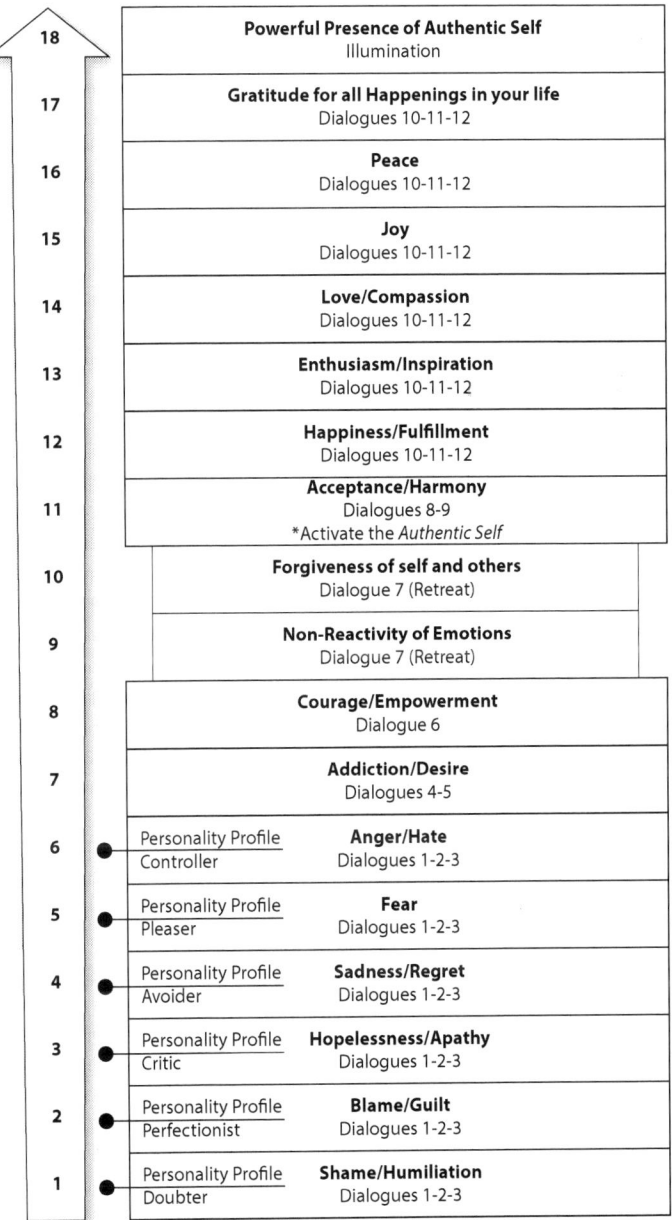

*Based on David Hawkins' Map of Consciousness from Power vs. Force

Chapter 14
Modern Miracles

Physicist David Bohm believes that everything can be explained by cause and effect of mind creating matter, not the other way around. As in Bell's proof of nonlocality, or the fact that electrons can communicate with each other through the energy field that surrounds us, we create our outer world through the thoughts and feelings of our inner world. What better reason to make sure we are in control and managing our inner world (Bohm, 1992)?

One of the most famous examples of people materializing "things" out of nothingness is a holy man from India named Sathya Sai Baba who can materialize objects, such as costly rings, jewelry, and food, out of the air. Thousands of people have witnessed this, and deception has never been noted. But it is hard to believe (Haraldsson, 1987, pp. 26–27).

Another Indian miracle producer is Paramahansa Yogananda, who died in 1952, but spent a lot of time in America to bring his message to the West. He describes meetings with many Hindu spiritual leaders who could materialize gold plates and other objects out of nothingness. He is quoted as saying, "Whatever your powerful mind believes very intensely instantly comes to pass" (Yogananda, 1973, p. 134).

These people have been able to tap into that vast sea of cosmic energy that Bohm claims fills every cubic centimeter of empty space. These may seem like magic, but it is just not what we are accustomed to seeing in the world (Bohm, 1986, p. 128).

GLOSSARY OF TERMS

Anterior cingulate cortex (ACC): The part of the brain that lights up when it does something of its own volition—the area that seems to contain the "I" that I feel we all have within us, the place where Divine Intelligence is stored. The ACC is located right behind the space between your eyes. Spiritual mystics have always called this space *the third eye*—the eye of God.

Authentic Self: Your Authentic Self is who you were created to be. It is the true you at the core of your being, a reflection of your own personal beliefs, values, and truths.

Bell's Theory of Nonlocality: (1964) Bell's Theory proved physical reality in one place can be affected instantaneously by an action in some faraway place such as our minds. The Universe is all connected by our thoughts. This has become known as Entanglement.

Conditioned Self: The Conditioned Self is the human mindset: it results in a lower energy level and negative mindset. It is the opposite of ipseity.

Copenhagen Interpretation: According to the Copenhagen interpretation, physical systems generally do not have definite properties prior to being measured, and quantum mechanics can only predict the probabilities that measurements will produce certain results. The act of measurement affects the system, causing the set of probabilities to reduce to only one of the possible values immediately after the measurement. This feature is known as wave function collapse.

Correspondence Principle: The correspondence principle states that the behavior of systems described by the theory of quantum mechanics reproduces classical physics.

Divine Intelligence: The unlimited creative potential in you.

Entanglement: Entanglement occurs when a pair of particles, such as photons, interact physically. In quantum physics, entangled particles remain connected so that actions performed on one affect the other, even when separated by great distances. The phenomenon so riled Albert Einstein he called it "spooky action at a distance."

God: The presence of Divine Intelligence in each of us; the Creator.

Hardwired neural pathways: Some of these automatic pathways are built into the brain from the beginning, while others are imprinted on the brain through emotional experiences. One example of a hardwired neural pathway is the fight-or-flight response. If a big, black bear bursts through your door, you don't have to think consciously about what to do; you will either fight or run. When neural pathways are hardwired into the brain, they do not have to be accessed consciously—they trigger an immediate response.

Heisenberg Uncertainty Principle: The Heisenberg Uncertainty Principle states the very act of observing alters the position of the particle being observed. Named after German Noble-laureate physicist Werner Karl Heisenberg (1901-1976) the Uncertainty Principle states that (in particle physics experiments) in science, that it is impossible to know simultaneously the exact position and momentum of a particle. That is, the more exactly the position is determined, the less known the momentum, and vice versa.

Ipseity: Ipseity is a sense of self without limits or restrictions, pure awareness before the brain has been wired with beliefs. It is your potential greatness. Neuroscientists use this term to mean "untouched by human imprint."

Light Frequency: Light Frequency is the degree of illumination or ability to create things out in the world. It is determined by the degree of our emotional positivity. If we can shine brightly out in the world with positive energy, we attract good things. For example, if a person feels positive and confident that he will get a job, he is at a higher frequency than when he is worried or fearful about paying his bills. Remember, everything in the Universe is connected with everything else, and like attracts like.

Meditation: The literal translation of the Sanskrit word "meditation" is "to familiarize," meaning that a person is familiar with his own mind. Science defines it as a state of neutral indifference, undisturbed by strong emotions or feelings.

Mirror Neurons: When we observe someone doing something like eating an ice cream cone, the same pattern of brain activation that allows that person to do what they are doing is mirrored in our brain. First seen in monkeys, scientists eventually found a set of "mirror neurons" in humans that mirror the behavior of someone who is being observed. Activations are seen in the premotor and parietal cortex of the brain: regions that prepare the body for movement and attention. Thus, our brains appear to mirror the actions of another person automatically.

Neural pathway: A neural pathway, or neural network, is a chain of neurons that is linked together by the generation of new ideas. Any time you learn to perform a new action or think a new thought, a string of neurons connects, end to end, to form a brand new neural pathway.

Neurons: Neurons, or nerve cells, are the long, narrow cells found in nerve tissue throughout the body. They are the building blocks of the brain, and about 100 billion of them are required to keep our brains working as they should. Each neuron is a small device or engine for transmitting electrical, chemical, or hormonal information from one end of the neuron to the other. A single neuron cannot transmit information very far or for very long. Fortunately, neurons can connect via synapses to allow for more intricate brain activity.

Neuroplasticity: The brain's ability to reorganize itself by forming new neural connections and create lasting changes to the brain throughout your life is known as neuroplasticity.

Neuroscience: Neuroscience is the scientific study of the nervous system. It is a multi-disciplinary field that includes psychology, biology, chemistry, and physics. It is the study of neurons, the spinal cord, and the brain.

Observer Effect: The Observer Effect means that the act of observing will influence the phenomenon being observed. For example, for us to "see" an electron, a photon must first interact with it, and this interaction will change the path of that electron. It was proposed by Erwin Schrödinger in 1935 in his famous cat experiment. It demonstrates how a system exists in super-position in all possible states until we observe that it is only in one specific state.

Positive Anchor: A Positive Anchor is a memory of a moment in time when you were successful. It is used to shift from a negative mindset to a positive one.

Power Potential: Power Potentials are untapped talents and abilities that create your Divine Intelligence. Everyone has at least twelve Power Potentials, but they are more developed in some people than in others.

Prayer: Prayer is the internal work of shifting to a higher mindset.

Quantum BioFeedback (QFB): Quantum BioFeedback uses a device to measure the amount of Light Frequency that is occurring in a particular, concentrated point in the body. The device gives us a score as to the amount of potential energy or Light Frequency we are accessing in different parts of our body in that moment. Then it helps uncover where light is blocked, as well as measuring where the blocks of energy are coming from, i.e. emotional, injuries, phobias, or nutritionally.

Quantum physics: The branch of physics that uses quantum theory—a theory of the mechanics of atoms, molecules, and other physical systems subject to the uncertainty principle.

Rewire Retreat: The Rewire Retreat is a tool used to ease the stress on the physical body caused by unconscious retention of negative emotions. The retreat, likened to a fast-track detox, cleanses the body of energy-draining, old emotions that prevent us from feeling good and being able to fight off disease.

Spiritual development: Spiritual development is the daily work of managing your emotional energy for the good.

Spiritual evolution: Spiritual evolution is a current movement toward understanding your inner life and working toward improving your mindset.

Spiritual maturity: Spiritual maturity is the willingness to accept responsibility for everything that shows up for you, including your emotions.

Spirituality: Spirituality is the movement in each moment of our lives from our human self to our divine self, or from our Conditioned Self to our Authentic Self. It is a constant motion toward the divine, expanding our Divine Intelligence with each small movement forward.

Synapses: Synapses are the connections that link neurons to one another. Because neurons are connected to each other, activating one can influence an average of ten thousand others. The number of possible activation combinations is staggering, which allows for an infinite creative process and incredibly high levels of thinking. When synapses link neurons together, they form neural pathways, also known as chains or networks.

Zero Point Field: The Zero Point Field is essentially the energy left in a space when all possible matter and energy are removed. This remaining field comprises a supercharged sea-of-light backdrop to everything, and physicists have theorized that if we learn how to tap it, it could become a limitless energy supply.

REFERENCES

Adler, A. (1964). *Superiority and Social Interest*. New York: Norton.

Allman, J. M., Hakeem, A., Erwin, J. M., Nimchinsky, E., & Hof, P. (2001). The anterior cingulate cortex: The evolution of an interface between emotion and cognition. *Annals of the New York Academy of Sciences*, May (935): 107–117.

Alper, M. (2008). *The God part of the brain: A scientific interpretation of human spirituality and God*. Naperville, IL: Sourcebooks.

Amen, D. G. (1998). *Change your brain, change your life*. New York: Three Rivers Press.

Arnsten A. F. T., & Goldman-Rakic, P.S. (1998). Noise stress impairs pre-frontal cortical cognitive function in monkeys: Evidence for the hyperdopaminergic mechanism. *Archives of General Psychiatry* 55: 362-368.

Atkinson, W. (2000). Strategies for Workplace Stress. Retrieved from http://www.riskandinsurance.com

Baierlein, R. (1992). *Newton to Einstein*. Cambridge, MA: Cambridge University Press.

Barna Research Group. (2007). A new generation expresses its skepticism and frustration with Christianity. Retrieved from https://www.barna.com/research/a-new-generation-expresses-its-skepticism-and-frustration-with-christianity/

Barnstone, W., & Meyer, M. (2003). *The Gnostic Bible*. Boston: New Seeds.

Baumann, T. L. (2006). *The Akashic light: Religion's common thread*. Virginia Beach, VA: A.R.E. Press.

Beilock, S. (2010). *Choke: What the secrets of the brain reveal about getting it right when you have to*. New York: Free Press.

Bergland, C. (2012, November 29). The neurochemicals of happiness: 7 brain molecules that make you feel great. [Web log post] The athlete's way. Retrieved from http://www.psychologytoday.com/blog/the-athletes-way/201211/the-neurochemicals-happiness

Blakemore, S. J., & Choudhury, S. (2006). Development of the adolescent brain: Implications for executive function and social cognition. *Journal of Child Psychology and Psychiatry* 47: 296–312.

Bohm, D. (1986). A new theory of the relationship of mind and matter. *Journal of the American Society for Psychical Research* 80 (2): 128.

Bohm, D. (1992). *Thought as a system.* London: Routledge.

Bohm, D. (2002). *Wholeness and the implicate order.* London: Routledge.

Bradshaw, J. (1994). *Family secrets.* New York: Bantam Books.

Butterworth, E. (1968). *Discover the power within you.* San Francisco: Harper.

Byrne, R. (2006). *The secret.* New York: Atria Books.

Cacioppo, J. T., Hatfield, E., & Rapson, R. L. (1994). *Emotional contagion.* Paris: Cambridge University Press.

Casey, B. J., Tottenham, N., Listen, C., & Durston, S. (2005). Imaging the developing brain: What have we learned about cognitive development? *Trends in Cognitive Sciences* 9 (3): 104–110.

Chergui, M. (2006). Controlling biological functions. *Science* 313: 1246-1247.

Chopra, D. (2015). *Quantum healing: Exploring the frontiers of mind/body medicine.* New York: Bantam Books.

Chopra, D. & Tanzi, R. (2015) *Super genes: Unlock the astonishing power of your DNA for optimum health and well-being.* New York: Harmony Books.

Course in Miracles. (2011). Omaha, NE: Course in Miracles Society.

Creswell, J. D., Taren, A. A., Lindsay, E. K., Greco, C. M., Gianaros, P. J., Fairgrieve, A., Marsland, A. L., Brown, K. W., Way, B. M. (2016, July 1). Alterations in resting-state functional connectivity link mindfulness meditation with reduced interleukin-6: A randomized controlled trial. *Biological Psychiatry, Volume 80, Issue 1*, pp. 53–61. http://dx.doi.org/10.1016/j.biopsych.2016.01.008

Crow, D. M. (2000). Physiological and health effects on writing about stress (Doctoral dissertation). Southern Methodist University.

Davidson, R.J. (2013). *The emotional life of your brain: How its unique patterns affect the way you think, feel, and live—and how you can change them.* Hudson, New York: The Penguin Group.

Davies, P. (1985). *Superforce.* New York: Simon and Schuster.

De Moor, C., Sterner, J., Hall, M., Warneke, C., Gilani, Z., Amato, R., & Cohen, L., (2002). A pilot study of the effects of expressive writing in a phase II trial of vaccine therapy for metastatic renal cell carcinoma. *Health Psychology* 21: 615–619.

Doidge, N. (2007). *The brain that changes itself.* New York: Penguin.

Dyer, W. W. (1994). *Manifest your destiny.* New York: HarperPerennial.

Einstein, A. (1956). *The world as I see it.* New York: Citadel Press.

Fehmi, L.G., Robbins, J., (2001, Summer). Mastering our brain's electrical rhythms. *Cerebrum*, (The Dana Forum on Brain Science), 3:3, 55-67.

Fels, D. (2009). Cellular communication through light. PLOS ONE 4(4): e5086. doi:10.1371/journal.pone.0005086

Flowers, B. S., Jaworski, J., Scharmer, C. O., & Senge, P. (2004). *Presence: Exploring profound change in people, organizations and society.* New York: Doubleday.

Ford, D. (2002). *The Secret of the shadow.* San Francisco: HarperSanFrancisco.

Fox, M. (1934). *The sermon on the mount: The key to success in life.* New York: HarperCollins.

Freke, T., & Gandy, P. (1999). *The Jesus mysteries.* New York: Three Rivers Press.

Freke, T., & Gandy, P. (2001). *Jesus and the lost goddess.* New York: Three Rivers Press.

Gaidos, S., & Fuller, N. R. (2009). Living physics: From green leaves to bird brains, biological systems may exploit quantum phenomena. *Science News* 175-26-29.

Gardner-Warlick, S. J. (1989). Family environment, lifestyle, and control factors of depressed adolescents and their parents (Doctoral Dissertation). University of North Texas.

Gawain, S. (1978). *Creative visualization.* Novato, CA: Nataraj.

Gibran, K. (2003). *The prophet: Freedom.* New York: Rupa.

Gilbert, P. (2010). *The compassionate mind.* Oakland, CA: New Harbinger.

Goldman, B. (2015, January 15). Environment, not genes, dictates human immune variation, study finds. *ScienceDaily.* Retrieved April 12, 2017 from www.sciencedaily.com/releases/2015/01/150115134715.htm

Goldt, S., and Seifert, U. (2017, January 6). Stochastic Thermodynamics of Learning. *Physical Review Letters, Volume 118.* DOI: https://doi.org/10.1103/PhysRevLett.118.010601

Goleman, D. (1995). *Emotional intelligence.* New York: Bantam Books.

Goleman, D. (2006). *Social intelligence: The new science of human relationships.* New York: Bantam Books.

Gottman, J. (1995). *Why marriages succeed and fail: And how you can make yours last.* New York: Simon and Schuster.

Grossman, C. (2010, October 14). Survey: 72% of millennials 'more spiritual than religious.' USA Today. Retrieved from https://usatoday30.usatoday.com/news/religion/2010-04-27-Amillfaith27_ST_N.htm

Hanh, T. N. (1995). *Living buddha, living Christ.* New York: Berkley.

Hanh, T. N. (2001). *Anger: Wisdom for cooling the flames.* London: The Berkley Publishing Group.

Haraldsson, E. (1987). *Modern miracles: An investigative report on psychic phenomena associated with Sathya Sai Baba.* New York: Fawcett Columbine Books.

Harpur, T. (2004). *The pagan Christ: Is blind faith killing Christianity?* New York: Walker.

Harter, S. (1988). Developmental processes in the construction of the self. In T. D. Yawkey and J. E. Johnson (Eds.) *Integrative processes and socialization: Early to middle childhood* (pp. 45–78). Hillsdale, NJ: Erlbaum.

Harter, S., Bresnick, S., Bouchey, H. A., & Whitsell, N. R. (1997). The development of multiple role-related selves during adolescence. *Development and Psychopathology* 9: 835–854.

Hawkins, D. (1995). Qualitative and quantitative analysis and calibration of the levels of human consciousness (Doctoral Dissertation).

Hawkins, D. R. (2002). *Power vs. force: The hidden determinants of human behavior.* New York: Hay.

Hawkins, D. (2007). *Discovery of the presence of God: Devotional nonduality.* W. Sedona, AZ: R. Veritas Publishing.

Herman, J. L. (1992). *Trauma and recovery.* New York: Basic Books.

Hill, N. (1960). *Think and grow rich.* New York: Ballantine Books.

Hoeller, S. A. (2002). *Gnosticism: New light on the ancient tradition of inner knowing.* Wheaton, IL: Quest Books.

Hoeller, S. A. (2004). *Jung and the lost gospels: Insights into the Dead Sea Scrolls and the Nag Hammadi Library.* Wheaton, IL: Quest Books.

Holmes, E. (1918). *Creative mind.* Radford, VA: Wilder.

Holmes, E. (1926). *The science of mind.* New York: Penguin Putnam.

Hughes, D. A. (2006). *Building the bonds of attachment: Awakening love in deeply troubled children.* New York: Aronson.

Hunt, V. (1990, January). Infinite mind. *Magical Blend,* no. 25.

Johnsen, L. (2002). *The complete idiot's guide to Hinduism.* Indianapolis, IN: Alpha Books.

Karen, R. (1994). *Becoming attached.* New York: Oxford University Press.

Keating, T. (1994). *Intimacy with God.* New York: Crossroad.

Kemeny, M. (1993). Emotions and the immune system. In B. Moyers (Ed.), *Healing and the Mind* (pp. 195–211). New York: Doubleday.

Khalsa, D. S. (1997). *Brain longevity: The breakthrough medical program that improves your mind and memory.* New York: Warner Books.

King, J. C. (2009). *The code of authentic living.* Fort Collins, CO: Word Keepers.

Klein, K., & Boals, A. (2001). Expressive writing can increase working memory capacity. *Journal of Experimental Psychology: General* 130: 520–533.

Kopp, M. S., & Rethelyi, J. (2004). Where psychology meets physiology: chronic stress and premature mortality—the Central-Eastern European health paradox. *Brain Research Bulletin* 62: 351-367.

Lazar, S. W., Kerr, C. E., Wasserman, R. H., Gray, J. R., Greve, D. N., Treadway, M. T., et al. (2005). Meditation experience is associated with increased cortical thickness. *Neuroreport* 16 (17): 1893–1897.

Leary, M., Tate, E., Adams, C., Allen, A., & Hancock, J. (2007). Self-compassion and reactions to unpleasant self-relevant events: The implications for treating oneself kindly. *Journal of Personality* 92: 887–904.

Lepore, S. J., & Smyth, J. M. eds. (2002). *The writing cure: How expressive writing promotes health and well-being.* Washington, DC: American Psychological Association.

Lipton, B. (2005). *The biology of belief: Unleashing the power of consciousness, matter, and miracles.* California: Elite Books.

Lutz, A., Dunne, J. D., & Davidson, R. J. (2007). Meditation and the neuroscience of consciousness. In P. D. Zelazo, M. Moscovitch, and E. Thompson (Eds.) *The Cambridge Handbook of Consciousness.* Cambridge, UK: Cambridge University Press.

Lutz, A., Greischar, L. L., Rawlings, N. B., Richard, M., & Davidson, R. J. (2004). Long-term meditators self-induce high-amplitude gamma synchrony during mental practice. *Proceedings of the National Academy of Sciences* 101 (46): 16369–16373.

Mabey, J., (Ed.). (2000). *Rumi: A spiritual treasury.* Oxford, UK: One World.

MacLean, P. C. (1990). *The triune brain in evolution: Role in paleocerebral functions.* New York: Springer.

Maslow, A. (1994). *Religions, values, and peak-experiences.* New York: Viking Press.

McCraty, R. (2015). Science of the heart, Volume 2: Exploring the role of the heart in human performance. Boulder Creek, CA; HeartMath Institute.

McEwen, B. S., & Seeman, T. (1999). Protective and damaging effects of mediators of stress: Elaborating and testing the concepts of allostasis and allostatic load. *Annals of the New York Academy of Sciences* 896: 30-47.

McEwen, B., & Lasley, E. N. (2002). *The end of stress as we know it.* Washington: National Academies Press.

McTaggart, L. (2008). *The field: The quest for the secret force of the universe.* New York: HarperCollins.

Meyer, M. (1992). *The gospel of Thomas: The hidden sayings of Jesus.* New York: HarperOne.

Miller, A. (1984). *Thou shalt not be aware.* New York: Meridian Books.

Miller, G. (2014, May 5). The unfinished science behind the new wave of electrical brain stimulation. *Wired.* Retrieved from https://www.wired.com/2014/05/brain-stimulation-science/

Mother Teresa. (1995). *A simple path.* New York: Random House.

Mother Teresa. (2009). *Everything starts from prayer.* Ashland, OR: White Cloud Press.

Moyers, B. (Ed.). (1993). *Healing and the mind.* New York: Doubleday.

Neff, K. (2009). Self-compassion. In M. R. Leary and R. H. Hoyle (Eds.) *Handbook of individual differences in social behavior* (pp. 569–573). New York: Guilford Press.

Nelson, R. D., Radin, D. I., Shoup, R., & Bancel, P. (2000). Correlation of continuous random data with major world events. *Foundation of Physics Letters* 15(6): 537–550.

Newberg, A., & Waldman, M. R. (2009). *How God changes your brain: Breakthrough findings from a leading neuroscientist.* New York: Random House.

Niedenthal, P. (2007). Embodying emotion. *Science* 316: 1002.

Norville, D. (2007). *Thank you power: Making the science of gratitude work for you.* Nashville, TN: Nelson.

Ochsner, K. N., Bunge, S. A., Gross, J. J., & Gabrieli, J. D. E. (2002). Rethinking feelings: An fMRI study of the cognitive regulation of emotion. *Journal of Cognitive Neuroscience* 14: 1215–1229.

Pagels, E. (1979). *The Gnostic gospels.* New York: Vintage Books.

Pagels, E. (2003). *Beyond belief: The secret gospel of Thomas.* New York: Vintage Books.

Passingham, D., Jueptner, M., Stephan, K. M., Frith, C.D., et al. (1997). Anatomy of motor learning. *Journal of Neurophysiology* 77: 1313–1324.

Peace Quarters. (2017). *Scientists found that the soul doesn't die—It goes back to the universe.* Retrieved from: https://www.peacequarters.com/scientists-found-soul-doesnt-die-goes-back-universe/?utm_medium=social&utm_source=facebook&utm_campaign=pafb

Pearsal, P. (1998). *The heart's code.* New York: Broadway Books.

Peeters, G., & Czapinski, J. (1990). Positive-negative asymmetry in evaluations: The distinction between affective and informational negativity effects. In W. Stroebe and M. Hewstone (Eds.). *European Review of Social Psychology,* Vol. 1. New York: Wiley.

Peirce, P. (2009). *Frequency.* Hillsboro, OR: Beyond Words.

Pennebaker, J. W., Kiecolt-Glaser, J. K., & Glaser, R. (1988). Disclosure of traumas and immune function: Health implications for psychotherapy. *Journal of Consulting and Clinical Psychology,* Vol. 56, pp. 239-245.

Pennebaker, J. W. (1990). *Opening up: The healing power of expressing emotions.* New York: Guilford Press.

Pennebaker, J. W. (2004). *Writing to heal: A guided journal for recovering from trauma and emotional upheaval.* Oakland, CA: New Harbinger.

Pennebaker, J. W., Hughes, C. F., & O'Heeron, R. C. (1987). The psycho-physiology of confession: linking inhibitory and psychosomatic processes. *Journal of Personality and Social Psychology* 52: 871–793.

Pennebaker, J. W., & Susman, J. R. (1988). Disclosure of traumas and psychosomatic processes. *Social Science and Medicine* 26: 327–332.

Pert, C. (1997). *Molecules of emotion: Why you feel the way you feel.* New York: Simon and Schuster.

Petrie, K. J., Fontanilla, I., Thomas, M. G., Booth, R. J. & Pennebaker, J. W. (2005). Effect of written emotional expression on immune functioning in patients with HIV infection. *Psychosomatic Medicine* 66 (2): 272–275.

Pophristic, V. & Goodman, L. (2001). Hyperconjugation not steric repulsion leads to the staggered structure of ethane. *Nature* 411: 565-568.

Popp, F. A. (2006). Coupling of Fröhlich-modes as a basis of biological regulation. In Hyland G. J., P. Rowlands (Eds.), *Herbert Fröhlich, FRS: A physicist ahead of his time* (pp. 139–175). Liverpool: The University of Liverpool.

Preidt, R. (2015, January 15). Environment trumps genes at shaping immune system: Study. *U.S. News & World Report.* Retrieved from http://health.usnews.com/health-news/articles/2015/01/15/environment-trumps-genes-at-shaping-immune-system-study

Pribram, K. (1971). *Languages of the brain: experimental paradoxes and principles in neuropsychology.* Englewood Cliffs, NJ: Prentice Hall.

Prochaska, J. O., Butterworth, S., Redding, C. A., Burden, V., Perrin, N., Leo, M., Flaherty-Robb, M., & Prochaska, J. M. (2008). Initial efficacy of MI, TTM tailoring and HRI's with multiple behaviors for employee health promotion. *Preventive Medicine* 46 (3): 226–231.

Ratey, J. J. (2008). *Spark: The revolutionary new science of exercise and the brain.* New York: Little, Brown.

Reynolds, J. (2005). *20/20 brain power.* Laguna Beach, CA: 20/20 Brain Power Partners.

Robinson, J. M. (1978). *The Nag Hammadi Library.* San Francisco: HarperCollins.

Ross, E. D., Homan, R. W., & Buck, R. (1994). Differential hemispheric lateralization of primary and social emotions: Implications for developing a comprehensive neurology of emotions, repression, and the subconscious. *Neuropsychiatry, Neuropsychology, and Behavioral Neurology* 7:1–19.

Sagan, C. (1980). *Cosmos.* New York: Random House.

Schore, A. N. (1994). *Affect regulation and the origin of the self: The neurobiology of emotional development.* Hillsdale, NJ: Erlbaum.

Schulten, K. (2000). Electron transfer exploiting thermal motion. *Science* 290: 61-62.

Schuyler, B., Kral, T., Jacquart, J., Burghy, C., Weng, H., Perlman, D., Bachhuber, D. R. W., Rosenkranz, M. et al. (2014). Temporal dynamics of emotional responding: Amygdala recovery predicts emotional traits. *Social Cognitive and Affective Neuroscience* 9.2 (2014): 176-181.

Schwartz, J. M. (2002). *The mind and the brain.* New York: HarperPerennial.

Segerstrom, S. C., & Miller, G. E. (2004). Psychological stress and the human immune system: A meta-analytic study of 30 years of inquiry. *Psychological Bulletin* 130(4): 601-630.

Seligman, M. (2006). *Learned optimism: How to change your mind and your life.* New York: Vintage Books/Random House.

Shantideva. (1997). *The way of the Bodhisattva: A translation of the Bodhicharyavatara.* Boston: Shambhala.

Siegel, B. (1986). *Love, medicine and miracles.* New York: Harper & Row.

Siegel, D. J. (1999). *The developing mind: How relationships and the brain interact to shape who we are.* New York: Guilford Press.

Siegel, D, J. (2007). *The mindful brain.* New York: Norton.

Siegel, D. J. (2011a). *The mindful therapist.* New York: Norton.

Siegel, D. J. (2011b). *Mindsight.* New York: Random House.

Smyth, J. M. (1998). Written emotional expression: Effect size, outcome types, and moderating variables. *Journal of Consulting and Clinical Psychology* 66: 174–184.

Spera, S. P., Buhrfeind, E. D., & Pennebaker, J. W. (1994). Expressive writing and coping with job loss. *Academy of Management Journal* 37: 722–733.

Stetka, B. (2014, December 16). Changing our DNA through mind control? *Scientific American.* Retrieved from https://www.scientificamerican.com/article/changing-our-dna-through-mind-control/?wt.mc=SA

Takamatsu, H., Noda, A., et al. (2003). A PET study following treatment with a pharmacological stressor, FG7142, in conscious rhesus monkeys. *Brain Research* 980: 275-280.

Talbot, M. (1991). *The holographic universe.* New York: HarperCollins.

Taylor, J. B. (2006). *My stroke of insight.* New York: Penguin.

Tolle, E. (1999). *The power of now.* Novato, CA: New World Library.

Tolle, E. (2005). *A new Earth: Awakening to your life's purpose.* New York: Penguin.

Tolstoy, L. (2006). *The kingdom of God is within you.* Minelo, New York: Dover.

Tulving, E. (1993). Varieties of consciousness and levels of awareness in memory. In A. Baddeley & L. Weiskrantz (Eds.), *Attention, selection, awareness and control: A tribute to Donald Broadbent* (pp. 283–299). London: Oxford University Press.

Vaish, A., Grossmann, T., & Woodward, A. (2008). Not all emotions are created equal: Negative bias in social-emotional development. *Psychological Bulletin* 134: 383–403.

Verrier, N. (1993). *The primal wound: Understanding the adopted child.* Baltimore: Gateway Press.

Walsch, N. D. (1995). *Conversations with God: Book one.* London: Hodder and Stoughton.

Woodland, L. (2007). Quantum spirit unlimited: Lynn Woodland's miracles course. Retrieved from: https://www.quantumspiritunlimited.com.

Yang, E., Zald, D., & Blake, R. (2007). Fearful expressions gain preferential access to awareness during continuous flash suppression. *Emotion* 7: 882–886.

Yogananda, P. (1973). *Autobiography of a yogi.* Los Angeles: Self Realization Fellowship.

Zajonc, A. (1993). *Catching the light: The entwined history of light and mind.* New York: Oxford University Press.

Zelazo, P. D., Moscovitch, M., & Thompson, E. (Eds.). (2007). *Cambridge handbook of consciousness.* Toronto: University of Toronto.

Zukav, G. (1989). *The seat of the soul.* New York: Simon and Schuster.

INDEX

accepting the self-discovery invitation
   coaching and self-examination, 44–46
   conscious change and real evolution, 49–50
   consciousness as conduit to DI development, 50–52
   DI concealment, 53
   key concepts, 55
   looking inward, 56
   narrative story, 41–44
   science and The Observer Effect, 47–49
   scientific basis of, 47–54
   self-directed change, 53–54
   Universal Spiritual Truth, 46–47
affective neuroscience, 149
Albigensian Crusade, 314
Allogenes, 185
Alper, Matthew, 198
Alpha brainwaves, 218
amygdala
   amygdala hijack, 149–52
   and emotional expression, 149, 329
   and emotional power, 162
Anderson, Robert M., Jr., 181
anger and Rewire Retreat, 186–87
anterior cingulate cortex (ACC), 197–99, 337
approach, not avoid, 328–30
Aspect, Alain, 128
as within, so without
   coaching and self-examination, 157–58
   Inside and Outside Wins, 253–56, 278
   key concepts, 166
   looking inward, 167
   narrative story, 155–57
   scientific basis, 160–65
   Universal Spiritual Truth, 159–60

authenticity, 287
Authentic Self
  and ACC, 199
  activation of, 175–76
  and Conditioned Self, 97–103, 257–58
  described, 70, 107, 337
  interview of, 248–53
  and The Observer Effect, 48–49
  recognizing, 75–78
  versus Conditioned Self, 108–9
Avoider/Worker
  emotional power levels, 335
  Personality Profile, 325

Beauregard, Mario, 198
Beckwith, Michael Bernard, 302
being in the flow, 218, 219, 241, 328
beliefs
  belief system formation, 85–87, 100–101
  and epigenetics, 129–31
  irrational, 87
  memories as key to belief system, 87–88
  rewiring our belief system, 207–8, 211–12, 213–15, 224
  See also limiting beliefs
Bell, John S., 163
Bell's Theorem (nonlocality), 162–63, 267, 284, 318, 337
Bergland, Christopher, 133
Beta brainwaves, 218
Beyond Belief (Pagels), 319
Biological Psychiatry journal, 220
The Biology of Belief (Lipton), 84, 129–30
birth star, 35–36
Bohm, David, 14, 128–29, 194, 279, 292–93, 336
Bohr, Niels, 48, 259
"The Bonding Molecule" (oxytocin), 133
brain
  anterior cingulate cortex (ACC), 197–99
  conscious change and real evolution, 49–50, 147–48

consciousness as conduit to DI development, 50–52
electrical brain activity, 194, 216–17
emotions as energy source for, 146–47
epigenetics, 129–31
evolution of images and understanding of God, 82–83
False Self and limiting beliefs, 108–9
Holographic Brain theory, 318
limbic system, 51, 147, 148
and locus of control, 164–65
meditation and self-care, 127–28
and the mind of God, 51
neural redesign, 213–15
neurochemicals, 133
and Rewire Retreat, 172–75, 179, 185–87, 190–92, 196, 198–99, 201, 211
teenage brain, 152
time required to rewire, 131–33, 247
triune brain, 50, 53–54, 82, 144–45
visceral brain, 51, 53, 55
and the world as a hologram, 128–29
See also amygdala; Authentic Self; Conditioned Self; thinking brain (neocortex)

The Brain That Changes Itself (Doidge), 195
brainwaves
  brainwave treatment research, 332–33
  changing with meditation, 219–22
  described, 194, 217–18
  power of, 216–17, 218–19
Buddha
  on accepting the self-discovery invitation, 46–47
  and Buddhism, 313
  and dying as transformation, 159–60
  on praise from others, 212
  retreat and transformation, 176
Butterworth, Eric, 32, 281

Cambridge Handbook of Consciousness (Zelazo), 36
Cathars, 314–15

358 DIVINE INTELLIGENCE

change
   resistance to, 182
   Trans-Theoretical Model (TTM) of change, 332
chi, 144, 285
Chopra, Deepak, 84, 130
The Chopra Center for Wellbeing, 84
Christianity
   dying as transformation, 159–60
   on light and God/inner divinity, 31, 63
Christos (follower of Christ), 31
coaching
   coaching *versus* therapy, 27–28, 321–22
   and DI Process, 20
   dying to human self as transformation, 192–93
   everything begins with you, 61–62
   finding the God within us, 27–29
   God is in everyone, 27–29
   holding no emotional violence, 142–43
   knowledge of self is knowledge of God, 174–75
   nothing is impossible, 256
   performing miracles, 278–80
   seek first who you are not, 103–6
   we are the Creators, 235–36
   what you are seeking is hidden within you, 78–81
   as within, so without, 157–58
   you are your own master, 211–12
cognitive intervention and learning from negative memories, 329–30
coherence and brain integration, 197
Conditioned Self
   compared to Authentic Self, 257–58
   as default personality, 111
   described, 70, 107, 337
   dying as transformation, 160
   false self and limiting beliefs, 109–10, 231–32, 236
   interview of, 97–106
   necessity of multiple deaths of, 111–12
   and need for self-care, 125
   Personality Profiles, 323–28

   and rebirth of Authentic Self, 175–76, 177–79, 214
   recognizing, 72–75
   versus ipseity, 108–9, 113–14
   voice of, 112–13
Conditioned-Self Thinking, 216
"The Confidence Molecule" (serotonin), 133
conscious creativity, 287
conscious evolution
   accepting the self-discovery invitation, 49–50
   creating our own best life, 183
   emotional connectedness and spiritual growth, 154
   inner divinity, 263
   internal locus of control, 167
   ipseity and inner divinity, 39
   looking inward, 56, 68
   performing miracles, 289
   release of limiting beliefs, 90
   resilience and mental shifting, 245
   Rewire Retreat, 201
   rewiring our belief system, 224
   self-care and brain change, 135
   separation from Conditioned Self, 116
consciousness
   as conduit to DI development, 50–52
   forgiveness and transformed consciousness, 176–77
   and light, 164
   physics of, 163–64
Constantine, 314
Controller/Leader
   emotional power levels, 335
   Personality Profile, 323
Conversations with God (Walsch), 238–39
Copenhagen interpretation, 337
Copernicus, 315
Correspondence Principle, 59, 317, 337
cortical rhythm, 217
Cosmos (Sagan), 35
Course in Miracles, 238, 281

creation and visualization, 238
creative capacity and views of God, 5–6
Creative Mind (Holmes), 167
Creative Visualization (Gawain), 212, 213–14
the Creator within, 13, 16–17, 27–29, 212–13, 271
   See also we are the Creators
Creswell, David, 220
Critic/Problem Solver
   emotional power levels, 335
   Personality Profile, 324
the Crusades, 314

Dalai Lama, 219, 283
Dalibard, Jean, 128
Damasio, Antonio, 36
Dan's story
   accepting the self-discovery invitation, 41–44
   and DI Process, 20
   dying to human self as transformation, 185–92
   everything begins with you, 57–61
   as evolutionary process framework, 2–3, 15–16, 300–307
   God is in everyone, 23–26
   holding no emotional violence, 137–42
   knowledge of self is knowledge of God, 171–74
   nothing is impossible, 247–56
   path to salvation, 117–23
   performing miracles, 265–78
   seek first who you are not, 93–103
   we are all connected and one with God, 291–307
   we are the Creators, 225–35
   what you are seeking is hidden within you, 69–78
   as within, so without, 155–57
   you are your own master, 203–11
Davidson, Richard, 36, 149, 219–20, 331
Davis, Hap, 329
default personality (Conditioned Self), 111
Delta brainwaves, 218
The Developing Mind (Siegel), 86–87, 108, 109–10

dialoguing
- changing the voices in your head, 113–14
- Conditioned-Self interview, 97–106
- described, 4, 64–65
- and DI Process, 61, 67, 186
- and neural redesign, 214–15
- Positive Anchor focus, 78
- Rewire Retreat, 172–75
- self-acceptance, 95–96
- and stress reduction, 65–66

Divine Intelligence (DI) Process
- activation of our DI, 215, 240–41, 242–43
- concealment of, 53
- consciousness as conduit to DI development, 50–52
- Dan's story as evolutionary process framework, 2–3, 15–16, 300–307
- described, 19–20, 337
- empowerment and relationship with the self, 3–5
- Gnostic Gospels as source of Universal Spiritual Truths, 8–10
- historical timeline of DI evolution, 313–20
- human energy field and DI Power Potentials, 285–88
- keeping our minds unlimited and open to all possibilities, 255
- and locus of control, 164–65, 166
- organization of book, 19–20
- search for divinity of the self, 1–2
- spirituality of, 10
- *See also* scientific basis of DI

Divine Intelligence Institute, 359–61

divinity of the self
- and anterior cingulate cortex (ACC), 197–99
- Dan's story as evolutionary process framework, 2–3, 15–16
- empowerment and relationship with the self, 3–5
- Gnostic Gospels as source of Universal Spiritual Truths, 8–10
- human energy field and DI Power Potentials, 285–88
- search for, 1–2

Doidge, Norman, 195

dopamine, 133

Doubter/Team Player

emotional power levels, 335
Personality Profile, 328
Dunne, Brenda, 163
Dunne, John, 36
dying as transformation, 159–60, 175
dying to human self as rebirth
   coaching and self-examination, 192–93
   key concepts, 200
   looking inward, 201
   narrative story, 185–92
   scientific basis, 194–99
   Universal Spiritual Truth, 193

Einstein, Albert, 6–8, 48, 128, 162, 267, 277, 311, 317
electrical brain activity. *See* brainwaves
Ellis, Albert, 76
Emerson, Ralph Waldo, 32
emotional energy
   and connection to our truth, 145–47
   dialoguing and stress reduction, 65–66
   emotional connectedness and spiritual growth, 142–43
   emotional power levels, 335
   integration of thoughts and emotions, 147–48
   and Light Frequency, 37, 174
   and memories, 88
   mirror neurons and the Field, 282–84
   and self-awareness, 64, 67
   See also holding no emotional violence
Emotional Intelligence (Goleman), 128
Emotional Non-Reactivity, 151, 211, 261, 286, 287, 330–31
emotions
   and amygdala hijack, 149–52
   charge test, 330
   integration of thoughts and emotions, 147–48, 160–61, 328–30
   our thoughts create our world, 162–63
empowerment and relationship with the self, 3–5
energy as God, 259, 272–73
epigenetics, 129–31

everything begins with you
  coaching and self-examination, 61–62
  key concepts, 67
  looking inward, 68
  narrative story, 57–61
  scientific basis of, 63–66
  Universal Spiritual Truth, 62–63
evolutionary growth
  God and the Creator within us, 296–300
  integration of thoughts and emotions, 147–48
  as within, so without, 309–11
externalization and voice of Conditioned Self, 112

Fall of Montségur, 315
false brain messages, 216
False Self
  described, 106
  limiting beliefs and Conditioned Self, 109–10
fathers, equating father with God, 79–81
feeling brain (limbic system), 51, 55, 82–83
Feynman, Richard, 33
Fillmore, Charles, 32
flow, being in the flow, 218, 219, 241, 328
forgiveness, 176–77, 331–32
Fox, Matthew, 257–58
functional magnetic resonance imaging (fMRI), 197–98, 242, 329

Gage, Phineas, 147
Galileo, 315
Gamma brainwaves, 218–19
Gandhi, Mahatma, 32, 316
Gawain, Shakti, 212
genetics and the biology of DI, 84–85
The Global Coherence Initiative (GCI), 301
gnosis, 9, 41, 117, 306
Gnostic Gospels, 8–10, 27, 46–47, 69, 93, 137, 203, 225, 291, 306, 310–11, 314, 316, 319
The Gnostic Gospels (Pagels), 9, 318

God
   conscious evolution and inner divinity, 39
   and the Creator within, 13, 16–17, 27–29, 212–13, 271, 295–300
   definitions of and search for, 41–44, 272–76, 338
   Einstein on cosmic religious feeling and God, 6–8
   energy as God, 259, 272–73
   equating father with God, 79–81
   evolution of images and understanding of, 82–83
   "God particle" (Higgs-Boson particle), 270–71, 319
   ipseity and inner divinity, 33, 36, 38, 39
   and Light Frequency, 34–36, 36–37, 38
   limiting beliefs about, 80–81, 82
   omnipotence, omnipresence, and omniscience of, 14–15
   prayer and talking to God, 227–28
   views of God and creative capacity, 5–6
   See also knowledge of self is knowledge of God
The God Gene (Hamer), 198
God is in everyone
   coaching and self-examination, 27–29
   key concepts, 38
   light and God, 31–32
   looking inward, 39
   narrative story, 23–26
   scientific basis of, 32–37
   Universal Spiritual Truth, 29–32
The God Part of the Brain (Alper), 198
Goleman, Daniel, 128, 282, 330
Gospel of Mary Magdalene, 316
Gospel of Matthew, 225, 311
Gospel of Philip, 137, 203, 291, 306
Gospel of Thomas, 69, 93, 314, 316, 319
Gospel of Truth, New Testament Apocrypha, 27
gratitude
   as divine mindset, 259–60
   "gratitude is the heart's memory," 251
   power of, 260–61
Gray, Robert, 329

Hamer, Dean, 198
Hameroff, Stuart, 35
Harter studies, 110
Hasidism, 316
Hawkins, David, 37, 49, 179, 260, 282, 294
Hay, Louise, 259
health and negative emotions, 144–45
HeartMath Institute, 146, 282
Hebb's Law (wiring with fire), 150, 180
Heisenberg, Werner, 48, 317
Heisenberg Uncertainty Principle, 38, 317, 338
Henry, Richard Conn, 12–13
Herman, Judith Lewis, 180
Hickerson, Jane C., 152
Higgs-Boson particle ("God particle"), 270–71, 319
Hinduism
    japa, 214
    on light and inner divinity, 30, 31, 63
    origins of, 313
    and performance of miracles, 282
Hippolytus, on inner divinity, 57
holding no emotional violence
    coaching and self-examination, 142–43
    key concepts, 153
    looking inward, 154
    narrative story, 137–42
    scientific basis, 144–52
    Universal Spiritual Truth, 143–44
Holmes, Ernest, 32, 167, 238, 317
hologram, the world as a hologram, 128–29
Holographic Brain theory, 318
The Holographic Universe (Talbot), 194, 285
How God Changes Your Brain (Newberg and Waldman), 82
Hubble, Edwin, 14
human (False Self) vs. divine (True Self), 106–7
Hunt, Valerie, 163, 194

inner voice, 161, 179, 231, 253
Inside Wins, 253–56, 278
internal attunement, 287
International Coach Federation, 319
interview of Conditioned Self, 97–106
Intimacy with God (Keating), 106
ipseity
   and the brain, 52
   described, 338
   of infants, 85
   and inner voice emergence, 161
   light and God/inner divinity, 33, 36, 38, 39, 258
   and unlimited potential, 94–95, 97
   versus Conditioned Self, 108–9, 113–14
Irenaeus, 314
irrational beliefs, 87
Islam on inner divinity, 30, 31

Jahn, Robert G., 163
James, William, 239, 316
japa, 214
Jesus
   on accepting the self-discovery invitation, 46
   birth and life of, 313–14
   and dying as transformation, 159–60
   and forgiveness, 176–77
   on inner divinity, 30
   on kingdom of Heaven within us, 23
   on light and inner divinity, 63
   limiting beliefs about, 81
   on performing miracles, 265, 281
   retreat and transformation, 176
John Paul II, Pope, 319
Josephson, Brian, 164
journaling *versus* dialoguing, 64–65
Judaism, 30–31, 315
Jung, Carl, 107, 316

Kabbalists on light and inner divinity, 31
Kandall, Eric, 88
Keating, Thomas, 106, 107, 193, 318
key concepts
    accepting the self-discovery invitation, 55
    and DI Process, 20
    dying to human self as transformation, 200
    everything begins with you, 67
    God is in everyone, 38
    God within us, 38
    holding no emotional violence, 153
    knowledge of self is knowledge of God, 182
    nothing is impossible, 262
    path to salvation, 134
    performing miracles, 288
    seek first who you are not, 115
    we are the creators, 244
    what you are seeking is hidden within you, 89
    as within, so without, 166
    you are your own master, 223
kinesiology, 163–64, 194
The Kingdom of God Is within You (Tolstoy), 32
Knights of the Templar, 315
knowledge of self is knowledge of God
    coaching and self-examination, 174–75
    key concepts, 182
    looking inward, 183
    narrative story, 171–74
    scientific basis, 177–81
    Universal Spiritual Truth, 175–77
Kuhn, Alvin Boyd, 213

Languages and the Brain (Pribram), 129
Lashley, Karl, 129
light
    and consciousness, 164
    as form of energy, 33–36
    human energy field and DI Power Potentials, 194, 268–69, 285–88

and inner divinity, 29–30, 31–32
ipseity and inner divinity, 36–37, 38
Light Frequency, 34–36, 36–37, 38
Light Frequency
  and activation of our DI, 215, 240–41, 242–43
  and brainwave power, 218–19
  conscious change and real evolution, 49
  described, 338
  and emotional energy, 37, 174
  and inner divinity, 34–36, 36–37, 38
  and limiting beliefs, 81–82
  measurement of, 141, 189, 254–56, 293–94, 322–23
  and release of negative emotions, 178–79, 188–90, 192–93, 214–15
  and self-care benefits, 126–27
  and transformed consciousness, 177
limbic system (feeling brain), 51, 55, 82–83, 151, 180–81
limiting beliefs
  about God, 80–81, 82
  Conditioned Self and, 72–75, 109–10, 321–22
  confronting, 231
  False Self and, 108–9
  and holding no emotional violence, 138
  release of, 90, 175–76
  and teenage brain, 152, 153
Lipton, Bruce, 84, 129
Living Buddha, Living Christ (Nhat Hanh), 159
locus of control, 4, 164–65
looking inward
  accepting the self-discovery invitation, 56
  and DI Process, 20
  dying to human self as transformation, 201
  everything begins with you, 68
  God is in everyone, 39
  God within us, 39
  holding no emotional violence, 154
  nothing is impossible, 263
  path to salvation, 135

performing miracles, 289
seek first who you are not, 116
we are the Creators, 245
what you are seeking is hidden within you, 90
as within, so without, 167
Love, Medicine and Miracles (Siegel), 181
luminosity, 287
Lutz, Antoine, 36

MacLean, Paul, 50, 144
magnetic resonance imaging (MRI), 318
Magus, Simon, 213, 310
Maslow, Abraham, 281
Massy, Gerald, 311
Maxwell, James Clerk, 63–64
McCraty, Rollin, 146
McTaggart, Lynne, 294
meditation
   and changing your brainwaves, 219–22
   described, 338
   and self-care benefits, 125
memory
   Authentic Self and positive memories, 75–78
   cognitive intervention and learning from negative memories, 329–30
   Conditioned Self and limiting beliefs, 72–75, 109–10, 321–22
   as key to belief system, 87–88
   memory retrieval rewriting our own histories, 180–81
   Positive Anchors, 75–78, 189, 233–34, 236, 241–42, 303, 340
   working, 65
mental shifting, 216, 239–40
The Mind and The Brain (Schwartz), 215
The Mindful Brain (Siegel), 195
mindfulness, 287
The Mindful Therapist (Siegel), 196
Mindsight (Siegel), 128
miracles. *See* performing miracles
mirror neurons, 282–84, 319, 339

Molecules of Emotion (Pert), 178–79, 195–96
"Monday effect" and rewiring the brain, 131–33
Muktananda on conscious evolution, 68
multiple deaths of Conditioned Self, 111–12
Murray, William Hutchinson, 62

Nag Hammadi Library. *See* Gnostic Gospels
Nakshatra (birth star), 35–36
nefish, 285
negative information, 111, 112
neocortex (thinking brain)
   and amygdala hijack, 149–52
   approach, not avoid, 328–30
   described, 52, 55
   development of, 87, 89, 113
   integration of thoughts and emotions, 147–48, 328–30
   and the limbic system, 53, 82–83
neural redesign, 213–15
neurochemicals, 133
neuroplasticity
   described, 12, 339195–97
   and hardwired neural pathways, 338
   and meditation, 219–20
neuroscience
   affective neuroscience, 149
   brainwaves, 194, 216–22
   mirror neurons, 282–84, 319, 339
   and release of negative emotions, 177–79
   and Universal Spiritual Truths, 11–12
neutrinos, 34, 36
A New Earth (Tolle), 193
Newton, Isaac, 315
Nhat Hanh, Thich, 159
Nicene Councils, 314
9/11, 293
nonjudgmentalness, 287
nonlocality (Bell's Theorem), 162–63, 267, 284, 318, 337
nothing is impossible

coaching and self-examination, 256
key concepts, 262
looking inward, 263
narrative story, 247–56
scientific basis, 258–61
Universal Spiritual Truth, 257–58

O'Brien, Dan, 329–30
The Observer Effect, 47–49, 162–63, 339–40
obsessive-compulsive disorder (OCD), 215, 216
O'Leary, Denyse, 198
omnipotence, omnipresence, and omniscience of God, 14–15
Opening Up (Pennebaker), 159
openness and receptivity, 286
our thoughts create our world, 162–63
Outside Wins, 253–56, 278
oxytocin, 133

Pagels, Elaine, 9, 319
"pain body," 106–7
parents and development of Conditioned Self, 109–10
Parksepp, Jaak, 36
Pascual-Leone, Alvaro, 131–32, 214, 240
path to salvation
  key concepts, 134
  looking inward, 135
  meditation, 125
  narrative story, 117–23
  need for self-care, 125
  scientific basis, 127–33
  Universal Spiritual Truth, 126–27
Pennebaker, James, 65–66, 159, 334
Penrose, Roger, 35
Perfectionist/Talented
  emotional power levels, 335
  Personality Profile, 326
performing miracles
  coaching and self-examination, 278–80

key concepts, 288
  looking inward, 289
  narrative story, 265–78
  scientific basis, 282–87
  Universal Spiritual Truth, 281–82
Personality Profiles (Conditioned Self), 323–28
personality types, 97
Pert, Candace, 144–45, 178, 195–96, 319
physics of consciousness, 163–64
Planck, Max, 33, 317
Plato, 300, 313, 315
Pleaser/Intuitive personality
  Conditioned-Self interview, 97–103
  emotional power levels, 335
  Personality Profile, 327
Plotinus, 314
Popp, Fritz-Albert, 34, 318
Portenga, Steve, 329
Positive Anchors, 75–78, 189, 233–34, 236, 241–42, 303, 340
positive interactions, 111
positron emission tomography (PET) scans, 197–98
powerful presence, 287
Power Potentials, 279, 286–87, 340
Power vs. Force (Hawkins), 49, 260
prana, 144, 285
prayer
  discipline as prayer, 235
  scientific prayer, 238–39
  and talking to God, 227–28
Pribram, Karl, 129, 318
The Primal Wound (Verrier), 157
Ptolemy on *gnosis*, 41

Quantum BioFeedback, measurement of Light Frequency, 34, 36, 141, 189, 254–56, 322–23, 340
Quantum Entanglement, 162–63, 337–38
Quantum Healing (Chopra), 130–31
quantum physics

Bell's Theorem (nonlocality), 162–63, 267, 284, 318, 337
   and the biology of DI, 83–85
   and Correspondence Principle, 258–59
   and the world as a hologram, 128–29
quantum physics and Universal Spiritual Truths, 12–14

Ramachandram, Vilayanur, 198
random-number generators (RNGs), 293
Ratey, John J., 127–28
"reactionary personality," 148
rejection as invitation to grow, 59–60
Religious Science (Science of the Mind), 32
Religious Science magazine, 238
repetition and neural redesign, 214–15
resilience
   benefits of, 334
   DI Power Potential, 287
   and mental shifting, 216, 239–40
"The Reward Molecule" (dopamine), 133
Rewire Retreat, 172–75, 179, 185–87, 190–92, 196, 198–99, 201, 211
rewriting our own histories
   Rewire Retreat, 190–92
   and trauma recovery, 180–81
Roach, Paul John, 176
Roger, Gerard, 128

Sagan, Carl, 35
Saint (Mother) Teresa, 107, 179, 281, 311
Saint Augustine, 281
salvation. *See* path to salvation
Sathya Sai Baba, 336
Schopenhauer, Arthur, 8
Schwartz, Jeffrey, 215, 216
Science of the Heart (McCraty), 146
Science of the Mind (Religious Science), 32
scientific basis of DI
   accepting the self-discovery invitation, 47–54

dying to human self as transformation, 194–99
everything begins with you, 63–66
God is in everyone, 32–37
holding no emotional violence, 144–52
knowledge of self is knowledge of God, 177–81
nothing is impossible, 258–61
path to salvation, 127–33
performing miracles, 282–87
seek first who you are not, 108–14
of Universal Spiritual Truths, 10–11
we are the Creators, 239–43
what you are seeking is hidden within you, 83–88
as within, so without, 160–65
you are your own master, 213–22
scientific prayer, 238–39
search for divinity of the self, 1–2
The Seat of the Soul (Zukav), 126, 144
seek first who you are not
   coaching and self-examination, 103–6
   key concepts, 115
   looking inward, 116
   narrative story, 93–103
   scientific basis, 108–14
   Universal Spiritual Truth, 106–7
self-awareness, 286
self-care
   need for, 125
   path to salvation narrative story, 117–25
   and stress reduction, 130–31
self-compassion, 143–44
self-discovery. *See* accepting the self-discovery invitation
self-growth process, 43–46, 61–62
self-knowledge. *See* knowledge of self is knowledge of God
self-responsibility, 286
self-state, 108–9
self-talk, 113
Seligman, Martin, 319
The Sermon on the Mount (Fox), 257–58

serotonin, 133
the shadow, 107
Siegel, Bernie S., 181
Siegel, Daniel, 86–87, 88, 108, 109, 128, 195, 196, 197
Silvanus, 63, 247
A Simple Path (Mother Teresa), 311
Social Intelligence (Goleman), 282
Socrates, 313
soul's return to Universe after death, 35
sound waves and brainwave entrainment, 220–22
the source of all power lies within us, 258
Spark (Ratey), 127
The Spiritual Brain (Beauregard and O'Leary), 198
spiritual bypass, 47
spiritual development, 340
spiritual evolution, 160–61, 340
spirituality, 341
spiritual law of circulation, 213
spiritual maturity, 340
"spooky action at a distance," 163, 337–38
state of mind, 108
stress reduction, 130–31
Super Genes (Chopra and Tanzi), 84
synapses, 341

Tanzi, Rudolph E., 84
teenage brain, 152
Tesla, Nicola, 316
therapy, coaching *versus* therapy, 27–28, 321–22
Theta brainwaves, 218–19
thinking brain. *See* neocortex (thinking brain)
Thoreau, David, 32
Tibetan Buddhism, 219–20
time and integration of emotional experiences, 160–61
Tolle, Eckhart, 106, 193
Tolstoy, Leo, 316
transcendence, 256
Trans-Theoretical Model (TTM) of change, 332

trauma recovery and rewriting our own histories, 180–81
triune brain, 50, 53–54, 82, 144–45
The Triune Brain in Evolution (MacLean), 50

Unity Field Theory, 128–29
Universal Spiritual Truths
   accepting the self-discovery invitation, 46–47
   and DI Process, 20
   dying to human self as transformation, 193
   everything begins with you, 62–63
   Gnostic Gospels as source of, 8–10
   God is in everyone, 29–32
   holding no emotional violence, 143–44
   knowledge of self is knowledge of God, 175–77
   neuroscience and, 11–12
   nothing is impossible, 257–58
   path to salvation, 126–27
   performing miracles, 281–82
   quantum physics and, 12–14
   scientific basis of, 10–11
   seek first who you are not, 106–7
   the fifteen truths, 10
   we are the Creators, 237–39
   what you are seeking is hidden within you, 81–83
   as within, so without, 159–60
   you are your own master, 212–13

Valentinus, 117
Verrier, Nancy, 157, 208
visceral brain, 51, 55
visualization
   and creation, 238
   mental shifting and resilience, 239–40
   and rewiring our brain, 240
voice of Conditioned Self, 112–13
Vygotsky, Lev, 86

Walsch, Neale Donald, 238

we are all connected and one with God
   God and the Creator within us, 291–300
   Universal Spiritual Truth, 300–307
we are the Creators
   coaching and self-examination, 235–36
   key concepts, 244
   looking inward, 245
   narrative story, 225–35
   scientific basis, 239–43
   Universal Spiritual Truth, 237–39
what you are seeking is hidden within you
   coaching and self-examination, 78–81
   key concepts, 89
   looking inward, 90
   narrative story, 69–78
   scientific basis of, 83–88
   Universal Spiritual Truth, 81–83
Wheeler, John, 237
working memory, 65
the world as a hologram, 128–29
The World as I See It (Einstein), 7
writing *versus* dialoguing, 64–65

Yogananda, Paramahansa, 336
you are your own master
   coaching and self-examination, 211–12
   key concepts, 223
   narrative story, 203–11
   scientific basis, 213–22
   Universal Spiritual Truth, 212–13

Zahavi, Dan, 36
Zelazo, Philip David, 36
Zero Point Field (ZPF, "the Field")
   and acts of creation, 259
   and brainwaves, 218–19, 220–22
   described, 14, 341
   light and God/inner divinity, 32–33, 35

and mirror neurons, 282–84
power of recognition of, 285
as source of energy, 63–64
Zukav, Gary, 126, 144

ACKNOWLEDGMENTS

Thanks to all my writers. Renée, your faith in me was the driving force behind this new edition. Your diligence and insistence upon truth was an inspiration to this new edition. I am grateful for your time and effortless enthusiasm on this project. Lesley, you taught me I had to write this book myself! Sarah, your purity in writing down my words when I couldn't, started me off authentically. Janie, you added the spice; the God part of you blended it all together. Bethany, you read it at just the right time and gave me inspiration that I could continue to be me and write my way.

Kelley, your coaching made me realize the enormous message I have to spread and that, as you say: "You are something bigger than you think."

Sarah, Jamey, and Jessica, my dear daughters, you dared to take the process into your own lives to show me it was good. And the results are that your Authentic Selves are leading your lives. Thanks for believing in me enough to trust the process! You are the manifestation of the Creator within me.

To my sons, Matthew and Stephen, I can see the Creator in you! Thank you so much for allowing me to be a part of your unfolding lives. I love you both!

Mom, you were the first one to give me the idea that God is on the inside! Thank you from the bottom of my heart for creating me and making me who I am. I never think of you as a single entity, so I know Daddy was a part of this process also, in such a loving and caring way. You both love me so much. Know that I am forever grateful!

To the Mindset coaches who have trained to use this process: Thanks for having the courage and belief in my work to carry it out to the world. I cannot complete my mission without all of you. Thank you!

To my clients, your belief in and commitment to the Divine Intelligence Process and your personal successes are a constant source of inspiration.

To my readers, I appreciate your support and feedback, and I am grateful for your insights.

Dave, thank you for never doubting that I had the Creator in me, even when I did. You always see that divine part of me when at times it is lost to me. Thanks for being who you are. I am forever in love with you, and the Creator in us creates a union unlimited in love.

To the Creator within me—I bow down every day with thankfulness that I have found you!

ABOUT THE AUTHOR

As a Thought Leader with a distinct philosophy of self-help, ethical living and mind-power metaphysics, Dr. Jayne Gardner believes that thought can radically transform circumstances. When people move their minds, they move their world. The Divine Intelligence Process became successful only because she first tested it out in her own life and then in the lives of hundreds of clients.

Dr. Gardner has presented seminars and workshops all over the United States and has represented many prestigious groups, such as the International Coach Federation, Centers for Spiritual Living, Unity Churches, and the Young Presidents Organization.

She has presented her system for personal coaching on CNN's *Business Unusual,* as well as made several appearances on the *Good Morning Texas* show in response to current events.

She graduated with a Ph.D. from the University of North Texas in counseling psychology and is also a graduate of the Executive Coaching program at the University of Texas at Dallas (UTD). She is certified by the International Coach Federation as a Master Certified Coach (MCC), a designation awarded to fewer than 400 coaches worldwide. She has been on the faculty at Texas Christian University (TCU) and UTD and has coached Executive Master of Business Administration (EMBA) students at UTD. She owns her own coach training company called The Divine Intelligence Institute.

THE DIVINE INTELLIGENCE INSTITUTE

A Brief History

Started in 1995, and formerly called The Gardner Institute, The Divine Intelligence Institute™ grew out of the success of Dr. Jayne Gardner's Divine Intelligence Process™, a scientifically based, spiritual process for awakening the Creator within. This process offers step-by-step instructions for increasing a person's inner authority, thus, awakening their own creative potential.

The process's power as well as its challenge is to teach people how to reclaim their lives and take 100 percent responsibility for their personal and professional relationships, their health, and their well-being. The only true power is sourced from within. Nothing can do anything for us without a mental and spiritual shift within ourselves.

Dr. Gardner's passionate belief in the process's capacity to awaken the Divine Intelligence dormant in every person is behind the growth of the company. With the success of the Divine Intelligence Process over the last twenty-two years and growing demand, she developed a spiritual life coach training school where other life coaches could learn this transformative process for spiritual change. Joined by David Bauer as a principal in 1999, a certified (PCC) coach himself, their life coach training school flourished. In 2006, the spiritual life training school achieved the International Coaching Federation's accreditation. Since that time, more than 200 life coaches have been certified in the process.

In 2012, The Gardner Institute began to distinguish itself in the field of coaching by limiting admissions to those life coaches who wished to study a unique blend of spiritual coaching grounded in science. Spiritual coaching, unrelated to religion, is a deep, core, cellular transformation for finding the spirit within us, for uncovering our purpose, and for carrying the message that people are unlimited and connected to one another.

In September of 2013, The International Coach Federation awarded Dr. Gardner its highest designation in the coaching profession—the Master Certified Coaching Certification.

Confirmation of the process's effectiveness in individuals led them to begin offering it to groups via webinars in 2015. The virtual arena has expanded the process's reach, and the group format bolsters participant involvement by lending a feeling of support.

The vision of The Divine Intelligence Institute is to help 15 percent of the world's population (1.125 billion of the world's 7.5 billion people), the spiritual "tipping point," experience this life-changing process. The end result of what has occurred in the 2,243 people having taken the process is a decrease in their negative emotional reaction time to outside influences and an increase in their Light Frequency or their ability to maintain an emotional positivity. When this goal is reached, a shift in the world's emotional energy from the negative energy of anger, hatred, war and revenge to love, gratitude, acceptance and peace will occur, creating a more energetically balanced world.

Keeping true to their mission: to light up the human spirit one person at a time through this process, The Divine Intelligence Institute invites you to participate in raising the Light Frequency of the Collective Consciousness in our Universe by:

- Reading this book and passing it on to other spiritually-minded people
- Personal, one-on-one coaching through the process with Dr. Jayne
- Personal coaching through the process with a qualified Spiritual Life Coach taught by Dr. Jayne
- Participating in a 4-day workshop to discover your Divine Intelligence
- Taking the process via webinar in a group format
- Beginning coach training to become a Spiritual Life Coach

- Taking a free, Spiritual IQ assessment which provides a measuring scale for Divine Intelligence development; helpful ways to expand your DI accompany your quiz results

To learn more, please visit our website:
www.divineintelligenceinstitute.com

Or contact Dr. Jayne directly by email, phone, or mail:
drjayne@divineintelligenceinstitute.com
469-519-2727

The Divine Intelligence Institute
1333 W. McDermott, Suite 150
Allen, Texas 75013

Made in the USA
Lexington, KY
13 August 2017